**Land Use
Without
Zoning**

Land
Use
Without
Zoning

Bernard H. Siegan

Lexington Books
D.C. Heath and Company
Lexington, Massachusetts
Toronto   London

Library of Congress Cataloging in Publication Data

Siegan, Bernard H.
    Land use without zoning.

    1. Zoning - United States.   I. Title.
HT167.S5   333.7.7   72-4936
ISBN 0-669-82040-7

Published simultaneously in Canada.

Printed in the United States of America.

International Standard Book Number: 0–669–82040–7.

Library of Congress Catalog Card Number: 72–186339.

To Sharon

Contents

List of Figures

List of Tables

Foreword

The purpose of a foreword is in part to enable things to be said which the modesty of the author prevents him from saying and in part to appraise the work from a viewpoint broader than would be appropriate for the author of a specialized treatise. It is a task which, in the case of Mr. Siegan's book on Land Use Without Zoning, I am very happy to undertake.

Mr. Bernard H. Siegan has practiced as a lawyer in Chicago, specializing on real estate problems, for more than twenty years. This has given him an intimate knowledge of how zoning operates in practice. It was most fortunate that it was possible for Mr. Siegan to use this experience as a basis for a systematic study of zoning. In 1968 he was appointed a research fellow in law and economics at the University of Chicago Law School. His project was to investigate the effects of zoning. He knew how zoning worked and it was apparent that, in many respects, zoning led to results which were clearly harmful. But the question remained: might not any alternative to zoning have consequences that were even worse? To discover whether this was so, Mr. Siegan decided to study what happened in Houston, a city which had never had zoning, and, taking advantage of his experience, to compare this with what would probably have happened had Houston been a zoned city. Mr. Siegan's research was thorough. The results, first published in the *Journal of Law and Economics* in 1970, were unambiguous—and startling. The present book is an outgrowth of that earlier study. I will not attempt to steal Mr. Siegan's thunder. Suffice it to say that Houston not only secures many of the advantages which are supposed to be achieved only with zoning but manages to do so without some of the disadvantages which zoning brings with it.

Mr. Siegan's work is clearly a very important contribution to the literature on zoning. But it has a wider significance. At the present time it is generally agreed that government regulation in many areas is failing. And yet the almost instinctive reaction to the situation is to ask for more, or a different kind of, government regulation. This attitude represents what Dr. Samuel Johnson called, when speaking of another enterprise, a triumph of hope over experience. Of course, it cannot be denied that, on occasion, more or a different form of government regulation may be required. But it would be wrong to restrict our vision and narrow unduly the range of alternatives between which we choose. What Mr. Siegan shows, and it is this which makes his study of interest to a much wider audience than those professionally concerned with zoning, is that the market can be used effectively to solve problems which it is commonly thought can only be handled by government regulation. It suggests that the market might be used more often than it is at present to deal with other social problems. Of course, it is not possible, without careful investigation of how alernative social systems actually work, to say just what solution is best. This can only come from the kind of inquiry which Mr. Siegan has made for zoning and it is to be hoped that others, working on different social problems, will emulate Mr. Siegan's example.

It is a source of great satisfaction to me that Mr. Siegan's study, which is bound to have a considerable influence on our views on zoning, was carried out as part of the law-economics program of the University of Chicago Law School.

R. H. Coase
Musser Professor of Economics
University of Chicago Law School

Introduction

Since its inception in this country more than one-half century ago, local government has exercised through zoning an ever greater control over land use. Most people, expert or knowledgeable in this area, readily agree that the process and its consequences have been detrimental to the optimum use of the land. As a result, many legislators, planners and commentators in recent years have strongly advocated changes in existing powers and practices. These proposals usually have had one element in common: they maintain a large governmental presence in the use of the land.

An alternative which had not been given adequate attention was the elimination of most governmental powers over land use. Moreover, this alternative did not require abstract and theoretical contemplations; it could be pragmatically studied inasmuch as there are jurisdictions where zoning had never been adopted, notably Houston, Texas. The accomplishments and consequences of zoning could then be compared and evaluated. These considerations led to my appointment in 1968 as a research fellow in law and economics at the University of Chicago Law School to study Houston's system of "nonzoning."

This book is an extension and enlargement of my previously published papers on zoning and nonzoning. Like so many books these days, this book also is about the environment, but only about that portion that houses the people and supplies their material needs. This is by far the most important environment. It is not nearly as spectacular as the Alaskan tundra or Mineral King, subjects that attract the attention of many writers and politicians but have little meaning for a great percentage of the public. This book concerns instead, that huge portion of the population limited in its ability to change its environment, a group comprised principally of those of average and below-average income.

For most people, home is where the major part of life is spent. It is the place that occupies the time and attention of the wife and children most of each day. It is also the place where the husband spends most of his time when away from work and the major purpose for which he works. Its characteristics greatly influence the quality of one's life. For a family struggling to maintain financial solvency, a five or ten percent increase in the cost of housing is of vastly greater importance than the status of scenic wonders, regardless of one's feelings about nature and the wild. Similarly, for most people, a better neighborhood and greater convenience to work and shopping are most significant environmental goals.

For those concerned with the quality of life, housing and local environmental conditions merit the highest priority. I believe one means to achieve these objectives is to eliminate one of the principal barriers to production, zoning, and thereby allow the real estate market greater opportunity to satisfy the needs and desires of its consumers. My studies show that zoning is neither necessary to maintain or protect property values nor an aid to "planning"—its principal justifications. On the contrary, it has adverse effects on both. When it impedes the production of housing, it also impedes the achievement of better housing and housing conditions.

Those most expert at a task should be allowed to accomplish it, and in real estate those experts are builders and developers. Their livelihoods depend on their competency. Moreover, they are the only ones assigned this role in our society. We should remove those governmental restrictions that prevent them from maximizing the supply and competing with each other for our favor and benefit. Unfortunately, we have allowed one group in the population, local politicians, to gain dominance over land use, despite their lack of competency and even more important, socially desirable motivation. It is not a question of good or evil; the human condition prevails as much for the developer as it does for the politician: no segment of the population is exempt from scoundrels and grafters.

However, motivations and incentives do differ. The motivations of a builder and developer are to increase production, whereas those of the politician and planner all too often are to inhibit it, particularly in the roles they are assigned in the zoning process. The incentives of the profit system lead to more production; yet the rewards of public life frequently go to those who curtail production. The nation's suburbs provide ready evidence; the politician who advocates lifting restrictions upon real estate production does so at the risk of his political life—and therefore few do.

Unfortunately, many environmentalists also endeavor to have government restrict production under the mistaken belief that this will somehow enhance the environment; however, less production of real estate will tend to maintain present housing conditions, which for many are poor, and which will in time worsen. New opportunities will be denied many for a new home or apartment. It will be more difficult to achieve the goal of a decent home for everyone. By making daily life more pleasant for more people, maximizing production, not limiting it, will best serve the environment. This in itself should be the strongest argument in its favor.

BERNARD H. SIEGAN

Chicago, Illinois
June 1, 1972

**Land Use
Without
Zoning**

Part I
Zoning and Nonzoning

1

Zoning: Politics and Planning

Zoning is not just an expansion of the common law of nuisance. It seeks to achieve much more than the removal of obnoxious gases and unsightly uses. Underlying the entire concept of zoning is the assumption that zoning can be a vital tool for maintaining a civilized form of existence only if we employ the insights and the learning of the philosopher, the city planner, the economist, the sociologist, the public health expert and all the other professions concerned with urban problems.

. . . In exercising their zoning powers, the local authorities must act for the benefit of the community as a whole following a calm and deliberate consideration of the alternatives, and not because of the whims of either an articulate minority or even majority of the community. . . . Thus, the mandate of the Village Law . . . is not a mere technicality which serves only as an obstacle course for public officials to overcome in carrying out their duties. Rather, the comprehensive plan is the essence of zoning. Without it, there can be no rational allocation of land use. It is the insurance that the public welfare is being served and that zoning does not become nothing more than just a Gallup poll.[1]

The foregoing observations were made by Judge Keating of the New York Court of Appeals in a zoning case decided in 1968. They may not be the best or most accurate explanation for zoning, but there are few who would want to quarrel with the ideals and objectives set forth by the judge. Man's reason must serve man. We should indeed have the best reason and knowledge before we place governmental limitations on one's freedom to use his land and property.

The zoning system that prevails in this country is custom-designed to frustrate these most noble goals. The judge's criteria are self-defeating; by telling us what should be done, he makes it clear that it cannot be done. Even the most sophisticated computer could not possibly program all of these various and highly subjective elements. What then can we expect when we entrust them to a system dominated by the political apparatus of a community? In this chapter, I shall attempt to explain the process by which land and property is regulated in the zoned communities. It will be apparent that there is virtually no relationship between what Judge Keating says should occur and what actually does occur.

There are four distinct phases in the establishment and operation of zoning. I shall refer to them in the subsequent discussion as (1) planning, (2) public participation and decision making, (3) amendments and change, and (4) implementation. Before a zoning ordinance is adopted, it must be

3

prepared by technicians, discussed and considered by the public, and voted upon by the local legislative body. A similar procedure must be followed in order to amend the ordinance, either comprehensively or specifically. The courts may also change the ordinance when the local legislators refuse to do so. Once passed, the ordinance has to be interpreted and enforced by the staff of the local government. Let us now proceed to a discussion of each of the phases enumerated above.

Planning

The first step in the adoption of an original zoning ordinance or a general amendment thereto is the preparation of its text and accompanying maps showing the location of the various zoning districts. In the suburbs and smaller cities, this usually involves the employment of a professional planning firm to draft both documents. In the larger cities, the planning department might be assigned this task, and it might hire private consultants, or possibly a special commission and experts might be appointed. The project usually commences with a study of existing land uses. Thereafter, the input can be as unlimited as Judge Keating suggests it should be, but it never is.

Although there are differences in many specifics, and in draftsmanship and form, there is a great similarity among the zoning ordinances of affluent suburbs. This, despite their being located throughout a large country with many sectional differences and employing the services of a great many different planners. The explanation for this is simple: planning has been used to accomplish the common objective of suburbanites everywhere of maintaining a single-family character for their community. In this respect, when you've seen one suburban ordinance, you've seen them all. When a professional firm is hired to prepare a zoning ordinance, it has no option but to produce a document responsive to the desires of its client. Any other efforts would be wasted since the proposal must be adopted by the local legislature to become law.

The proposed ordinance and maps will provide for predominantly single-family usage, divided probably into several districts. A comparison of zoning provisions of suburbs in the Chicago metropolitan area shows a great amount of variation in the number of districts, minimum lot sizes, density, and height, and this holds true elsewhere. Being on one side or the other of a boundary line can make a substantial difference for a property owner and for future development of that property. It is also important where in the suburb the property is located; one section may be zoned for minimum lot size of one acre whereas another is zoned for half that amount. Were the property two hundred or three hundred feet away from its present location, it might be in another suburb where the requirements would be much different.

Many different firms are involved in this business: employing professional planners, architects, or engineers. Because the drafters are planners and not lawyers, the ordinance frequently carries with it an important defect, poor draftsmanship. Defects of this sort may, of course, be remedied by the legal staff of the municipality, but there is another remedy that is more certain of success. It is the likelihood that even the most legally doubtful provisions will never be challenged in the courts; the legal process is too costly and time-consuming for most property owners.

Over the years, the ordinances have grown much longer and definitions and explanations have become much more detailed. There is much emphasis in recent years on discretionary devices, such as special uses and planned unit developments, PUDs. (These will be discussed in Chapter 8.) Essentially, suburban ordinances in the relatively affluent sections of the country do not differ in the basic objective of using the vast bulk of the land for single-family lots, and limiting all other uses to areas where they are least likely to be objectionable to homeowners. The more recent ordinances tend to give great discretion to the municipality on the location of the unpopular uses—gas stations, motels, nursing homes, even townhouses and apartments. An effort will be made to accommodate the original zoning (or a comprehensive rezoning) to existing uses, but small, scattered nonresidential uses may be zoned residential and made "nonconforming" with established time limits within which the nonresidential use is to be terminated.

The usual pattern in Suburbia places the closest-numbered residential districts next to each other, that is, R-1 next to R-2, R-2 next to R-3, and so on. Apartment uses will be placed on major thoroughfares, or next to railroads industrial, and commercial, to buffer single-family homes. Commercial and industrial districts will usually be placed in or adjoining the downtown area and in the environs of the railroad stations. Some corners of major intersections and portions of major streets will be zoned commercial, and some "high grade" industrial zones may be created some distance from any existing homes.

The planners do not operate in a vacuum. Pressures may be exerted by those who hired the planners to have certain properties zoned for certain uses, and these pressures may prevail. It is usually neither difficult nor necessarily detrimental to the plan to accede to such requests, for many areas can be zoned to accommodate many different uses without disturbing what appears to be the basic "plan." Unless surrounded by homes, nearly any substantial area on a major thoroughfare and adjoining an intersection can be zoned for commercial or apartment use as well as for homes, without encountering significant problems. There is also minimum difficulty in zoning sizable remote tracts for "quality" industrial and possibly multi-family use.

As the preceding suggests, the foremost guide to planning in the suburbs is to please the customer. Market surveys are too expensive in most instances, and the client usually has little interest in the market in any event. Generally there is little or no coordination between or concern for land use and planning by adjoining municipalities, except possibly with respect to properties contiguous to the border. Little purpose would be served in any event, since the neighboring suburb or city has no zoning responsibility save to its own residents.

Planning is enormously more complex in the larger cities. The areas are greater, the population is diverse, life styles vary, and the objectives are much different. Unlike the suburbs, there is no one standard by which every proposal can be measured. The input can be truly enormous, much greater than that which Judge Keating suggests. Questions of compatibility, economic feasibility, property values, existing uses, adjoining and nearby uses, traffic, topography, utilities, schools, future growth, conservation, and environment have to be considered for countless locations, covering hundreds of square miles.

This cannot possibly be accomplished. Just to determine economic feasibility for certain uses at any one site for any one period of time would require a market survey costing possibly thousands of dollars, and this largely eliminates survey use. How does one decide on the priority of the various factors, that is, which are most and which are least important? That there is practically no limit to the number of factors pertinent to decision making nor any guide as to how they rank in importance allows for maximum discretion on the part of the planners. They can consciously or unconsciously accept or reject criteria and data almost at will. There are relatively few standards that confine their determinations except those which they establish for themselves. And, of course, in the big cities, unlike the suburbs, there is no predominant life style which planning must serve, except perhaps that of the city administration.

As can be expected, there are considerably different approaches among professional city planners. When guidelines such as operate in the suburbs are not present, the resulting product may depend considerably on the orientation of the planners. It is possible that tacit understandings have been reached with the city administration, but the vastness of the undertaking will still allow for considerable impact by the planners. Brooks has categorized planners into six different groups, and the label he designates for each discloses the disparities in approaches: (1) the hard-line physical planner, (2) the socially sensitized physical planner, (3) the social service planner, (4) the advocate planner, (5) the urban social planner, and (6) the radical planner.[2] There are bound to be one or more subgroups under each category.

In the broader context of the function and concept of planning, planners are beset by the same intellectual limitations and dilemmas confronting the rest of society. How should land be used? Each of the professions referred to by Judge Keating might give a vastly different response. One's ideological orientation may control his answer. The country is presently in the midst of a great controversy on the issues of growth and development, and the responses of these protagonists differ greatly. Much day-to-day planning revolves about the core issue of the extent to which government should protect the values and desires of homeowners and other property owners. Thus, in his very detailed study of apartment zoning practices there, Professor Mandelker found that the planners and zoning agencies in King County, Washington, "were caught between a desire to handle what they saw as land use externalities, and a desire to implement a plan for the future of the physical environment."[3] Jacob Ukeles adds this further insight:

Each category or type of decision includes a series of choices involving knowledge of the city as it presently is and as it is likely to become in the future. Most zoning issues cannot be resolved solely by knowledge of existing conditions and trends, but require the application of values and judgments. What a city *ought* to become is as relevant a zoning question as what a city is likely to become. Even so-called technical studies, especially the mapping of zones, involve many value judgments as well as judgments of fact. The question of the appropriateness of an area will appear differently to different observers depending on their view of what the city and the particular locality ought to become. The decision that a given commercial strip or factory area is a menace to neighboring residents while a second such area is not, is rarely a "technical" decision.[4]

There appears to be an accepted format for a zoning ordinance of the large city that requires the division into many zoning districts. Thus, under the 1957 Chicago zoning ordinance, there are two single-family districts, six multifamily districts, seven business districts, four commercial districts, and three industrial districts. Many of these districts have many subdistricts and the number of zoning classifications for Chicago is over seventy. For each, the planners must establish permitted and prohibited uses, special uses, and height, area bulk, and parking requirements. They must determine locations and sizes for every classification and the proximity of one to the other. The total area of Chicago is about 145,000 acres, each of which should be carefully studied, in whole and in part, for a rational and reasonable determination of how its use should be regulated. And since demands and desires and needs in our society are constantly changing, the decision should be constantly subject to re-evaluation. This objective can only be achieved through periodic overall amendment, which unfortunately appears too costly and time-consuming a process to be engaged in as needed. It may also create much conflict and turmoil among the many groups and organizations that comprise a large city. Thus it is interesting that the last comprehensive amendment to Chicago's zoning ordinance, adopted in 1957, requires the planning department annually to review zoning extensively and recommend changes. This provision has been ignored, according to the head of the group that drafted the comprehensive amendment.

The zoning process is basically a negative device, although on occasion it has been used in a "positive" manner to accomplish certain specific and limited objectives. Incentive zoning has been used effectively on occasion, but it is far more the exception than the rule in present zoning practice. It cannot be otherwise. To promote and produce developments within areas of the city as desired would require a sophistication in real estate economics far beyond the most able economists, let alone city planners, who do not usually specialize in economics. In addition, rigid controls and implementation would be required, and this is not normally possible in the politicized atmosphere of local government—and probably is incompatible with a system of private ownership. Consequently, efforts at directing development through the negative process of restriction usually accomplishes no more than compounding the restrictions. Furthermore, the existence of many different municipalities each with its own zoning powers also reduces or eliminates the power of any one to influence "positively" land development.

An additional problem faced by a planner is that his plans must be consistent with the laws which regulate zoning. The planners may decide that there are sufficient gas stations within an area, and therefore reject zoning any corner of a major intersection for a gas station. This might be a largely futile exercise since the courts are likely to overturn this decision. David Heeter has suggested three other problems created by legal limitations on the zoning power:[5]

1. If a parcel on several sides adjoins apartments or commercial establishments, the courts may not uphold a regulation that zones the parcel for homes even though the neighborhood is already "glutted" with apartments or commerce.
2. One cannot be granted the privilege of carrying out an activity denied to his neighbors.
3. Enforcement of the regulations is an all or nothing proposition. Either they comply with the legal test of validity or they cannot be enforced.

A zoning classification must be established for every single parcel—whether vacant or improved—in the city; such a requirement demands an enormous amount of decision making under serious limitations and without sufficient knowledge. Thus, land use planning in the cities is such an inherently difficult process that for most vacant land little more than guesswork establishes the zoning. This assumes that the planners have been left alone to meditate and contemplate. But again, they, like their suburban counterparts, do not operate in a vacuum. They or their superiors may have been appointed by certain influential people and, therefore, may be directly or indirectly beholden to those people. There is simply too much money and power at stake in land usage for the planning process to be completely removed from political pressures. Much can be gained in having the planners recommend a particular use rather than having that use adopted through amendment in the public phase of zoning, for there is an aura of respectability given any land use recommended by planners, and certainly much less public suspicion and scrutiny.

When changes are made in a proposed zoning ordinance to satisfy particular interests, the effect spreads. It may be necessary to offset the change by changing someone else's property from a more valuable to a less valuable use. For example, if density is to be limited within a certain area, giving more density to a favored property will require reducing the density of one less favored, even if the latter is more suitable for high density by the established standards. And, of course, there are limitations to the amount of any particular zoning that can be established within certain sections.

On the whole, the role of the planner in the zoning process must necessarily be a limited one for these reasons:

1. He is the paid employee of the locality and cannot be expected to espouse with any degree of consistency policies contrary to those of his employers. The basic rules are established by officials elected to govern. A planner who strongly advocates high density housing in suburbia may not last much longer than his first paycheck. Confrontations are probably rare because a planner is not likely to be hired or seek employment if his basic orientation appears to differ substantially from that of his prospective employers. Disagreements will occur and be tolerated—within limitations.

2. Even if a proposed plan appears to accord with the general desires of the legislators and may even have been commissioned by them, it still must be acceptable in significant respects after hearings and debates to at least a majority to be adopted. Amendments required for passage can easily change the meaning and impact of the legislation. The "perfect" plan is likely to be quite imperfect by the time it emerges from the legislative process, whether it be on a local or higher governmental level, and it might be ravaged further as administered. And, it is possible, the courts ultimately may lay much of it to rest.

Public Participation and Decision Making

Public participation is an integral part of zoning. The zoning ordinance (or a general amendment thereto) drafted by the planners must go through a process of formal public hearings (and necessarily much informal discussion) prior to adoption by the local legislature. The text of the ordinance will create some interest but the focus of attention will be on the maps showing the zoning proposed for all properties within the municipality. Once presented to the public, the proposed ordinance will obviously be the subject of much public and private activity, and it is difficult to assess which is most effective, the public or private. Many property owners will quickly consult with *their* city planners, the political precinct workers; and it may happen that certain legal or planning firms become known as the "right" ones to be hired to obtain desired zoning classifications.

In the more affluent suburbs, the controversy will be between resident and absentee vacant landowners and some business interests (mostly non-voters) on the one side, and resident homeowners and some civic and political groups (all voters) on the other, and this usually turns into a very one-sided contest. There are no such limitations in the bigger cities, where a great many persons and groups, ranging from the local delicatessen owner, whose livelihood may be at stake, to the League of Women Voters, whose members, livelihoods rarely are, will want to have their say. How land and property is utilized is of concern to a great many within a large city, and much time may be devoted to the public hearings. As much or more time, however, may be spent informally or privately trying to influence the councilmen.

Nevertheless, whether it be the suburbs or the city, "participatory democracy" is not an appropriate description of the public phase of zoning, even given the broadest definition of that concept. More people proportionately will be represented in the suburbs, but tenants, small businessmen, and employees will not usually be involved even though each has a significant interest in the outcome. More important, the zoning ordinance may directly or indirectly affect a great many who do not live in the suburb and who may not even be aware of the proceedings. These include potential homeowners and tenants as well as consumers and employees of companies that might want to locate there. The suburbs may be "tight little islands," but what they do with respect to land use affects many mainlanders.

Nor are many individuals in the city likely to participate unless they belong to some organization that enters the hearings, for although the public hearings bring out a great many interest groups and individuals, particularly those that exist for or thrive on such "civic" activities, they are of little concern to most of the people who do not feel affected by the proposed ordinance. The hearings, naturally, revolve about the proposed ordinance, and consider whether it should be amended and if so, how. One who might suggest that there should be no such ordinance in the first place might well be ruled publicly out of order—or worse! Yet, were participatory democracy truly involved in the sense of a public election or referendum on the question of adopting zoning, all views would have to be considered, and it might be that the proposed ordinance would suffer a premature death. As will be discused in the next chapter, zoning has not done well in public elections, and it is doubtful that so many cities would have zoning if they had subjected the question to the purest form of participatory democracy, a referendum.

In making a decision on zoning, the city council or other governing board may be motivated by one or any number of considerations. It may vote from what may be considered the "highest" motive, the health, safety, and welfare of the "people" as conceived by its members, or it may vote for the basest of reasons, the payment of graft. And there certainly are many other possibilities in between.

It will be in an atmosphere of considerable controversy that a great many land use decisions will be made by the councilmen in the bigger cities. Politics, money, public relations, personal business, and friendships may well be on the line in many votes. The recommendations of the planners will be one element in the mix and probably an unimportant one when political considerations enter. Considered as a whole a compromise document will emerge that will duly satisfy the obligations of the legislative process in a representative society but will have little relationship to any rational criteria for the use of land.

Political and economic considerations will reduce if not totally eliminate those concerns which Judge Keating and many others tell us should be dominant in zoning. In fact, the criteria most determinative are the ones least likely to meet reasonable standards for restricting one's right to use his land. How many people favor and how many oppose? *Who* supports the zoning of the site and *who* objects to it? Accordingly, when the final vote

comes, most if not all legislators will vote for reasons that have no relationship to maximizing production, satisfying consumer demand, maintaining
property rights and values, or planning soundly.

Zoning has given enormous powers to local politicians, who frequently
have minimal or no qualifications for this trust. Measured in overall effect,
the power local legislators have over land use is probably the most important one they possess. Decisions regulating the use of property in
suburban and rural areas have affected substantial portions of the population who never had any participation in the selection of the decision makers.
Biographical sketches of local legislators are not likely to inspire confidence
that they as a group have the competence or motivation for such responsibility. While there probably are notable exceptions, the office of alderman,
or trustee, or member of a zoning board is not likely to attract many individuals with any special knowledge or technical competence in the field
of land use planning. The result is that these powers are vested in many
who would not possibly be hired for this task by private industry. Yet they
are exercising powers far greater than those exercised by any builder or
developer. Even when they have some expertise, it may have to be sub-
ordinate to the commitments they must make to obtain and hold public
office. How is it possible, therefore, for a municipal legislature to "measure
prophetically the emerging and receding tides by which business evolves
and grows, to foresee and map exactly the appropriate uses to which land
shall be developed and the amount necessary for each separation . . ."?[6]

Amendments and Change

Proposals for comprehensive amendments are relatively rare events, but
petitions for and objections to specific zoning amendments and zoning
variances have become important features of life in many cities and suburbs. Across the country, thousands of petitions are filed annually, and
many more thousands of citizens become involved in their disposition. Zoning controversies are frequently the major source for news in local newspapers. For many, the show of the week is not on TV but at the Village
Hall.

The issues are much narrower and the amount of public interest much less
than in proceedings involving comprehensive amendments, but the nature
of the pressures and considerations are not much different. Planners, politicians, landowners, homeowners, and civic groups are also participants in
these proceedings. Judge Keating's objectives are no more likely to be
achieved in a proceeding for a specific zoning change than they were with
respect to an original ordinance or a comprehensive amendment. Again,
what should and what does occur differ greatly.

Amendments that could not be accomplished in a comprehensive rezoning may be sought subsequently. As these and other pressures for change
build up in the big cities, amendments will be adopted for a variety of rea-

sons. A good description of the process and its consequences is contained in a study, made in 1969 by the Committee on Zoning Practices and Procedures of Los Angeles, of zoning practices in that city. A county grand jury investigation into a zoning case involving alleged improprieties prompted its formation and a report was issued after more than a year of hearings and investigation. These are some of its conclusions:

The term "zoning" has lost much of its significance in the City of Los Angeles, for it has come to mean promiscuous changes in the zoning pattern rather than adherence to consistent, comprehensive zoning. Procedures in actual practice have frequently become so loose that even the limited requirements of the City Charter have not been met in numerous variance cases. . . .

Zoning practices in Los Angeles do not now sufficiently reflect sound planning objectives. Piecemeal or spot zoning is resorted to in place of zoning on an area-wide basis. Individual rights are sometimes restricted or privileges granted on the basis of personal circumstances and pressure, rather than on the basis of serving the public interest. . . .

The Zoning Code lags, rather than leads, City development. There has been no comprehensive, over-all review of the Code since 1946. Since then there have been over 300 amendments to the text of the Code and several thousand changes in the Zoning Map, mainly as a result of individual requests and specific problems.[7]

The author has no way of knowing whether these conclusions are warranted by the facts, but it is apparent that they could have occurred in most zoned cities. The comments quoted appear to be more descriptive than critical. The practices described are inherent in big city zoning. Los Angeles has had a tremendous growth since 1946, and no one could possibly have envisioned the demands for land use that would result in the subsequent twenty years. Would it have made much difference if the city had comprehensively amended its ordinance in the interim? Dallas comprehensively amended its zoning in 1965 (more than two years after its city council adopted a resolution for such purposes). Yet, by early 1969, so many changes had been made that zoning became an important issue in the city election of that year.

Lest the reader consider the problems as solely one of incompetency or venality, these comments by the authors of a seventeen-month study of a county zoning board in Kentucky involving 167 cases are relevant:

Our general conclusion is that the board has not operated in such a manner as to assure citizens equal protection of the law. It has not, during the seventeen months of our study, produced a pattern of consistent, sound and articulate judgments. Nor have its operations assured the public that the comprehensive plan is not being thwarted through the variance device. We do not mean by this to imply any personal criticism of the individual members of the Board. To the best of our knowledge, they are honest men and good citizens, serving without pay in a thankless job. Our criticism goes to the institution which we find is functioning badly.[8]

The critics should be delighted that the communities have not adhered to *the* plan. If they had, the results would have been worse. Probably the most constant event in society is change—mostly unpredictable change. Plans militate against accommodations to change. Consider the New York experience in this perspective:

The draftsmen of the 1916 zoning code of New York City began their work in 1913 and it lasted without substantial revision until 1939. Like all zoning plans it was drawn in the light of technology generally available some years earlier and it was addressed to problems set in motion decades or centuries earlier and then apparent. The decent motives of those draftsmen and their competence are unquestioned but their forward vision had to be small. Their image of the ideal city was heavily tinted by their memories of a more bucolic and less populous city of their youth. They were constrained to protect the future as a virtually straight-line extension of the past. They simply could not (nor could anybody else) anticipate and plan for the tumultuous events of the next 23 years; United States entry into World War I, the virtual cessation of immigration after 1924, the Great Depression, the ubiquitous and ferocious automobile, airconditioning, the supermarket, penicillin.[9]

It is always intriguing to inspect zoning maps of large cities and contemplate the reasons why any one or more individual parcels happened to be given particular zoning classifications. Even the curiosity of the most indifferent may well be tempted by some of the printed maps such as that of Chicago's zoning ordinance which are virtual galaxies of letters and numbers (see Figs. 1–1 and 1–2).

Was it to promote the public health, safety, and welfare? Was it to enhance property values—and whose? Perhaps it was bought and paid for. Was it upon advice or recommendation of a planner, political committeeman, or the "right" lawyer? Would many or any other planners have given similar advice? Was it pressure from the homeowner's association? Was it because two, twenty, or two hundred people appeared at a hearing to express opposition? Or again, a court may have ordered it contrary to the wishes of the city council.

A research report prepared in 1968 for the Douglas Commission contains some statistics as to what occurs subsequent to the adoption of zoning procedures.[10] Information was requested from a stratified sample of local governments with populations in excess of 5,000 as to (1) how many rezoning petitions were approved in whole or in part during the preceding twelve months, and (2) how many zoning variances were approved for the same period. Rezoning petitions acted upon averaged 11 per reporting government, and about 73 percent of those petitions were approved wholly or in part. Requests for zoning variances averaged about 24 per reporting government, and about 78 percent of these were approved. For the forty-seven largest cities that reported, each with a population in 1960 of 250,000 or more, the survey indicated an average of 1,030 rezoning petitions acted upon per city with 72 percent of these approved wholly or in part; and 2,713 requests for zoning variances handled per city with a 76 percent rate of approval.

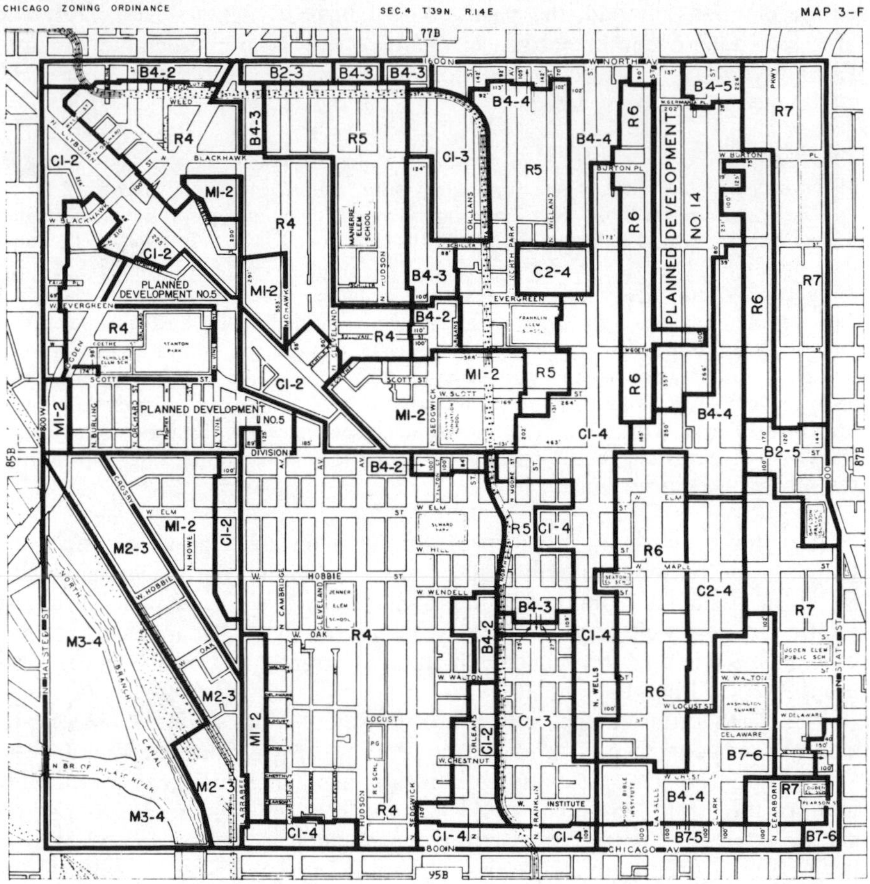

Figure 1-1. Zoning map of a near north section of Chicago. Source: *Chicago Zoning Ordinance,* 1963, p. 86B (Chapter 194A, Municipal Code of Chicago).

Professor Haar reports the following statistics with respect to variances:[11]

City	Period	Application or Requests	Number Granted	Approximate Percentage Granted
Cincinnati	1926–1937	1,940	1,493	77
Philadelphia	1933–1937	4,800	4,000	83
Cambridge				
(Use Variances)	1952	57	48	84
(Bulk Variances)		59	51	86

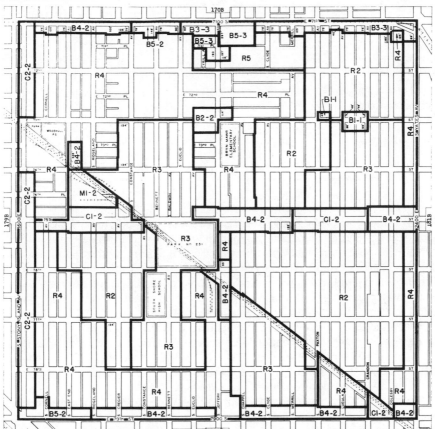

Figure 1–2. Zoning map of a South Shore section of Chicago. Source: *Chicago Zoning Ordinance,* 1963, p. 180B (Chapter 194A, Municipal Code of Chicago).

Another study of Philadelphia's Zoning Board of Adjustment shows that during September and October of 1956, it granted 143 applications unconditionally and 49 conditionally, or a total of 75 percent in 256 cases.[12] For the year spanning 1960 to 1961 the Board of Adjustment of Fort Worth, Texas, granted 95 out of 153 applications for variance, or about 62 percent.[13] The City Council of Austin, Texas, granted 80 percent of 378 applications for rezoning submitted from 1956 to 1958, inclusive.[14] Lexington-Fayette County Board of Adjustment (Kentucky) in the period from January 1960 to May 1961 granted 79 percent of 165 petitions.[15]

In Chicago, the record of Zoning Board of Appeals, as revealed by a number of different studies, has been as follows:[16]

Period	Applications	Number Granted	Approximate Percentage Granted
(a) 1923–1937	4,124	2,379	57.7
(b) 1951			70.0
(c) 1957–1961 (subsequent to passage of comprehensive amendment)	489	466	95.0
(d) 8-month period, 1965	269	253	94.0
(e) Hearings for Jan. 24, Feb. 14, and Feb 21, 1967.	33	32	98.0

It is difficult to evaluate the precise meaning of these figures. Thus, where the local legislature has made it clear that it will not approve petitions for certain purposes such as apartments or mobile homes, few petitions are filed for these uses and then largely by those prepared to institute litigation. On the other hand, a known policy favorable toward certain uses or exceptions may encourage the filing of petitions. Nor do the figures show how many "major" and "minor" matters were involved.

When the foregoing evidence is considered within the context of the prior discussion, at least two conclusions are warranted: (1) So many zoning changes in so many communities would not occur if there were general adherence to some form of master planning, and (2) control of property through zoning is more chaotic than it is orderly.

There is a story about a stock analyst who was alleged to have recommended stock purchases on the basis of darts he threw into a target while blindfolded. This technique seems even more appropriate for zoning. One might suspect, however, after an inspection of big city zoning maps that this method is already in use.

The principal criticism of zoning today, however, is not that it allows for too many changes but that it does not allow for enough. Amendments affecting large portions of land and many people are neither made nor for that matter ever requested owing to the likelihood that they will be denied. To a large extent this inflexibility is due to the proceedings required for the adoption of amendments. These proceedings appear to be clouded with fictions from conception to completion. Notice and publication is required to commence a petition for rezoning; yet of necessity neither is likely to inform many who have an important interest in the outcome, such as those who might want to live in the proposed development. Participation at a zoning hearing usually comes from the local residents and their representatives, on the one side, and the nonresident landowner and his representative, on the other. If the matter proceeds to a court trial, the contestants become the municipality (representing, in theory at least, its residents) and the same nonresident landowner. In these circumstances, it is not difficult to view a zoning contest merely as a conflict between "property rights" and "human rights" and thereby to help justify consciously or unconsciously a decision against the landowner. In most instances, however, such a view is not appropriate to the interests that are actually involved. In fact, in the aggregate, the number of people who do not appear and the extent to which they are affected may often surpass in both categories the ones who do.

An obvious illustration of this is any request to rezone land for an apartment or townhouse project. In such cases, the potential occupants of the proposed development may have as much at stake in the outcome as the local homeowners who are represented in the proceedings. Thus, the equities, purely in terms of "human rights" are much more equal, often even favoring the would-be renters. It is not difficult to further pursue this argument to include other occupants of housing accommodations in the region who would benefit from the filtering process and the added competition in housing. One newspaper writer has termed a housing controversy as an up-to-date version of the classic Western feud between the ranchers (represented by local property owners) and the homesteaders (represented by the developer).[17]

Thus, although zoning cases involving housing are in essence a conflict between existing residents and nonresidents, there is little opportunity within the zoning process for an appropriate weighing of the issues.

Public participation makes it most difficult to obtain a detached analysis and evaluation of the issues. In the hearings, the input from the public may run the gamut from professional analysis to hysterical outbursts with considerable doubt as to which is more effective. Questions involving municipal finances, law, and economics are much too complex for most laymen, yet their conclusions in these matters may be most critical in deciding the controversy. However, for local legislators concerned about the approval of their constituency, the most important factors probably are the amount and composition of objections to the petition. Thus a study of the Philadelphia Zoning Board of Adjustment in 1955 showed that the single most important variable in determining a petitioner's success was the presence of objectors.[18] In the forty-six cases where protesters appeared, only eleven variances were granted. A study of a seventeen-month period of work by the Lexington-Fayette County Zoning Board of Adjustment (Kentucky) in 1960–61 shows that 63 percent of petitions were granted in the presence of objectors while 85 percent were granted in their absence.[19]

The property owner who is denied relief by the municipality can seek redress in the courts. However, as I have suggested before, there are limitations in obtaining relief in the courts. In some states, the municipality is rarely overruled; but regardless of the law of the state, zoning has allowed the municipalities, as a practical matter, to be usually the final arbiter as to what can be built (and often who can live) within their borders. The reasons for this are that, on the whole, plaintiffs are not very plentiful and the courts are not very receptive to them. Any potential plaintiff must have considerable funds and time and be prepared for a long struggle with a municipality that may, in good or bad conscience, carry the case to the highest appellate level. Even when the facts are favorable, the larger or most affluent developer may not find such litigation a reasonable business risk.

Implementation

The substantial advantage thus accorded the zoning edicts of local government carries over into the enforcement process. It is sometimes too costly to challenge an official decision in matters of small consequence even before the zoning board. One's future relations with the municipality might suffer. Generally, zoning officials, in keeping with recognized bureaucratic standards, will tend to take the safest position, that is one clearly consistent with the terms of the ordinance, or the prevailing political climate. Although it is difficult to determine how rigorously zoning is enforced, there are examples suggesting that enforcement in the larger cities may frequently be correlated to the wishes of the inhabitants of the area concerned. On the other hand, smaller cities are frequently unable to employ personnel capable of administering and enforcing a technical legal document, so as a result, zoning procedures may be on a more or less informal basis. Enforcement in the more affluent suburbs seems to be much more strict, sometimes even to the extent of disregarding the wishes of the immediate area and adjoining owners. There is the case of the dentist who wanted to use his home for both an office and residence, which was agreeable to his neighbors but not to the suburban municipality, which successfully prevented his doing so, and whose wishes prevailed in the courts.[20]

Because of problems with enforcement in Chicago, the state of Illinois adopted legislation in 1969 authorizing an owner or tenant of property who is within five hundred feet of an alleged violation and who is "substantially affected" by it to bring an action for compliance, and if successful, to recover his attorney's fees.[21] Other states have statutes permitting neighboring owners to sue a violator to compel compliance with the zoning ordinance. However, to be entitled to bring such an action, the plaintiff must usually show damage to himself, different from that generally suffered by property owners.[22]

Zoning provisions that give most discretion to enforcement officials are, of course, also the ones that would most likely precipitate the most problems. Performance standards for determining eligibility for location within industrial districts provide a relevant example. The following excerpt from the Dallas zoning ordinance should explain to the reader the enormity of the problems involved in interpreting performance standards:

"(a) Emissions of odorous matter from a source of operation in the I-1, I-2 and PD districts shall not exceed the odor threshold at or beyond the bounding property line of the tract on which such use or operation is located." Sec. 10-432. "(a) Emission of odorous matter from a source of operation in the I-3 district shall not exceed a concentration at the bounding property line or any point beyond which when diluted with an equal volume or any point beyond which when diluted with an equal volume of odor-free air exceeds the odor threshold (two odor units)." Id., sec. 10-433. "Odor threshold—the concentration of odorous matter in the atmosphere necessary to be perceptible to the olfactory nerve of normal persons." Id., sec. 10-501 (16). "The odor threshold as herein referred to shall be determined by observation by a person or persons. In any case where the operator of an odor-emitting use may disagree with the enforcing officer where specific measurement of odor concentration is required, the method and procedures specified by American Society for Testing Material ASTMD 1391–57, entitled 'Standard Method for measuring odors in atmosphere' shall be used. . . ." Id., sec. 10-434.

Some Summary Conclusions

The experience of the city of Chicago with respect to its business zoning classifications provides a useful summary of the zoning process. The last comprehensive amendment to the zoning ordinance adopted in 1957 evolved at a period that I consider the high point of land use planning, when many seriously accepted the notion that land uses could be successfully planned and controlled on a relatively minute and rigid basis. This kind of enthusiasm has worn off considerably but not entirely. It is still accepted by some planners with whom I have spoken. Basically, the procedure of enumerating and separating remains in form the same. Zoning ordinances continue to separate business uses into distinct categories for various and sundry reasons. Given the high degree of subjectivity involved, however, it is doubtful if any two ordinances in the major cities are much alike.

The planners' task is indeed enormous! The objectives of (1) separating the permitted and special uses for each business district (there are over one hundred businesses listed in the Chicago ordinance), (2) determining the sizes of the areas to be included within the various districts and their locations, and at the same time (3) protecting property values within and without the districts seem nothing short of monumental. In Chicago, for example, under the amended ordinance adopted in 1957, there are seven business districts, B-1 to B-7, consisting of "local retail," "restricted retail," "general retail," "restricted service," "general service," "restricted central business," and "general central business" districts. In addition, there are four commercial districts, C-1 to C-4, which allow uses somewhere between business and industrial uses. Permitted in the B-1 district (local retail) are, among other things, barber shops, beauty parlors, clothes pressing establishments, colleges and universities (but not business college and trade schools), drugstores, grocery stores, bakeries, delicatessens, shoe and hat repair stores, and variety stores. Prohibited in B-1 but permitted in B-2 (restricted retail) are art and school supply stores, art galleries, books and stationery stores, candy and ice cream stores, gift shops, hardware stores, and shoe stores, and about fifty other uses. According to the text of the ordinance, the latter are forbidden in B-1 because it is "designed solely for the convenience shopping of persons residing in the adjacent residential areas to permit only such uses as are necessary to satisfy those limited basic shopping needs which occur daily or frequently and so require shopping facilities in close proximity to places of residence." For the same reason, the size of businesses are kept in B-1 to a maximum floor area of 6,250 square feet.

On its face, it appears doubtful whether the uses have been separated to accomplish the stated purpose; delicatessens, bakeries, drugstores, barber shops, and beauty shops may very well cater to customers who do not live within walking distance, especially if they contain 6,000 square feet of area, and may bring a substantial influx of traffic. They may well have to, for many B-1 districts adjoin low-density, single-family areas. In any event, whatever visions the planners had for B-1 of serene, quiet shopping areas intended primarily for "Ma and Pa" stores were probably shattered with the arrival in Chicago in the early 1960s of the "minisupermarkets," such as Convenient, Open Pantry, and 7–11 stores. These require less than 3,000 square feet of space and depend almost entirely upon automobile traffic from the hours of 7:00 or 9:00 A.M. to about 11:00 or 12:00 P.M. As grocery stores, they are permitted uses in B-1. If there ever was any meaningful difference between B-1 and some other districts, it was erased by the continual traffic generated by these stores.

Assuming even that there is some basis for the difference between the districts, the next problem for the planners is where to put the various districts, how close to the other business districts, and how much area each district should encompass at any particular location—all matters involving an evaluation of demand for goods and services in countless locations (227 square miles in the case of Chicago). Probably equally important in the adoption of a proposed ordinance or comprehensive amendment thereto are the pressures that will be exerted by the owners, the neighbors, competing business interests, and even trade associations. Thus, the relative infrequency of B-1 zoning in Chicago is probably due less to the prudence of the planners than the persuasiveness of property owners who successfully defended their economic interests. However, at the insistence of owners of many small grocery stores and delicatessens, B-1 uses were the only business uses permitted to remain in residential districts after passage of the comprehensive amendment despite earlier drafts thereof which required their gradual elimination as nonconforming uses over a period of years.

The "mistakes" of zoning should not be surprising. The zoning process is limited in its effect on business since ordinarily it can only decree what business cannot do, not what business will do. That zoning allows a business to locate in a certain area is meaningless if economic conditions dictate against it. What the regulations set forth for a particular district is one thing; what actually occurs may be considerably different. Further complicating the problem is the continual change with the passage of time in business methods and consumer preferences. Even if they were appropriate when made, studies on which planning decisions are based will be less applicable and finally irrelevant in future years although the zoning provisions will still be in force.

Although rezoning is available to rectify errors, it does not appear to be a satisfactory remedy. A change in zoning may appear unfair to an adjoining owner who relied on the zoning when acquiring his property. He then would have more reason to object than his counterpart in Houston who purchased next to unrestricted land. Further, changes in zoning do not always come about easily. Consider the owner of land zoned B-3 who wants to erect something that is authorized in B-4. Although the distinctions between the uses permitted in the two districts by the regulations may be perceptible only to their authors, the owner will still have to obtain a rezoning, and this will probably involve submitting the full details of what he proposes to the local legislature through a public hearing. He is not likely to obtain relief unless the councilmen—and, if there is opposition, often their constituents—approve of what he wants to do. The opportunity offered for graft (without sleepless nights) is apparent. He may also have to buy off any opposition that has developed, which is legal unless the payees are the city fathers. If his request is still denied his only recourse will be to the courts, a costly and often lengthy procedure, and one not suited for the less affluent. But this has not deterred the more affluent, such as the major oil companies who have obtained many of their gas stations in Illinois and other states by decree of court. In fact, suits to permit gas stations may hold the record for zoning litigation in any single category.[23]

Chicago, of course, should not be considered as an isolated example of what can occur in the differentiation of land uses. Nor is its ordinance considered a "bad" one; on the contrary, I have found that many planners consider it among the better and more "advanced" ordinances. When first adopted, it received praise for its new and different approaches to many zoning problems.[24]

Thus, it seems land and property is being regulated almost merely for the sake of regulation under an apparent assumption that no matter how unreasonable, inequitable, and irrational the process, its absence would only make things worse. The following chapter will be devoted to a discussion of what occurs when there is no zoning ordinance, and the reader should then be able to make some judgment as to this alternative.

2

Nonzoning: Economics and Consumers

What has transpired in land use and development when zoning controls have not been imposed on a municipality? How does the real estate market operate in the absence of zoning? These are the questions that led to my study of the land use experience of Houston, Texas, the only major city in the country that has never adopted zoning. I also studied other nonzoned cities of Texas and they generally confirm the land use experience of Houston. In a general sense, what happens in the real estate market in Houston is not unique to it. Everywhere, developers and builders have to follow rules and standards of the market place to maximize their profits. Supply is produced and demand is satisfied in certain and similar ways in real estate, whether the location is Houston, New York, or Chicago. Governmental rules can substantially influence but can never cancel the law of supply and demand. Consequently, Houston discloses what presently occurs in the nonzoned areas and what is likely to occur in zoned areas if zoning were to be removed.

I conducted this study as a research fellow in law and economics at the University of Chicago Law School. It began in April of 1968. The results of that period of study conducted under my research fellowship were published as an article in the April 1970 issue of the *Journal of Law and Economics*. The balance of this chapter is largely an updated version of that article.

Houston

To understand its system of nonzoning, some background knowledge of Houston is desirable. Houston is today the nation's sixth largest city in population and the third or fourth largest in land area.[1] It has grown from a population of 385,000 and an area of 73 square miles in 1940 to a population, as of January 1, 1972, of over 1.3 million and an area of about 450 square miles. Measured in total tonnage shipped and received, it is the nation's third largest port. From 1960 to 1970, inclusive, it has annually ranked either as the third or fourth city in dollar volume of total construction. It is a leading manufacturing center of the Southwest.

Houston has big-city skyscrapers, "sprawling" single-family subdivisions and garden apartments similar to those found in suburbs, and rural areas—if the existence of farm buildings and grazing of cattle within city limits is any criterion. Within the borders of the city are nine small separately incorporated and zoned "bedroom" municipalities not subject to its jurisdiction, the largest of which contains over 3.6 square miles. Few doubt that Houston's population and area will continue to grow. There is much unincorporated land surrounding the city which can be annexed. The city presently exercises extraterritorial rights within five miles of its corporate limits, or over about 2,000 square miles of unincorporated land adjoining its borders. Within this territory, there may be neither incorporations of new municipalities (except under special circumstances) nor annexations of land by any other cities or villages without the approval of Houston. All of this land is also subject to Houston's subdivision regulations. The city may already be big enough to qualify as a "region," as envisioned by the proponents of regional planning, although, ironically, planning in this instance, would exclude zoning.

Although Houston has never adopted a zoning ordinance, it does have subdivision controls, a minimum housing ordinance, a building code, and traffic ordinances. The subdivision regulations contain controls over land development, controls similar to those considered generally common elsewhere in the country. These controls were first adopted in 1940, and over three-quarters of the built-up area, estimates City Planning Director Roscoe H. Jones, were subject to them. The city has a building code typical of those in its region, and a housing ordinance establishing relatively minimal standards was adopted in 1969 as a result of a straw vote.

Notwithstanding the absence of zoning, Houston has had since 1940 a city planning department which otherwise functions in ways comparable to such departments in other large cities. It makes studies and recommendations for the location of streets, parks, public buildings, public utilities, waterways, examines plats of subdivision, and so on. Planning for the location of streets and other thoroughfares began at a time when the ownership of the automobile had become common, and most of the city is accessible to other parts by way of major streets and expressways. Traffic appears to be exceedingly well regulated and engineered. Houston does not have a rapid transit system, and the bus system does not provide regular service for many sections. Any potential developer has to take into consideration the proximity of his property to an entrance or exit on an expressway, for these are the sole means for travelling considerable distances in a "reasonable" time. Accordingly, it is most difficult to compare the physical composition and appearance of Houston, which has tended to grow horizontally, with the larger cities of the North in which vertical growth has been more important; the more appropriate comparisons are with cities that have similarly grown with the automobile.

In Harris County, in which Houston is located, the absence of zoning ordinance is not unique. The county itself does not have such an ordinance, and neither do at least eight of its municipalities in addition to Houston. These include such cities as Pasadena, with a population of about 100,000, and Baytown, with a population of about 45,000. However, more than a dozen cities and villages within and adjoining Houston are zoned.

Zoning Elections

Both Houston and Baytown are unusual in that their decisions not to adopt zoning were a result of public elections. Houston is apparently the only major city in the nation to have permitted its citizens to directly decide this matter. In fact, there have been two such votes, and on each occasion those voting rejected it. Prior to each vote, the city held extensive public hearings on the proposed zoning ordinance. In each instance, the ordinance would have in effect frozen the most predominant uses of property existing at the time it was drafted.

In 1948, only property owners were allowed to vote, and the result was 14,142 to 6,555. In 1962, when there was no such restriction on voting, the vote was 70,957 to 54,279; approximately 48.5 percent of those qualified voted.

The most recent expression of voter sentiment toward zoning in the Houston area occurred in Baytown on May 20, 1969, when a referendum was held on the adoption of a proposed comprehensive zoning ordinance. The voters rejected the ordinance by a margin of 2,977 to 1,345 with only a 30 percent turnout of eligible voters. Baytown lies about ten miles east of the city limits of Houston at the entrance of the ship channel leading to Houston, and is an industrialized city containing chemical, synthetic rubber, and petroleum refining industries. Residential properties are largely single-family with ownership distributed among almost all income categories; as of March 1968, single-family dwellings constituted over 90 percent of all residential units. An analysis of the vote shows that the only precinct voting in favor of zoning contained primarily middle-middle– and upper-middle–income single-family homes built within the last fifteen or twenty years. The strongest opposition in terms of percentages was found in the precinct containing largely black voters. The other nine precincts containing various mixtures of income levels also voted against.

Another Texas city that decided against zoning through the voting process is Wichita Falls. It has a population of about 100,000, and is located about 400 miles northwest of Houston. More than 75 percent of the housing there consists of single-family dwellings encompassing income categories from highest to lowest.

The question of zoning was submitted in Wichita Falls to popular vote on four occasions. The zoning ordinance enacted by the city council in February 1948 was voted out about a year later by a close margin of 2,570 to 2,555. In 1958, the voters rejected zoning by a vote of 1,225 to 880, but approved it in 1961, 5,067 to 3,487. In neither of the latter elections was a proposed zoning ordinance prepared prior to the election. However, when such an ordinance was drafted pursuant to the vote in 1961, it was defeated in 1963, 4,144 to 858.

A proposed zoning ordinance was defeated by a 70 percent margin in Beaumont, Texas, in 1948, 3,389 to 1,279; however, the council subsequently adopted zoning in 1956.

While there may have been local or philosophical issues involved, in

(Houston, Baytown, and apparently elsewhere, the predominant pattern of voting shows that higher-income precincts (middle-middle to upper, inclusive) in the newer areas of the city generally supported zoning and that the lesser-income precincts (lower and lower-middle) in the older areas generally opposed it.) In general, restricted areas wanted zoning, whereas unrestricted areas rejected it. The more affluent voters turned out in greater numbers to vote, with the strongest support coming from middle–middle– to upper-middle–income homeowners in areas having the newest homes. Yet even in these precincts almost one-third of the voters rejected zoning. Table 2–1 is a detailed analysis of the 1962 straw vote. It shows an exceedingly high correlation between the voter's record in the straw vote and the voter's economic status as indicated by median value of home owned or average monthly rental.

There is much reason to believe that the less affluent homeowners oppose zoning because they are disinterested in or reject strict homogeneous single-family living. They may reject zoning because of a belief that it is exclusionary towards them. It may be also that they do not have the same aesthetic standards as their wealthier counterparts. The risks in terms of values may be as different for each group as perhaps are their tastes. They may want the right to use or sell their property for commercial or apartment purposes and perhaps do not believe that the elimination of such opportunity will enhance their property values.

Differing life styles make for differences in aesthetics and values. The existence of so-called "incompatible" uses may well increase rather than decrease the viability of a lesser-income area. The elimination of small commercial enterprises within the subdivision, such as groceries and even auto repair shops, can both inconvenience the family with one or no car and seriously reduce the desirability of that area for most of its residents. Such commercial uses, therefore, may be neither incompatible nor undersirable in these circumstances. Their elimination may frequently be more harmful than helpful.

Houston's Land Use Controls

Although Houston has no zoning ordinance, it has adopted some controls over land uses that are ordinarily found in zoning ordinances. These are extremely modest when compared to what is contained in most zoning ordinances. Houston has few regulations that set forth specific restrictions on the uses that may be established on any property, the essential ingredient of zoning authority. Unless it is subject to an enforceable restrictive covenant limiting its use to single-family dwellings, there are relatively few legal limitations on the use of any given tract, whether it be for a mansion or for a heavy industrial factory, or for most other purposes.

The Rules for Land Subdivision adopted by the Houston City Planning Commission, which must approve all the land subdivisions within Houston and the contiguous unincorporated areas lying inside its extraterritorial limits, contain some controls which generally appear in zoning ordinances. These regulations apply only to those subdivision plats submitted for approval and have had no effect upon existing uses or existing subdivisions. A subdivision plat is required for all single-family construction and may be required for an apartment or a commercial or industrial development, depending upon its proximity to a public street and whether a thoroughfare for public use is involved.

For those properties affected within the city, building permits will not be issued unless the lots are part of a subdivision or resubdivision approved by the commission. With respect to properties located in the unincorporated areas outside of Houston, but within its planning jurisdiction, the Texas statutes require approval by a City Planning Commission as a condition for the recording of lots. Subdivisions outside of the city must also be approved by the County Flood Control District. Questions of flood control are considered by the City Planning Commission when it approves plats for properties in the city.

The following is a brief summary of most land use control regulations presently in effect:

1. Regulations (adopted in 1963) resembling zoning provisions apply to subdivisions for individually owned (*not* rental) townhouses. They provide for, among other things, minimum lot areas of 2,500 square feet per unit, a minimum building setback line of 20 feet, and various minimum dimensions for open courts and inside streets. They also require screening in specified instances. These standards are not quite as liberal as those allowed by some zoning ordinances (such as Chicago's) for similar structures, but are more consistent with those in zoned cities of the Southwest.

2. Trailers are also now subject to some location and density restrictions. The city council in early 1972 adopted an ordinance entitled "Mobile Home Code," similar for the most part to the "Recommended Ordinance Governing Mobile Home Communities" prepared by various federal agencies in cooperation with the Mobile Home Manufacturers' Association. The code provides density controls and forbids location of mobile home parks in two fire zones covering portions of the central business district and some adjoining areas. Individual mobile homes will no longer be allowed to locate outside a mobile home park or mobile home subdivision except by temporary permit issued by city officials. The code also establishes license requirements and fees, utilities and maintenance standards, resident "responsibilities," and fire protection rules. A mobile home park must consist of a minimum of two acres and not less than ten sites, and the minimum for a mobile home subdivision is four acres and twenty lots.

3. Abattoirs and slaughterhouses are prohibited by another city ordinance from locating within 3,000 feet of a church, public park, school, hospital, college or university or any dwelling resided in by anyone other than the abattoir or slaughterhouse owner or employees. Rendering plants are excluded from areas within 600 feet of the same structures (and also of "established eating places"). Convalescent homes are not permitted within 300 feet of a school, church, or public playground. The location of kennels and farm and other

Table 2-1
Houston Straw Vote, 1962: Voter Socioeconomic Characteristics

Area[a]	Voting Record[b]					Socioeconomic Description[c]				
	Percentage Voting Against Zoning	Straw Vote Percentage Voting	Gubernatorial Election			Area Race by Percentage[d]	Approx. No. Owners[e]	Median Value[f]	Approx. No Renters[e]	Ave. monthly rental[g]
			Dem.	Rep.	Percentage Voting					
Group I — Areas casting more than 72% of vote against zoning										
Lindale, Melrose	84.3%	43.1%	56.6%	42.3%	52.1%	10% black	2/3	$ 7200–9700	1/3	$ 52–55
Little York	82.7	49.3	53.3	45.9	57.1	white	5/6	8200–10600	1/6	$ 61–62
Magnolia Park	79.8	30.7	68.3	30.9	45.7	white	4/9	6700–6900	5/9	$ 44–47
Heights	76.5	42.3	52.1	47.2	53.4	10% black	1/2	7500–9000	1/2	$ 47–60
Negro	72.3	28.3	95.3	4.4	53.5	black (10% white)	1/3	6600–12000	2/3	$ 42–80
Group II — Areas voting between 45–62% against zoning										
Park Place Pecan Place	62.0	51.9	45.4	54.1	63.6	white	2/3	12,300	1/3	$ 75
Mason Park Kensington	61.5	51.2	42.5	56.9	61.7	white	3/5	7,800–9,900	2/5	$ 55–68
Garden Oaks Oak Forest	58.7	55.7	36.6	62.7	65.7	10% black	6/7	11,300–12,300	1/7	$ 62–86
Freeway Manor	56.2	47.0	43.8	55.6	60.9	white	almost all	11,300–12,900	few	$ 63–95
Golfcrest South Park	49.3	54.9	44.2	55.3	63.4	10% black	6/7	9,900–13,000	1/7	$ 79–107
Southland Hermann Park	46.7	50.7	41.4	57.9	59.8	white	1/2	9300–16,500	1/2–	94–129
Group III — Areas voting between 31–42% against zoning										
Westheimer Post Oaks	41.9	63.3	22.9	76.7	73.0	10% black	5/7	$13,800–25,000+	2/7	$ 78–132
River Oaks Tanglewood	41.1	60.5	20.0	79.9	70.6	white	2/3	25,000+	1/3	107–132
Memorial Spring Branch	39.3	59.8	25.0	74.6	71.0	white	almost all	11,700–25,000+	few	85–171
Westbury	35.0	64.5	30.9	68.8	73.1	white	almost all	18,300–22,600	few	115–134
Sharpstown	31.7	65.3	25.4	74.3	72.1	white	almost all	15,600–16,600	few	123–124

*a*These are the area designations given by the *Houston Post* in its report of the election of November 6, 1962. The Negro area is scattered among numerous voting precincts on the east side of Houston. Concentrations occur just east of the CBD and in both northeast and southeast quarters.

*b*Voting results of the zoning straw vote and the gubernatorial race are also from the *Houston Post* of November 7 1962. The percentage of eligible voters voting, also as presented in the *Houston Post*, November 7, 1962, are found in the columns headed "Percentage Voting." In this election, the Democratic candidate for governor was Connally, the Republican, Cox. Carswell, who also ran, generally received less than one percent of the votes cast in each of the above-designated areas, accounting for the Democratic and Republican vote totalling just under 100%.

*c*The data under Socioeconomic Description has been taken direct or derived from the 1960 U.S. Census Tract Profiles. For this table, the census tracts used were those falling completely or predominantly (approximately 2/3 or more) within a designated voting area. Since the census tracts and voting area boundaries seldom coincided, there are some portions of voting areas unaccounted for; likewise, the census data may include some persons outside the voting area. Consequently, the data presented in this caetory are approximations and not precise.

*d*Race. One area was designated "Negro" by the *Houston Post*, although the precincts included within it ranged from a few in which whites were almost evenly matched with blacks to most which were almost exclusively black. The total "Negro area," as selectively sampled by the *Post* includes approximately 10% whites. In this table, the term "white" is used for purposes of simplification to characterize those areas in which 98% or more of the residents are caucasoid. There were some areas with approximately 9:1 white to black ratio and these are shown as "10% black" in this table.

*e*Owner v. Renter. The breakdown between homeowners and renters is deliberately broad, again reflecting the limitations of the data as described above. The fractions indicate rough approximations so that a 2/3 may perhaps range from 64 to 68% and 1/3 from 36 to 32%. In those instances where "almost all" is noted, the incidence of ownership was in the 90% range in those census tracts included.

*f*Median Values is the census tract term used to identify the value of owner-occupied housing units for each census tract area. Where more than one value is shown, more than one (often several) separate census tract areas are represented. Only the high and low medians are indicated in this table. In the case of the black area, the high median ($12,000) is quite unrepresentative. The homeownership in the single census tract area in which this value was found was only about 10% of that area and fell to a negligible 1% of the entire black area homeowners. The next highest median value was $9,000, which also showed low frequency in terms of population representation. The high concentration of median values for this area was within the $7,000–8,000 range. The large spread manifest in the median values recorded for Westheimer-Post Oaks area reflects two distinct socioeconomic groupings: About two thirds of the sample from this area are white (98% or more) and own homes valued upwards of $25,000 (median value). The remaining third live in a census tract area in which more than one-fifth of the population is black and the median home values are $13,800.

*g*Average Monthly Rentals are again based on census tract area figures with a range indicating high and low rentals for the designated voting area. They are subject to the same kinds of error as are median home values. In the case of the Negro area, the $80 rental figure is skewed. Only one census tract shows so high a figure (far above the next highest), and the number of renters represented is less than one-tenth of that tract's population and accounts for less than 1% of the total number of renters for this area. All other monthly rental averages fall within the $42–55 range. The wide range in Westheimer-Post Oaks rentals also reflects the phenomenon already discussed under median home values. One third of that area's population live in the "mixed" census tract and it shows an average rental of $78. This tract, however, is predominantly composed of homeowners.

animals is also controlled within 100 feet of a residence and certain institutions. There are location requirements—with respect to churches, schools, hospitals, and charities—for liquor dealers, amusement parks, and motion picture theaters. There are fencing requirements for auto wrecking yards and possible other uses.

4. Minimum lot sizes: 50 feet wide, 100 feet deep, 5,000 square feet of land area where the lot is served by a sanitary sewer line and 7,000 where it is not; greater width for some corner lots and greater depth for lots adjoining major thoroughfares than for those on inside streets.

5. Building lines: for single-family dwellings, 25 feet at the front, and also 10 feet on the side for corner lots; 35-foot building line when facing or 20 feet on the rear or side when backing or siding on major thoroughfares. For apartments, 20 feet in front, and also 10 feet on the side for corner lots. For all commercial and industrial property, 10 feet in front, and also 10 feet on the side of corner lots, but 25 feet in front when facing residential property.

6. The city has adopted an off-street parking ordinance requiring one and a fraction or more off-street parking spaces of specified dimensions for each dwelling unit constructed or altered, depending upon the number of bedrooms in the unit. There are no parking requirements for commercial and industrial uses.

7. In an effort to regulate the location of subsidized multifamily housing projects provided for under Section 236 of the National Housing Act, the city council in March of 1971, adopted a resolution ratifying the appointment of a four-member Neighborhood Analysis Committee to review and report on all applications for 236-projects, on the basis of a wide variety of land use criteria. Unlike prior housing subsidy legislation, the 236-program does not give veto power over these projects to local government, and the committee was appointed as a result of public demands that arose when a number of 236-projects were erected on nonrestricted land adjoining single-family subdivisions. The committee's recommendations or those of the city council are not binding on land use and can be overruled by the Department of Housing and Urban Development. The department, however, consistent with its policy of not forcing 236-projects on local governments, has agreed with the mayor to consider these recommendations before issuing commitments. City officials believe that this understanding gives local control over 236-projects. At least a dozen 236-projects had been commenced in the city since the adoption of the ordinance and prior to the end of 1971. (My impression is that organizations promoting subsidized housing and development in the city were not displeased and probably favored the adoption of the ordinance. As of the beginning of 1972, at least, they apparently did not believe it had handicapped their endeavors. There were no significant controversies concerning 236-projects during this period.)

8. The city has nuisance ordinances, and, of course, all use and development activity is subject to the common law of nuisance. Suits may be filed by private individuals or by the city to enforce nuisance laws. Many activities which would be precluded by zoning can also be precluded or terminated through use of the nuisance laws.

9. Measured in time and money, the main efforts of the city in land use control are directed toward enforcing the countless restrictive covenants covering the bulk of single-family dwellings within the city—covenants privately drafted

for the most part without any desire or belief that the city would ever have any role in their enforcement. This effort began in 1965 when the Texas legislature, by a statute intended solely for application in Harris County, allowed the city to participate in the enforcement of residential restrictive covenants to about the same extent as if it were the owner of property subject to them. Thus, Houston was given authority to sue to enjoin or abate the violation of a restriction effecting a subdivision within the city. In another statute, applicable only to Houston, it was also authorized to withhold certain city permits when the use for which the permit was sought would violate covenants restricting the property to single-family use. The city council has adopted ordinances pursuant to these statutes, and maintains a program of enforcement.

In a memorandum to the mayor submitted to the Department of Housing and Urban Development as part of its application for model city funds, the city attorney stated that between September 1, 1965, and December 6, 1968, about 2,300 violations were abated through action of his department and 38 lawsuits were filed. He further stated that some "affirmative action" was taken in approximately 250 subdivisions. During the next three years only 38 more suits were filed. It seems to be the practice of most subdivisions to enlist the aid of the city, even those with resources readily available for this task, and it should not, therefore, be inferred that the city's aid was essential in each instance to combat a breach of a covenant.

Although no detailed analysis is available of the violations abated, most seem to have concerned a use contrary to the covenants, but apparently many involved breaches of aesthetic and construction restrictions. The majority of *use* violations complained of apparently involve home occupations. Any uses requiring financing are rarely a problem because the mortgage company or other lender will not make funds available where the proposed use may possibly be enjoined.

Some perspective for these figures is presented by the experience of Chicago with respect to violations of zoning restrictions. Chicago's population is about 3.4 million, or almost 2.6 times the population of Houston, and, of course, all property, not just single-family subdivisions, are subject to zoning enforcement. (According to the 1970 census, both cities have almost the same number of single-family dwellings.) The following statistics are for the year 1971 for Chicago:

total complaints received for zoning violations	5,187
notices mailed	4,920
lawsuits filed to compel compliance	481

A more precise indication of the city's role in the maintenance of the covenants is furnished by Pasadena, Texas, which has been enforcing restrictive covenants under an ordinance adopted in March 1968. Unlike Houston, Pasadena requires a written complaint, and from March 1968 to November 1, 1969, only nine complaints had been filed, of which only one alleged a use that was not in violation of the covenants. The volume of complaints apparently did not increase for the subsequent period terminating in January 1972 although precise figures were not available to me. Pasadena has about 22,000 single-family dwellings, largely middle-income, the vast majority of which are still subject to restrictive covenants. It was and still is a rapidly growing city, having increased by 40,000 in population since 1960, when it had less than 60,000 inhabitants. Most of the units built in the city within recent years have been apartments, suggesting that there is a demand for such use in single-family areas. Four of the complaints (for the period from March 1968 to November 1969) involved alleged use violations: the use of a house for an antique shop on a high traffic street; the use of a house for a drive-in grocery on the same street; a continuous garage sale in a house on an interior street; and parking a trailer on a lot on another interior street. Two of these instances were in areas of the subdivision where the covenants were probably no longer enforceable. The other four complaints involved a fence erected in violation of the building line; the erection of a storage shed; questionable architectural design of a portion of the house; and continual parking of a trailer in a driveway. An attorney for the city told the writer that many of the complaints were prompted by disputes between neighbors. But, of course, some would-be complainants may be deterred by "neighborliness." The experience of Pasadena may perhaps be more revealing than that of Houston because the data is more precise. If so, it suggests that the ordinances in question may not be of great consequence to the maintenance of the covenants.

There have been serious doubts as to whether a statute authorizing the city to enforce privately established restrictions is valid under the Texas constitution.[2] Without going into the merits of this controversy, it is apparent that at least for the time being the city is engaged in "policing" the existing single-family areas as long as the covenants are enforceable in much the same way for use violations as it might were these areas zoned for such use. It is also enforcing aesthetic and construction requirements that frequently will not be of concern in zoning enforcement.

Restrictive covenants governing the use of land in a subdivision can generally be enforced by any owner in that subdivision whose property is subject to such restrictions. The existence of almost countless "unviolated" single-family subdivisions created many years prior to 1965 attests to the fact that the city's aid is not essential to such maintenance, and that if the Texas courts held the enabling legislation unconstitutional, most subdivisions would be affected only by an increase in their enforcement costs. There are also many neighborhoods where the covenants have expired but the uses still remain homogeneous or largely so owing to the absence of any economic pressures for diverse uses. The covenants have probably expired (or never existed) in the poorest areas (which are also the oldest) so that the groups occupying such areas are likewise not affected by the city's policies.

The effect and significance of the city's enforcement policies vary from subdivision to subdivision and may be summarized as follows:

1. The more affluent subdivisions have the means to compel compliance. While now relying on the city for aid, they can take care of themselves if necessary.
2. The same is probably true of the less affluent subdivisions, provided they have maintained their residential character and still have a viable property owners' organization. This is especially true for the larger subdivisions that can raise substantial sums from dues collections.
3. It is the less affluent areas that lack these characteristics and the small sub-divisions of, say thirty to forty homes or less, that will be most affected by the city's program. This would be especially important if the covenants have become legally vulnerable, inasmuch as this fact might not deter the city as much as it would a privately financed group. However, the less affluent subdivisions are more likely to be in areas where there are minimal pressures for diverse uses, and as a result the absence of enforcement (or even of the covenants) may not be very important.

Restrictive Covenants

Officials in Houston estimate that there are from seven thousand to eight thousand (perhaps as many as ten thousand) individual subdivisions and separate sections of subdivisions which may be subject to restrictive cove-nants of varying kinds. There is general agreement that at one time or another the vast majority were probably subject to restrictive covenants and that most of these covenants are still in force. The size, form, and content of documents establishing the individual covenants differ with the developer and/or his lawyer and the time of execution. They vary from one hand-written page at the turn of the century to the dozen or more carefully and minutely detailed pages of more recent days. Apparently a number of the earlier restrictive covenants were poorly drafted or otherwise technically insufficient, with the result that they could not be enforced.

Even the valid ones may become unenforceable unless they are diligently enforced. Each case stands on its own facts. As a general legal proposition, failure to take action against a single breach (unless it is of "major" conse-quence) in a particular area of the subdivision will not necessarily preclude abatement of other breaches in the same area, on the theory that despite the one violation, the balance of the area has a substantial economic interest in maintaining the covenants. If subsequent violations for such and other uses occur, it will become increasingly difficult and ultimately impossible to uphold the restrictions in the area. The courts could then hold that the area has changed and no longer has the character and environment envisioned when the restrictions were imposed. There is, thus, little or no property interest in the covenants left to be protected. Courts in some states apply this rule when there has been a substantial change in conditions in an adjoining area. Or they could rule that by failing to take action, the owners have waived or abandoned enforcement of the covenants.

Violations in one area of the subdivision may have little or no economic significance in other areas. Such reasoning would frequently enable restric-tions for homes on interior streets of the subdivision to remain enforceable even if those for homes along major thoroughfares become unenforceable. Because use restrictions are more likely to break down on the heavily travelled streets, where economic pressures are far greater, a separation of areas of the subdivision on the basis of economic interest can be of importance to the maintenance of homogeneous single-family use.

The terms of the covenants are determined by the developer and often his mortgage lender, and the covenants are recorded prior to the sale of any lots. If either FHA or VA approval is desired, its recommendations on covenants will have to be observed. The only other control over provisions of the covenants rests with the marketplace, whether they will be acceptable to potential purchasers. Once there has been a sale, the developer loses all power to make changes without the approval of each purchaser (unless otherwise provided, which is rare). Accordingly, unless there is a provision to the contrary, any change in the covenants requires the approval of all owners in the subdivision. Such consent might, of course, have to be purchased.

Frequently, covenants contain controls not normally found in zoning ordinances. Provisions governing architectural requirements, cost of construction, aesthetics, and maintenance of the lot and exterior of the house found in covenants are rarely found in zoning or other city ordinances and might be illegal if they were. Zoning does not, however, preclude property owners from imposing such restrictions if they desire. Nor does the adoption of a zoning ordinance nullify existing restrictive covenants. The FHA even recommends such covenants in zoned areas "as an important supplementary aid in maintaining neighborhood character and values."[3]

Almost all the covenants contain specific termination dates, and it is these provisions that could affect the future character and development of Houston. When restrictions expire, so do virtually all controls over land uses in these areas. As can be expected, the content of termination provisions varies from one subdivision to another. There are no statistics presently available as to the probable expiration dates of these covenants. Some of the older restrictions were drafted to run in perpetuity and some for the life of the grantor plus twenty-one years, to cite but two examples. However, it appears that the vast majority of restrictions recorded between 1950 and the present time, a period of enormous growth for Houston, contain the "automatic extension" provision. (The 1950 census showed 122,000 single-family homes; the number increased to 288,000 in 1970.) The covenants are to run with the land for a specified period of time, typically twenty-five to thirty years, and are renewed automatically at ten-year intervals *ad infinitum,* unless 51 percent of the owners of lots (or frontage) decide to cancel or amend them prior to the end of the original or any subsequent ten-year period. One reason this provision is so commonly used is that the FHA and VA require it for all subdivisions they accept. It would seem, therefore, that fears that the bulk of covenants will expire within the near future are unfounded. The provision in question limits the subdivisions covered to single-family usage for substantial periods of time to come, provided only that this remains the desire of a majority of the owners in the subdivision.

Because enforcement of deed restrictions has become part of home-ownership in Houston, many subdivisions have organized a civic club to act in their behalf (and sometimes for those in adjoining subdivisions) in this and other matters. The city planning director estimated that there are about from 150 to 200 civic clubs. Some of these organizations were created in the same document imposing the restrictions, and they were often given power to make assessments on individual lots for common purposes. Members of these organizations pay fees or dues that may be used for enforcement costs and for such other matters as maintenance and operation of common areas, recreational facilities, vacant lots, insect control, and even the hiring of policemen. Organizations of homeowners also exist, and some undertake similar activities in zoned areas.

The imposition of restrictive covenants is not confined in Houston to residential property. Developers of industrial parks in the area have also established restrictions resembling in style and amount of detailed control the current residential covenants. As in zoned areas, a townhouse development for individual ownership is always subjected to very detailed restrictions. Since space in shopping centers is leased, the lease agreement ordinarily serves to control uses within the center.

Thus, to summarize in part, homeowners in an area subject to restrictive covenants who so desire can ordinarily relieve the area of such controls prior to their expiration in three ways: (1) by permitting breaches of the covenants to be successful, making them in time unenforceable; (2) by having a majority agree against renewal or extension, where it is so provided, when the original or subsequent terms end; and (3) by unanimously agreeing at any time to rescind them. Failure to abate violations may often reflect the will of most owners in the area against continuance since the apportionment of attorney's fees and other costs can minimize individual costs. Under the city's program of enforcement, the city has largely preempted such opportunities to dispense with the covenants inasmuch as it will act upon a complaint of any one owner who by himself might be unwilling to carry the financial burden. Because of the city's policies, the covenants will probably remain in force through at least the original term unless there is unanimous agreement for prior termination. This latter possibility is not as unlikely as it may seem, since as has happened, an entire subdivision may be purchased by a developer. An example of this is presented in Chapter 5.

How does this compare with what can occur under zoning? Violations can also be abated by the city, either on its own initiative or upon request. However, that a majority seeks a change in zoning at any time after the subdivision has begun may or may not result in such a change being made. Legally, there must be a change in "conditions" warranting an amendment. Moreover, it may not occur if there is opposition by owners in adjoining areas, who might regard the change as adverse, and their opposition may require that the amendment be carried by a two-thirds (in Illinois) or three-quarters (in Texas) vote of the council. Because zoning decisions are legislative decisions, there can be no certainty that the will of a majority of owners will necessarily prevail. The purchase of an entire subdivision may also not come about as readily under zoning, if at all, as in its absence.

When the Covenants Expire

When covenants terminate in a single-family subdivision, changes to other uses occur in accordance with economic pressures. There are substantial areas along interior (or local) streets in Houston where, despite the absence of covenants for long periods, single-family remains almost the sole use. This is because there are no economic pressures for any other uses, or if there are, they are perhaps inadequate to overcome the owner's reluctance to offend some of his neighbors. In many other interior areas, a relatively small percentage is being used for multiple-family and commercial purposes. Where there is proximity to industry, some industrial uses may have also developed.

Interior streets (including that portion adjoining properties fronting on major thoroughfares) occupy close to 80 percent of the total lineal mileage of all of the thoroughfares within the city. Owners of businesses which require high accessibility and substantial traffic have no interest in locating on an interior street. Since most businesses require such conditions, relatively few wish to locate there, and prefer instead the more heavily travelled streets. Similarly, despite the apartment booms of the early and late 1960s (limited to "low rise" two- and three-story buildings in the Houston area), many areas of the city are still not attractive for apartment development, and these areas remain almost free of such use despite the absence of any covenants.

To determine what actually does occur in "interior" areas never or no longer restricted, surveys were made in December 1969, of three areas; the first is in and somewhat above the lower-income category, and largely immune from the apartment boom; the second is middle-income and subject to strong demand for multiple-family sites; and the third is of an income level between the other two, and the demand for multiple-family sites is likewise intermediate in intensity.[4]

The first area surveyed, "Denver Harbor" (one of the oldest sections of the city), is a rectangular section, three blocks wide on the north and south, and thirty blocks long on the east and west. It is bounded on the north by Wallisville Road, on the east by Harbor Street, on the south by Palestine, and on the west by Boyles. It is divided into two parts by Interstate Highway 10. Except for Wallisville and two frontage roads adjoining the expressway and one other street (Lyons), its streets are interior ones almost all of which are paved. The area is four to five miles from the downtown center and northeast thereof. There is one city park, an elementary school, and five

churches. Adjoining the survey area on the north and at its southwest corner
are heavy industrial areas. Homes largely similar in character adjoin the
other three sides. Asking prices for homes (in 1969) ranged from about
$7,000 to $11,000 and an unknown number were rented. The homes are
largely of frame construction, some with partial brick exteriors. The area is
largely white and many inhabitants are of Mexican-American origin.

The area was first subdivided in 1911, and the balance in 1913. None
of it has ever been subject to restrictive covenants creating use or building
requirements. (There were, however, racial restrictions.) A sampling of
property tax records shows that houses in the survey area were built in each
decade beginning in 1930 and up to and through the 1960s. There are
probably also some which date back to earlier than even 1920.

This area has afforded maximum opportunities for the entry of non-
single-family uses, but actually relatively few have entered. On interior
streets, there were over 950 structures and about 13 percent of the land was
vacant. Approximately 7 percent of the structures contained home occupations and commercial uses, about one-third of which were either automobile
repair shops or grocery stores. Duplex and apartment uses constituted 5
percent and trailers about 2 percent. (This included trailers parked in a
sort of a trailer park which was on several residential lots.) Industrial uses
constituted about 1 percent, but they were of somewhat greater significance
in terms of area. Most of two separate, but not adjoining, blocks (out of
over eighty-five blocks) were being used for equipment storage and metal
fabricating. The existence of such industrial uses seems to reflect the proximity of heavy industry to the area. These uses may have been complementary to those in the industrial areas, or may have "split over" from such
areas. Interestingly enough, many homes had and still have fences, but these
are usually only about three feet high and of chain-link variety, which suggests that they were and are used principally for defining ownership rather
than for privacy or aesthetic reasons.

About 30 percent of the commercial and industrial uses were on Harbor
Street, which, until the construction of the expressway within the preceding
ten years, was apparently a relatively important traffic street in the area.
One of the two larger industrial uses referred to was on this street, and the
other was about one lot removed therefrom. The expressway divided the
street into two sections, and thus limited its accessibility. Both the proposed
1948 and 1962 zoning ordinances classified all property in the survey area
adjoining Harbor as commercial, which, along with the existence of these
commercial uses, suggests that at one time it may have had a greater traffic
count than the usual interior street. Most (if not almost all) of these commercial, as well as industrial, uses or their predecessors were developed
prior to the expressway.

In November 1969, the writer discussed with a real estate broker, two
homes for sale in an area of Denver Harbor, within one mile of the area
surveyed. There were several commercial uses nearby. One of the homes
was sold within sixty days after this conversation, at about the asking price,

Homes constructed in the late 1960s in the "Denver Harbor" section of Houston. The land on which these homes were built is part of a subdivision created before World War I. Lots in that subdivision were not subject to any restrictions controlling use and development. It has remained largely residential despite the absence of legal controls.

Figure 2–3.

according to the broker. The loan on it was guaranteed by the FHA. When I asked an FHA official over the telephone about this home and the area, he said that the area was "very stable," and in general there would be no difficulty obtaining an FHA commitment if the buyer were "qualified." However, I subsequently learned that houses next to or in the midst of certain commercial uses may not be acceptable to the FHA. The sampling of property tax records of eighty-eight homes revealed that at least five new homes were erected in about 1967 in the survey area of Denver Harbor. At least one was erected there in about 1968. (See Figs. 2–1, 2–2, and 2–3.)

These records also show many remodelings and additions to existing homes. Mr. Stauss, who surveyed the area, (footnote 4), states that there were a few instances of an owner totally destroying his old home and replacing it with a new one.

The second area surveyed lies in the Montrose area, which is clearly subject to the effects of the recent apartment boom. The survey area is also rectangular in shape, running from east to west; it is three blocks wide by fifteen blocks deep, bounded by Sul Ross on the north, the Southwest Freeway on the east, Colquitt on the south, and Woodhead on the west. It is about two miles southwest of the downtown center. Major thorough-fares, which contain strip commercial areas, are located one block to the north and one block to the south. One street (Montrose) and the frontage road adjoining the expressway are the only noninterior streets within the area. One elementary school and St. Thomas University are in the area. The population is white. Homes generally sell on the basis of land area (asking prices on the residential streets were then from $3.00 to $4.00 per square foot), and single lots contain about 6,250 or more square feet. Restrictive covenants for subdivisions covering most lots in the survey area expired in 1936, and those covering the balance (except perhaps for a twenty-five home subdivision) appear not to have been enforced for a long but unknown amount of time.

The area contained two apartment complexes, each on about the equivalent of a square block, and a portion of a shopping center on about one third of a block extending from the major thoroughfare to the north. Of the remaining approximately 450 separate structures on interior streets, about 4 percent contained commercial uses, and more than 25 percent were duplexes or multiple-family dwellings with three or more units. About 4 percent of the land was vacant. The balance remained single-family. There were no industrial or "heavy" commercial (such as auto repair) uses. The apartment buildings appeared to have no more than two stories. As of the date of the survey, six of the homes appeared to have been recently improved suggesting (surprisingly perhaps) some confidence in the future of the area for homes. There apparently was no problem obtaining a mortgage for houses from fifty to sixty years old that were in good condition. See Figs. 2–4, 2–5, 2–6, 2–7, and 2–8, showing new construction in the survey area in 1972.

A third area, Riverside, was surveyed in the belief that all the covenants there had expired. Information obtained subsequently, however, showed that about one-half was still restricted and that the restrictions on the balance had expired in 1950. The unrestricted area is bounded by South-more on the north, Velasco on the east, Dowling on the west, and Riverside and North MacGregor on the south. It is about three miles south of the downtown center. The area was about low-middle–income and was then populated by blacks; it was at one time a white area. Asking prices in the survey area and nearby unrestricted areas ranged from $9,000 to $19,000. MacGregor, Riverside, and Southmore were the only heavily travelled streets. About 5 percent of the approximately 240 structures on the interior

Figure 2–4.

Figure 2–5.

Figure 2–6.

Figure 2–7.

Garden apartments constructed in recent years in the "Montrose" section of Houston in the midst of older homes. Restrictive covenants covering most lots in the areas shown expired in the mid-1930s. The demand for apartments in the Montrose area is among the strongest in the city. A high degree of aesthetic compatability has developed between the old and the new without the compulsion of any legal authority.

Figure 2–8.

streets had home occupations or other commercial uses. There were no industrial or "heavy" commercial uses. About 20 percent of the land was used for duplexes or apartments, and about 2 percent was vacant.

In the 1962 straw vote on zoning, those precincts of Denver Harbor which encompassed the survey area (62 and 79) voted against zoning by a margin of 995 to 205. The precincts of Montrose, which contained this survey area (60 and 123), also voted against, but by a much smaller margin, 862 to 784. The precinct containing all the Riverside area surveyed (136) voted for zoning 456 to 248.

Houston contains so many subdivisions that it is difficult to be sure that the areas surveyed are representative. However, sufficient information seems available to allow for some conclusions with respect to those portions of a subdivision fronting on local streets. First, there is no reason to believe that the termination of restrictions will inevitably lead to large numbers of changes in uses. Second, substantial changes will only come about if there is strong demand for multiple-family sites in the area. Third, in the absence of such demand, changes to other uses will be relatively small in number and will probably be confined to the following categories: (1) businesses established in response to demand for goods and services within the area; (2) home occupations; (3) businesses complementary to or "spill over" from nearby commercial (including major thoroughfares) and industrial areas; (4) businesses which do not need high accessibility and traffic count; and (5) other types of living accommodations.

The effect upon values of the termination of restrictions within an entire subdivision may be summarized as follows:

1. Once unrestricted, homes on thoroughfares with relatively high traffic counts will be available for commercial or apartment use, and their values, depending upon location, should, at worst, remain about the same, and, at best, greatly appreciate. Some houses will be used "as is" or be converted for commercial purposes, while others, of course, will be demolished for the new uses.
2. Owners of homes on interior streets in areas where the demand for apartment sites is substantial will also generally profit, although possibly not to the same extent as owners of homes on the major thoroughfares, since the latter can also be sold for commercial purposes. Inasmuch as apartment land sells on a square-foot basis, the home owner with a large lot and "inexpensive" house will benefit the most. The owner of an "expensive" house on a small lot will have more difficulty profiting from the change unless it is usable as part of a larger development. The higher- and medium-priced homes appear likely, but not necessarily, to be in areas where there is a substantial demand for multiple-family sites, and the low-priced homes are in areas where such demand is minimal. One reason is that values tend to be greater in the predominately white areas of Houston than in the more mixed or black or Mexican-American sections; and the demand for apartment sites is much larger in the white areas in part because of greater availability of financing.
3. Thus, currently, the values of many homes on interior streets are supported by their potential as apartment sites, even assuming that values are injured

by entry of diverse uses. In the lower-cost areas with small or no demand for apartment sites, there is somewhat less certainty as to the effect on values of the termination of restrictions. At the very least, however, there are lower-income sections of Houston, such as Denver Harbor, which contain both diverse uses and relatively stable property values. It is probable that the entry of small businesses catering to people within the area augments its desirability and, therefore, property values.

4. Among those who will also gain are the relatively few who desire to use homes entirely or partially for business purposes. Areas of diverse use have served well the interest of some small or beginning businesses.

5. Those who may be most adversely affected are the owners of homes backing up to those on major thoroughfares in areas where there is a minimal apartment demand. If the latter homes are replaced by or used for strip commercial purposes, values may be jeopardized for such adjoining homes. (An analogous situation can occur in a zoned city if the property on a major thoroughfare is rezoned from single-family to commercial, which of course does happen.)

6. There also may be adverse effects on homes within restricted subdivisions adjoining or across a thoroughfare from the subdivision on which the covenants expire.

Areas where covenants have expired provide a test of the traditional argument in support of zoning: that the entry of diverse uses will destroy values of houses and often lead to blight and slum conditions. Because values there will tend to appreciate, areas subject to strong apartment demand are generally immune from such dire consequences. Where there is little demand for apartment sites, however, it is difficult to believe that a relatively small number of diverse uses will inevitably lead to these conditions in neighborhoods that are at least twenty to twenty-five years old.

Most zoning ordinances would probably allow some of these uses, inasmuch as "home occupations" are often a permitted use in single-family areas, and such use could be commenced from the inception of the subdivision. This is likewise true with respect to churches, which generate considerable traffic. The enforcement machinery of zoning is also not always certain to abate violations. Thus the Board of Zoning Appeals of Chicago, during the years from 1936 to 1938, collected evidence of 264 violations of the ordinance. Most of these involved beauty parlors, grocery stores, or tailor shops in residential areas; few, if any had been eliminated as of 1941.[5] One reason for this failure was "that most zoning violation cases in Chicago are continued time and time again until the prosecution is finally dropped."[6] In a study of Cleveland, it is estimated there were between seventeen hundred and two thousand nonconforming uses in residential districts in 1954.[7] The large percentage of variances generally granted would also suggest the existence of many diverse uses in areas zoned for single-family use (see Chapter 1).

As a subdivision grows older, differing uses may be less objectionable than when it was new. When the subdivision has reached a "mature" age, many of the homes may not be well or "desirably" maintained. The small grocery store, beauty shop, or even plumber's office may not stand out as dramatically against a background of twenty-five-year-old homes as against five-year-old ones. The garden apartment building and townhouse might even blend in (see Figs. 2–4 through 2–8). In fact, any of the foregoing might be an improvement over a neighboring house. Distance of the home from a commercial or industrial use may also be a factor. For example, one row of houses buffering strip commercial development may provide virtually complete separation. A study of a middle-to-upper-middle–income suburb of Chicago has shown that the concern of homeowners there about proposed rezoning faded out almost in proportion to their distance from the site.[8] Thus, the grocery store or beauty shop, or auto repair shop, might be an asset if it were a block away; but, in any event, possibly not "harmful" at that distance. And, due to limited demand, a grocery store a block away may make for the absence of any other such use within one's own block. The Zoning Appeals Board in Philadelphia took the position that the effect of a variance usually does not extend any further than the same block.[9] A study of some older areas of Pittsburgh suggests that home prices in such areas may not be affected by uses considered as "adverse" or "incompatible" by planners.[10] On the other hand, there are a great many for whom diverse uses anywhere in the neighborhood, excluding perhaps strip property, would probably make it undesirable. But, even for some of those with such tastes, a desirable location or its ethnic or cultural orientation may tend to make diverse uses a secondary or even unimportant consideration.

The economic class of the individual will also affect his views as to how he regards nearby uses. When a major oil company attempted to build on unrestricted property at an intersection of Memorial Drive in Houston, in an area of expensive homes, adjoining owners and other residents in the area made a determined effort to induce the company to abandon the project. They even burned their credit cards. In another section of Memorial, similar pressures were applied against a proposed shopping center. If the residents had been of a lower-income level, the protests, if any, would probably have been only from adjoining owners. Similar controversies apparently have not arisen in less affluent areas, although gas stations have undoubtedly been built in comparable locations of such areas. The convenience of having a gas station nearby is much more important for the lesser-income groups.

For the family that does not own an automobile, the existence of a nearby grocery store (with possibly liberal credit terms) may be a great convenience, if not actually a necessity. The same may be true for the family whose one car is used by the husband during the day. Because the car may be old and often require repairs, it is desirable to have an automobile repair shop a block, rather than a mile or more away. The local shops are also likely to give better values than does the franchised dealer. They may offer better credit terms and employ used parts. Given the choice between "garden city" aesthetics and the convenience in both time and money of a neighboring car repair shop, the owner of an older car in an automobile city may well choose the latter. Houston's application to HUD for model cities' funds in 1968 proposed the creation of a controlled "diverse land use district" for the areas involved, on the theory that separated uses are "out of place in near-city locations because of the lack of mobility of low-income residents."[11]

It should by now be recognized that the *gemutlichkeit* of garden-city living is simply not shared by all homeowners. In Houston, Baytown, and Wichita Falls, probably most homeowners voted against zoning in areas where covenants were no longer enforced or were soon to expire. Apparently there are many of middle-income level who prefer living in the Montrose area and along major thoroughfares next to commercial uses. These appear to be among the many who seem to reject the amenities commonly associated with single-family subdivisions. Persons with such tastes may not find satisfactory accommodation in the strict separation of uses.

Thus, many homes in the oldest section of Westheimer Road, a major thoroughfare, are still occupied for residential purposes, although their value for non-single-family use is much greater. The area in question began to change to commercial in 1951. This though should not be surprising; tastes differ greatly. Even grass lawns may not appeal to everyone.[12] Nor is there unanimity about the common amenities inside a building. Some people prefer community kitchens to eliminate loneliness and induce friendships and mutual adjustments.[13]

A story in the *Wall Street Journal* epitomizes the differences in values and tastes. It describes a class in futuristics at Cornell University; in the class the students designed a city of the future to satisfy the needs and comforts of slum residents. On viewing this project paradise, the ghetto dwellers laughed. Explained the instructor, "the actual ghetto residents said they simply wouldn't want to live the way the students had mapped out their lives for them."[14]

For those who desire to continue living in a homogeneous community, it is, of course possible for new covenants to be created prior to or after the expiration of the old. The difficulties involved in accomplishing this are not as great as might appear. It has happened that most and even all owners within areas where covenants have expired have entered into new covenants. (These situations will be more fully discussed in Chapter 15.) Possibly an area smaller than the original might be restricted, omitting properties adjoining certain streets and corners. In addition, to satisfy some owners, the new covenants may have to allow for more dense residential use; that is, for garden apartments and/or townhouses.

Some Comparisons with Zoned Cities

How does Houston compare in appearance with zoned cities? Has the absence of zoning created ugliness and visual disorder and disarray? Although some have attempted to answer these questions,[15] it would seem impossible to evaluate the aesthetics and physical composition of over 450 square miles of real estate and compare such a determination with a similar area elsewhere. There certainly are a great many areas of single-family occupancy that look identical to the "idyllic" areas of the zoned cities. There are also mixtures of uses available for those wishing to demonstrate the ill effects of nonzoning. Frequently, however, the same mixtures exist in cities that are zoned. Thus, it is not uncommon for apartments to be permitted next to commercial uses for a variety of "sound" planning reasons. For example, under the Chicago zoning ordinance, gas stations and apartments are both permitted in six of its eleven business and commercial zones. Similar provisions can be found in the zoning ordinances of Dallas and Los Angeles, and probably most large cities.

In comparing Houston to zoned cities an attempt might be made to be more specific, and to make a comparison with some other city. If there were a "like" zoned city, it might be possible to make a precise determination as to the effects of nonzoning. The problem arises in finding a city with similar characteristics. Such a comparison is further complicated by the differences between zoning ordinances and the dates of their adoption. Provisions contained in different zoning ordinances may differ considerably. Zoning is a product of legislative decision, and what may have prompted one city council to adopt a particular provision may well have caused another to reject it. An additional difficulty is that some cities adopted zoning ordinances in the late 1920s or 1930s after substantial portions of their areas had been developed, and perhaps made major changes in their ordinances in the 1950s, after much more had been built.

Nevertheless, zoning has been a significant influence in the use and development of property. In the balance of this chapter, an attempt will be made to compare the operation of zoning and nonzoning, using the Houston experience as the basis for the discussion. Comparisons will be made on the basis of various categories of land use: how each develops under zoning and nonzoning. Readers should be aware that the writer's experience relates principally to Chicago and its suburbs and that perhaps some of his observations may be influenced by this.

Commercial Uses

Major Thoroughfares

Various uses may front on the more heavily traveled streets in Houston and the zoned cities. For distances on Kirby, South MacGregor, and Memorial drives in Houston, one can see expensive single-family homes with big lawns adjoining other expensive single-family homes with equally big lawns fronting on side streets. On the other hand, both sides of Westheimer consist of some single-family dwellings and countless and different commercial and apartment uses, in back of which may be more of the same or residential developments. Driving down Stella Link Road south of Bellaire Boulevard to the expressway, one can observe many blocks restricted to middle-income homes, some corners with shopping centers, a school, and a park. Northerly portions of Gessner provide an example of a more recently developed, heavily travelled street: both sides of it consist almost entirely of apartment and business uses and vacant parcels awaiting such usc, and to their rear are relatively new single-family and townhouse developments. This "strip" or "ribbon" pattern of commercial development interspersed with "nodes," as on Westheimer and Gessner, is evident in most zoned cities to a greater or less extent, depending upon the city.

"Strips"

Houston and zoned cities confront different problems in connection with the development of property adjoining major streets. There is clearly a market for homes adjoining major streets, as is apparent in Houston and elsewhere, but because the land in Houston can be used commercially and for apartments, the price may be too high for homes. Further, houses may not be built on such streets unless there is certainty as to the use of neighboring land, both across the street and adjoining. Zoning and covenants may provide such assurances. A private developer may find it too costly to buy the adjoining property or covenants restricting it. The homes built on the major streets of Houston are frequently part of a larger subdivision. Sometimes the other side of the street is also part of the same subdivision. Often these subdivisions were planned before the streets became important arteries.

As covenants affecting such property expire, some will be used commercially or for apartments. Violations of the covenants for commercial uses are much more common on the major thoroughfares than on interior streets, sometimes to such an extent that the covenants became unenforceable for all property within the subdivision fronting on the thoroughfare. Accordingly, it is likely that there is, or will be, more property available on major thoroughfares for other than single-family uses than would have been the case had Houston adopted zoning.

At the same time the absence of zoning restrictions—including those for signs and billboards—should allow for maximum development of strip areas. Because of the apartment booms of the 1960s, a considerable portion of "strip" property has been, and will be, destined for apartment use. The existence of such a supply of land along major thoroughfares should relieve pressure for the development of commercial and apartments within single-family subdivisions. It may account in part for the absence of diverse uses in some subdivisions where the covenants have expired.

Location of Uses

If some of the nonrestricted "strip" and "node" areas adjoining major streets in nonzoned cities were zoned for business use, at least two things could be accomplished: (1) local law would thereafter prohibit industrial uses that are obnoxious in terms of smoke, odor, and noise from locating in such areas, and (2) the city could separate all of the various business uses into a number of districts to be placed at different locations on the basis of some kind of "compatibility" criteria. The authors of the early zoning ordinances who were primarily concerned with the protection of residential property were generally satisfied to achieve only (1) and at times did so by making the use-groupings referred to in (2) on the basis of potential harm to adjoining residential areas. More recently, uses have been separated for this but also for many other reasons. The early drafters were probably wiser than their successors, and neither has been more so than the Houston "nondrafters."

The FHA, in Houston, has required in nonzoned areas that if there is common ownership of both the strip and the adjoining property designated for residential use, a covenant be recorded on the strip property forbidding only "obnoxious" industrial uses. In the writer's conversations with FHA officials in 1969,[16] he was advised that this requirement was due largely to the government's desire for assurance (or reassurance), which could easily be achieved in the instance of common ownership, and that to their knowledge nothing more harmful had been built in any strip areas than gas stations (which they do not consider obnoxious). They are probably correct, and, of course, the FHA policy in itself will reinforce this conclusion. In instances of common ownership and development, private lenders might also require such a covenant, or, at least, some such understanding. If not, the interests of the developer during the period in which he is selling homes could be relied upon to control uses for at least that period. Thereafter, the economic interests of the owners of the strip would probably control "obnoxiousness" thereon. One reason is that business and apartment users will generally pay much more for land than will industrial users, thus limiting the industrial market for such property. Even if the price were low enough for such industrial use, however, it is doubtful that an owner would sell any portion less than the whole and thereby jeopardize prospective sales for business and apartment uses for the balance. Furthermore, there are not likely to be many such industrial users because of the problems created for them by unhappy and complaining homeowners. (It might even cost less to install devices for odor, noise, and smoke reduction than to fight off the neighbors.) If some of the strip had already been developed with apartments or business, the owners of such properties (or those providing the financing) may have exacted an understanding at the time they purchased as to what would be permitted on the balance or the nearby properties. Owners of contiguous strip properties might also agree to uses as a matter of self-interest. Accordingly, it does not seem likely that industry with obnoxious characteristics will settle in the strip areas that were never restricted. If some do, the adjoining and nearby property owners and the city may obtain relief under laws against nuisance and pollution.

The foregoing analysis should also apply in general to strip areas where the covenants have expired. However, the much greater diversity of ownership makes it more difficult for common purposes to be achieved. Still, the likelihood is that obnoxiousness will be avoided for the reasons previously given.

What would happen in the absence of such restrictions separating business uses? An answer was provided by the Architecture Department at Rice University[17] in classroom studies made of Westheimer Road, a major east-west thoroughfare located in the southwest section of Houston. These studies suggest that there is inherent in the marketplace a planning mechanism that tends to separate and allocate business uses. For instance, although no municipal agency has ever controlled its development, this major road has evolved into what might be regarded in terms of business zoning as three, possibly four, separate use districts, broadly defined as being from "local shopping" to "regional shopping." At the eastern end of this street are many art galleries and antique shops and "night clubs" converted to these uses from old residences. About four or five miles to the west are grouped three large prestigious department stores creating one of the major shopping sections of the city. Still further west are located many different food drive-ins. Gas stations are largely at intersections; the older steel and enamel type prevalent in the east part of the street giving way to the brick residential types in the newer areas toward the western limits of the city. And, of course, there are areas or centers for local or general retail shopping. The results could well be attributed to the design of some central authority although the likelihood is that zoning restrictions could only have impeded this development. There is no reason to believe that such pattern of development is confined to Westheimer. A business will only be located where conditions are most suitable and this varies with individual business uses.

The Dallas zoning ordinance (and probably others) provides for two districts restricted to office buildings, provisions intended to induce the erection of and secure economic protection for such structures. For blocks along Richmond Road on both sides of Buffalo Speedway in Houston, there is an area containing large prestige office buildings, constituting in effect a self-created "district." Government restrictions could hardly have aided such developments, but certainly could have been detrimental.

Traffic

Before concluding this section on commercial uses, it would seem appropriate to discuss the relationship of traffic planning to the control of land uses. This discussion is also relevant to analyzing other important land-use concerns of communities. Houston's traffic department regulates all means of entrance and exit to and from properties fronting on public streets. Driveways, parking areas, and aisles are thus controlled for safety and traffic flow. If there are still congestion problems at a particular location, the city can require the installation by a new business of an auxiliary lane to channel traffic for it off the regular lane, or it may prevent left turns into the business by erecting small barriers. The Planning Commission requires substantial dedication of land by subdividers for rights-of-way for major thoroughfares. In older sections, new lanes will be added if sufficient land is available or can be acquired.

The *ad hoc* approach of zoning controls can hardly be more effective, either as a substitute for part of such a program or as a supplement to it. "Traffic" is, of course, but one of the many factors involved in the making of a zoning decision. The local legislator is advised about traffic considerations by the city's traffic department, and in many cases also by the petitioner's traffic engineer. He must evaluate this professional advice and weigh it alongside other considerations, including the many exigencies of the legislative process. When major commercial developments are proposed that are clearly burdensome to streets and expressways, "traffic" will be relegated to a minor consideration by the potential of additional local employment and revenues, and even prestige. The councilmen are more prone to act on alleged traffic problems related to strip locations, where such questions are much more conjectural. "Traffic" has probably often been employed as an excuse to cover other reasons for restricting uses (such as gas stations and car "washes"), which involve aesthetics and offensiveness of the use to nearby residents. When so used, it may even contribute to traffic problems. The very act of limiting the number of gas stations or car "washes" may be self-defeating in that the fewer the stations, the greater the congestion at each.

It should also be recognized that planners are limited as to what they can do in relation to any alleged traffic problem. Consider the use of land for a gas station. Suppose that the planners recommend that a site on a street with a low traffic count be zoned to allow gas stations, and a site on a high traffic street be zoned to exclude gas stations. The result will be that no gas station will be erected at either site. This situation will continue unless the "low" count street becomes heavily travelled (and, therefore, more of a "problem") and/or the oil companies and their planners and traffic engineers succeed in convincing the local legislature or the courts to rezone the site of the "high" count street. Ironically, the courts may find, contrary to the conclusion of the planners, that the "high" traffic count is at least one factor that makes the site suitable for such use. Often, probably, city planners make recommendations which accord with the desires of the oil companies. This is more likely in the larger cities, which generally are much more favorably disposed toward gas stations than the suburbs, particularly the bedroom ones. When this probability is added to the probability that sites rejected by planners will be ultimately zoned or rezoned for gas station use, the correlation may often be high between what occurs in a larger city with and one without zoning.

Single-Family Use

Although it might be difficult to detect in the more modern zoning ordinances that endeavor to control minutely all uses, a paramount reason leading to the adoption of zoning was the protection of the single-family residence. Considering how successful this battlecry was in spreading zoning to all parts of the country within the twenty to twenty-five years after it was first adopted in New York in 1916, it might be thought that the continued existence of the single-family home was once presumed in peril and that, were it not for zoning, the single-family subdivision might be by now something of the past. The Houston experience, however, does not bear this out; the single-family residence is hardly in jeopardy there. It would appear that on the average, and notwithstanding the termination of restrictions in many places, homes have had steady and substantial appreciation in value over the years, not unlike what has occurred elsewhere in the nation. Sales prices of FHA insured new and used homes in Houston for the last ten years, compared with those in the ten other largest cities in the country, reveal no significant difference in the pattern of appreciation of values in Houston for this period.[18]

It is difficult to perceive any differences due to the absence of zoning in the recent single-family subdivisions of Houston. Perhaps the only easily observable difference is in those subdivisions where the builder has covered most of the lot with the home, and has left room only for a small rear yard. Zoning ordinances generally require substantial front and rear yards. While a twenty-five foot front yard is mandatory under the subdivision requirements of Houston, there is no rear yard standard, and this has enabled some builders to keep distances between the backs of homes at a minimum. Alley lots or lots with no street frontage are not permitted under the subdivision regulations, but living structures adjoining alleys or rear lot lines are evident in the older sections of the city.

In many instances, rear yards are provided, and the covenants result in a subdivision essentially identical to what would have resulted under zoning. The minimum lot size permitted in new subdivisions is not unusual for a large city, although it is smaller than that allowed in many suburban areas. The Planning Director of Houston states that the outlying areas are comparable to the suburban areas of other large cities except that there is more "strip" development in Houston, and it is difficult to contest his conclusion. In 1966, there were about 270,000 single-family dwellings on a total of 62,062 acres, or an average of about 10,000 square feet per unit, which is twice the area then and now required for building sites in new subdivisions served by a sanitary sewer main and almost 1½ times the area required in the absence of such mains.

The average and median size of lots were smaller in Houston than in Dallas for those new and existing homes insured by the FHA during the four year period of the sixties for which statistics are available (Table 4–8). However, the floor area of the average new and existing homes insured by FHA from 1960 through 1969 inclusive, was usually larger in Houston (Tables 4–5 and 4–6).

During the period that the covenants are in force, an owner can generally rely on all of the land within the perimeter of his subdivision being used for single-family dwellings, or as otherwise provided by the terms of the covenants. Outside this perimeter vacant land can be used for almost any purpose unless it has been restricted by covenant. When the adjoining property is unrestricted, one might expect that lots and homes on the perimeter would probably sell for less than inside property to compensate for the risk assumed as to what will be erected thereon. What about the "innocent" purchaser? In practice, whether the purchaser is knowledgeable or not may be of secondary importance since mortgagees and mortgage insurers such as the FHA and VA, who guarantee mortgages close to the purchase price, also have a substantial stake and they are knowledgeable. They too will lose if the proverbial glue factory moves in as a neighbor. Since almost all houses will have mortgages, the market for perimeter homes adjoining vacant, unrestricted tracts should also, to some extent at least, reflect the decisions of the mortgage market, to the benefit of the buyer who lacks knowledge or is misled.

In actual practice, there is probably comparatively little difference in price for perimeter property for lower-cost homes, except where the evidence of likely non-residential use is relatively clear (such as on a strip adjoining a thoroughfare). This appears to be the opinion of the FHA officials with whom the writer spoke, as well as many others in the real estate business in Houston. This is probably not true, however, for higher-priced properties, which are subject to greater fluctuations in values. The market for perimeter property reflects the risk assumed by the buyers. Purchasing a home next to unrestricted property does not involve the assumption of great and undefinable risk as to the future of such property. The substantial viability of the single-family market in the nonzoned cities supports this conclusion; it would indeed be in jeopardy if the developer, mortgagee, and buyer could not predict with some certainty the likelihood of use for adjoining unrestricted property. The location of a gas station is an obvious example of such predictability; it will only locate on a major thoroughfare, preferably an intersection, regardless of where it is permitted to go. This can be better understood by analyzing the problems confronted by a home developer in the Houston area, of, let us say, one hundred acres with frontage on a major thoroughfare and contiguous on the remaining three sides to unrestricted acreage, as in Fig. 2–9. In perhaps most instances, the frontage to a depth of about from 150 to 300 feet will be used for strip commercial development with the balance for single-family homes. The usual pattern of development requires that perimeter home lots on all four sides face inward, backing up to the unrestricted property. The strip may remain unrestricted, although the FHA may require that it be restricted only against "obnoxious" type industry.

Property Adjoining the Strip

What is the effect of the strip development upon the value of contiguous homes and those further away? Commercial uses such as gas stations and supermarkets in addition to being unwanted neighbors to some may also

Figure 2-9. Land use expectations in the absence of zoning.

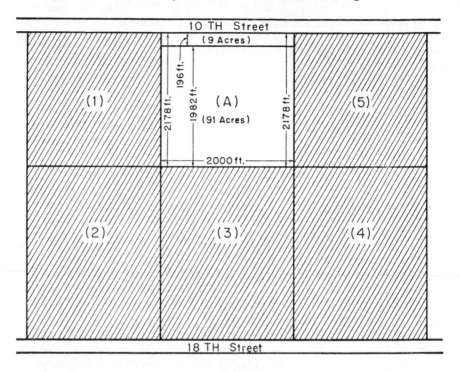

Assume that Tract A in Figure 2-9 is a 100-acre tract fronting on 10th Street with nine acres adjoining 10th unrestricted, and the balance of 91 acres restricted for single-family dwellings and subdivided for 400 lots. Assume that Tracts 1, 2, 3, 4 and 5 are each 100 acres or more and are not restricted. Assume also that both 10th and 18th are major thoroughfares and that Tract A is in Houston or the unincorporated area of Harris County, three to five miles to the expressway intersection and fifteen to twenty miles to the downtown center of Houston.

In this case, the predictability of site selection for Tracts 1, 2, 3, 4 and 5 would seem to be as follows:

Use	Likelihood of Such Use for Each Tract	Explanation
Large, Heavy Manufacturing Plant	Most unlikely	1. No railroad, waterway or expressway interesection adjoins or is proximate to any of the tracts.
		2. Presence of adjoining or near homeowners may impede operations of plant.

Use	Likelihood of Such Use for Each Tract	Explanation
		3. Each of the tracts would be priced for single-family and strip commercial use, largely because property adjoining or nearby is being developed for homes. This price would be excessive for heavy industrial usage.
		4. Area in question may not be in intrastate "commercial" and "switching" zones, resulting in increased delivery and shipping costs.
		5. Such use is relatively small compared to that for residential subdivisions. In 1966, within city limits, single-family dwellings occupied 96.9 square miles, and manufacturing (light and heavy), 7.6, or about 1/12 as much area. Since this is, at best, a secondary area for such use in terms of desirability, possibility of location is statistically remote.
High-Rise Apartment* Complex	Most unlikely	Very few high-rise apartments have been erected in Houston area and, then, on an individual basis. Each tract would, therefore, be too large for such use, particularly in view of "soft" demand for apartments in the location in question.
Office Building* Complex	Most unlikely	1. Demand for offices in such locations would be too minimal to warrant such a development.
		2. No major thoroughfare or expressway intersection adjoining or proximate.
		3. Not close enough expressway intersection.

Use	Likelihood of Such Use for Each Tract	Explanation
Major Shopping Center	Most unlikely	1. No major intersection.
		2. Not close enough to expressway intersection.
		3. Infrequent use of land since one major shopping center will serve large area.
Light Industrial* Park	Unlikely	1. No railroad, waterway or expressway intersection adjoins or is proximate to any of the tracts.
		2. Possible problems with adjoining or nearby homeowners.
		3. Location in question may not be in "commercial" or "switching" zones.
		4. Few such developments compared to new subdivisions. (See explanations for heavy manufacturing and also below this chart.)
Large, Light Industrial Plant	Unlikely	Same considerations as for light industrial park, except item 3 may not be as important for some plants.
Motel*	Unlikely	1. No major thoroughfare or expressway intersection adjoining or proximate.
		2. Not close enough to expressway intersection.
		3. Each tract is too big. It would have to be divided, and balance used or sold for single-family or multiple-family usage.
Two-To-Three-Story Garden Apartments* Or Townhouse Developments*	Least unlikely	1. Because of limited demand for multiple-family units in more distant areas, price of such large tracts generally would be too expensive for apartment and to a lesser extent townhouse developments.

Use	Likelihood of Such Use for Each Tract	Explanation
		2. The likelihood of for apartment use is statistically remote. The yield for 91 acres would usually be from 2,000 to 2,500 apartments. Total number of multiple-family units erected in non-zoned areas of Harris County in 1969 did not exceed 21,000, and the bulk of these were erected about 10 miles of downtown center. Very few major apartment complexes have been developed in the locations in question. Similar analysis is probably applicable to townhoues.
		3. Portion of a tract might be used for such development, and balance for homes. This is more likely to occur as demand for multiple family use increases in this location.
		4. Distance from expressway may deter such use in this location.
Single-Family (and strip) Development as in Tract "A"	Likely	Of all possibilities enumerated this is most likely. This is probably the principal use of land in the area. There are no "incompatible" uses adjoining.

*Use suitable for location in the strip areas.

By inserting expressways, railroads or thoroughfares at other locations and/or altering the size or location of the various tracts, the possibilities will vary as to where other uses might go in relation to Tract "A." The above criteria should provide the reader some guides as to what could happen under a different set of geographical conditions.

The above enumerations appear to be most of the principal factors in site selection. But there are numerous others, either on an individual or general basis. For example, a topography of rolling land is suitable for residential construction, but not desirable for industrial buildings, which may cover much land and need flat terrain. Demand will be an important factor: if the demand becomes extremely great for industrial sites, there will be more industrial parks. As of

1968, according to the Chamber of Commerce (whose list may not be complete), of the 31,000 acres that were originally within industrial parks in the Houston metropolitan area, approximately 18,000 acres were still available for sale. This would suggest that, at least for some period thereafter the existing demand could be partially satisfied by existing industrial parks, and there would be little demand for secondary sites such as the tracts shown. Certain of the uses shown can be developed on the commercial strips when these are created, and thereby satisfy some of the demand for such use. Source: *Journal of Law and Economics*, Vol. 13, No. 1 (April 1970) pp. 144–147.

be noisy, keep late hours, and create dust and dirt for many others. Accordingly, it is generally assumed that at least in the new subdivisions most people will not want to live next to them, and the price of adjoining property should be less. (Prices everywhere else in the subdivision however may be enhanced by the commercial uses.) This will be no different, of course, in the zoned areas except that a zoning ordinance might be more revealing concerning possible uses of vacant property in the strip. Consistent with this approach, the row of houses adjoining the strip will be treated differently than the balance of the homes. For example, the FHA in Houston requires that a six-foot-high wood fence be built along the rear of these lots to provide separation (similar fencing is not unusual in zoned municipalities). And it will probably value the lot and house with this fence less than comparable properties in the rest of the subdivision. Some developers at the beginning of subdivision activity may proceed to build and sell at a lower price such houses as a buffer to provide protection for the rest, while others will erect less expensive homes there.

Inasmuch as many subdivisions have not been, or will not be, submitted for FHA approval, it would seem pertinent to make some determinations as to what has been erected generally in Houston on land adjacent to strip commercial development. For this purpose, the author selected, for sample, developments that were contiguous to all of the Chevrolet, Ford, and Plymouth dealerships located within the city limits—which in total were twenty-four as of December 1, 1969. I selected for this purpose automobile dealerships for two reasons:

1. They are a use considered by many planners as more "offensive" than the ordinary business use because of their sales, repair and service operations and unenclosed sales lots. (Thus, under the Chicago ordinance, dealerships are largely restricted to "commercial" districts, which permit uses between business and industrial. However, Chicago's ordinance—as well as probably many others—does allow apartments in the same districts in which dealerships are allowed.)
2. They are scattered, and allow for a random selection.

Land use sketches were made of the dealerships and nearby properties.[19] All front on major thoroughfares and fourteen adjoin two or more. Apartments adjoined or were across a street from seven of the dealerships.

Five were located within the downtown area, each on most or all of a block. If homes were near, they were probably temporarily being used for residential purposes, if at all. *Nine* did not adjoin or were not across any street or thoroughfare from single-family use (except for one "stray" house surrounded by other uses). *One* was across a major thoroughfare from a single-family subdivision which had erected a wood fence six or more feet in height with hedging along the thoroughfare. *Three* adjoined on the rear single-family subdivisions, two of which were separated by a creek and heavily wooded area. The third was separated by the dealer's chain link fence; some of the homes also had chosen to install some hedging. *One* was across a major thoroughfare from a single-family subdivision which had erected an eight-foot brick fence along the thoroughfare; but also across a local street from this dealership were two frame houses in the midst of a commercial strip. *One* was, as its rear, across a local street from three old frame houses which were the only residential uses on a block containing a grocery store, a church and its annex, a playground, and parking lots. Commercial uses were also in an adjoining block making these homes contiguous to the church on one side, and adjoining or across the street from commercial uses on the other sides. *One* was across a major thoroughfare and a minor street from houses, all of which also adjoined (or were part of) some strip commercial uses, and were probably destined for commercial usage regardless of the existence of the dealership.

Except as indicated, none of the above-mentioned dealerships were otherwise contiguous directly or across a street from any houses. It is difficult to conclude that any depreciation in single-family values occurred as a result of the erection of any of these twenty-one dealerships. Most owners of businesses and apartment buildings and their mortgagees are competent to evaluate the economic advantages or disadvantages involved in such contiguity. Inasmuch as one or more major thoroughfares abutted each site, few could have been surprised by the location of a use requiring heavy traffic. In any event, I believe virtually all of the adjoining uses on the thoroughfares would be allowed in zoned districts that permit dealerships.

What about the remaining three dealerships? One adjoins a very low-income area where the frame houses are of minimal quality and the streets are not paved. There is little value left to depreciate in such structures, and the existence of the dealership may add value. Both of the remaining two dealerships adjoin lower-income frame houses. In the first instance, the houses are across a local street and at the rear of a shallower strip commercial area. This latter strip appears to be fully developed in the section adjoining these homes. The values of these houses may have been adversely affected by the erection of the dealership, although it is possible that they may in time be used for commercial purposes (and their present value may reflect this). There are also homes adjoining on the rear of this dealership. No fence has been erected for separation. The lone remaining dealership of this survey faces, across a local street, homes on a strip location which are probably destined for commercial use in the future. There are also some frame houses across another local street adjoining the rear of this dealership and these houses are contiguous to some apartments. If these houses are sold for apartment use, the dealership may not have affected their values, although the presence of the dealership might have lowered the price of these properties as apartment sites.

The conclusion seems warranted, with respect to the foregoing dealerships, that the private market has worked out favorably: they have located on sites well-suited to the carrying out of their business, and, on the whole, there has been little, if any, injury to values of adjoining properties. It is difficult to see how zoning could have helped. But it does not strain the imagination to envision the problems that zoning controls could have created for some dealers, and even other property owners.

The Other Three Sides

When asked if their practices for the homes bordering unrestricted property on any of the other three sides of the subdivision was similar to that for property adjoining the strip, the FHA officials replied in the negative. They will generally appraise such perimeter property at about the same as interior homes in the belief that if the location of the subdivision is acceptable, there is little likelihood that "adverse" uses, as they define the term, will occur on the adjoining unrestricted property. By acceptable location they appear to mean (1) that the area does not have an existing commercial or industrial orientation, and (2) that it is likely that the adjoining property will not be used "adversely." The FHA apparently (at this time) does not consider garden apartments as having adverse effects on adjoining homes for the lower-income level, with which it is principally involved. While high rises may have such effects, they are not very common in Houston and their likely location is predictable. Commercial uses such as shopping centers, office complexes, and motels require maximum traffic opportunities, and it would seem possible to predict whether a particular location is suitable for such use (see Fig. 2–9). If a commercial use appeared likely to locate on the unrestricted property adjoining the subdivision, fencing, as above described, might be required because a condition similar to a node in strip development would probably be involved. Industrial use is also considered as unlikely for the unrestricted property, as will be explained in the discussion on industrial uses. Regardless of the positions of the FHA and VA, however, the developer and his lender will have a financial interest in the well being of the subdivision for many years after sales begin; the developer until all the houses are sold, and the lender for many years thereafter. Therefore, if there is some question as to whether the adjoining unrestricted property will be used adversely, the developer may purchase, or may be required by the lender to purchase, either (1) a covenant restricting some or all of such property to residential use, or (2) a buffer area for such purpose.

One may conclude that economic forces cause a homogeneity of single-family areas in Houston, not unlike that which might take place under zoning. This statement is not contradicted by the fact that a large tract in an older section adjoining a single-family subdivision may be developed for garden apartments. An examination of the proposed 1962 zoning ordinance for Houston shows that a substantial number of areas zoned for single-family adjoined tracts on which the erection of apartments was permitted. Furthermore, even if many of these tracts had been zoned single-family by a prior ordinance, it is questionable whether it would have made very much difference.

It is difficult to believe that zoning in Houston, or any other major city, aside from the bedroom suburbs, could have withstood, or would have wanted to withstand, the enormous pressures of the apartment boom and keep its single-family subdivisions isolated therefrom. Zoning might, however, have placed some restrictions on apartment development for the benefit of adjoining single-family homeowners. If so, it would have been at the expense of the apartment dwellers, as will be explained later. In addition, requiring substantial separation of apartment developments from existing houses may limit the densities of such developments. This may result in the erection of more apartment projects, and it is possible that there will in time be a greater amount of proximity between the two uses.

For most of the newer single-family subdivisions, it would appear that the limitations on land use and development in Houston are roughly comparable to those of zoning, except that the controls are managed by different groups. As a practical matter, the homeowner in the newer subdivision is in much the same position he would have been in were the area zoned. In terms of future protection, the errors of the old subdividers in drafting inadequate restrictions seem to have been rectified. Values of homes appear to be secure. Instead of coming from the city council, the restrictions governing use and occupancy were created by private developers and investors, often with some direction from the FHA and VA, and are being enforced by the city. With respect to many subdivisions, perhaps most, it is very possible that the location of the subdivision, and the size of its lots, would have been the same if there had been zoning. Zoning might have increased in time, however, minimum lot sizes, and enabled some subdivisions to occupy land now used for multifamily development.

Industrial Use

Many homes are, of course, erected next to existing factories, and when prices reflect such proximity, it is difficult to see that anything other than a planner's sense of symmetry has been harmed. A problem may arise for other reasons: (1) a factory may be built on a vacant lot or tract next to an existing home and this risk was not discounted in the purchase price of the home; (2) the existence of some factories may discourage development of homes in nearby areas; and (3) the existing factory may begin to do things, such as emitting odors and fumes, not anticipated when the adjoining home was purchased. Although it might seem that government regulation is needed as protection against these problems, there is much reason to conclude that, on the whole, home values have not suffered more in Houston because of industrial development than they would have under zoning. In the subsequent discussion, this conclusion will be elaborated upon with consideration to: (1) the proximity of industrial use to residential areas, (2) the existing pattern of industrial location, and (3) controls over industrial uses. It will be assumed that the proximity of apartments (and, of course, commercial) to many industrial uses is acceptable to investors, and usually to planners, judging from the experience of zoned cities, where it is common.

Proximity

When plants are concentrated within an area (as in zoned districts), there is less likelihood of proximity to other uses than if each is separately located. An inspection of land use maps of Wichita Falls,[20] Pasadena,[21] and Baytown[22] shows that industry has tended to group and separate itself. Whether the percentage of total land used by industry is about 1·1 percent, as in Baytown, or 4 percent, as in Pasadena, or 5 percent, as in Wichita Falls, proliferation of industry is small. This lack of proliferation is not as clearly evident in the land use map for Houston, although it is apparent that the bulk of industry is confined within certain areas. The statistics of land use for Houston also suggest a minimum of industrial proliferation. The most current land use survey of the city was conducted by its planning department in 1966. The amount of land used for manufacturing, single-family, commercial, etc., was compiled for each 1960 census tract within the city in accordance with the definitions contained in the *Standard Land Use Code Manual,* adopted for purposes of national uniformity by agencies of the federal government.

The 1966 survey shows the following amounts of manufacturing use of land (which includes both "light" and "heavy" industry) based on 132 census tracts entirely or partially within the city limits: 37 tracts encompassing about 25 percent of land area contained no manufacturing use; 32 tracts with about 23 percent of land area contained between zero and 0.5 percent of manufacturing use; 18 tracts with 26 percent contained about 1 percent; 21 tracts with about 12 percent contained approximately 2 or 3 percent. The remaining 14 percent of land area contained the balance of manufacturing, or about 68 percent of manufacturing use within the city. (Use of statistics based on census tracts to determine proliferation of industry would tend to weight the figures in favor of greater proliferation than has actually occurred, since a census tract is based on population. There could, therefore, be no census tract which would show exclusively the existence of industry and nothing else, even though the amount of land devoted largely to industry may be greater in some instances than the land area of some census tracts covering sections of high population density.)

Moreover, the land use summary of 1966 suggests that whatever industrial proliferation has occurred, it has had a minimal effect on home values. It discloses that single-family areas occupied approximately 23 percent of the total land area of the city, and manufacturing uses approximately 2 percent (43 percent and 3 percent, respectively, of developed area). If, as it appears, two-thirds of the manufacturing is concentrated within its own areas, the likelihood of the industrial uses on the remaining 0.66 percent of the land area having been erected adjacent to homes after the latter were built is exceedingly small, especially considering that much of this remainder is probably separated from homes by vacant land, other uses, major thoroughfares, and expressways, which in the aggregate account for over 70 percent of the land area of the city. Furthermore, a comparison of the city's 1959 use map with that of 1968 reveals that some industry was erected prior to the time that residential development occurred adjoining or nearby.

That in the larger cities industrial uses exist next to residential properties should not be considered as necessarily a failure of zoning, since they may predate the ordinance. In addition, the earlier zoning ordinances did not prohibit residential uses in industrial districts. It would be extremely difficult to determine accurately whether industry in Houston is more scattered than is generally the case in zoned areas. The large areas involved and differing definitions of what is industry make precise comparison extremely difficult between major cities. It is possible that compared to major cities and their suburbs, Houston's industry, because of the vast area of the city, may be less scattered. Chicago, in an area about one-half of the size of Houston, has many industrial sections, and most of the suburbs surrounding it have at least one. While industry in Chicago and each of these suburbs may be segregated, taken as a whole there may be as much proliferation, or possibly more, within an area of comparable size as in Houston. The same also appears to be true for the Dallas area.[23] Zoning is hardly an iron-clad guarantee for homeowners against industrial encroachment. In unduly limiting an industrial district in one area, it may force some industry elsewhere. By creating districts it may even cause location that would otherwise not be selected by those industries that desire to be in a general area but to whom precise location is unimportant. For those industries which would not object to locating in or near a residential area, there are other reasons that tend to reduce the importance of zoning in eliminating industrial proliferation: (1) despite the strenuous efforts of a municipality to exclude them, courts have on occasion ordered industrial uses next to single-family houses,[24] and vice versa;[25] (2) because of the existence of many local governments, it is possible that a "homogeneous area is zoned for industry on one side of a municipal boundary line and for high-class low-density residential uses on the other side";[26] (3) the desire of local governments for added tax revenues may cause them to zone an area industrial contiguous to a scattering of homes, and this area may enlarge as such pressures multiply; and, (4) of course, the legislative and subsequent enforcement processes can be subjected to sundry political pressures.[27]

Existing Patterns

The land use maps of Wichita Falls, Pasadena, and Baytown evidence the tendency of industry to segregate itself. The maps disclose the principal reason for this: industry requires proximity to transportation facilities, that is, important thoroughfares, expressways, railroads, or waterways. Some plants may also find it advantageous to be near others with whom they can trade; and the proximity of the labor supply is a consideration in the larger cities. An additional explanation is that industry requires separation from homes or other uses which might impede its operations. This latter consideration is of considerable importance in current practices of much of large- and average-scale industry in determining site location. They do not wish to operate in areas that would adversely affect their production and reputation. Such industries either avoid residential area entirely, or, if possible, make their development at least "compatible" with residential areas.[28] To a substantial extent, this reasoning also accounts for the location of smaller industry, which often must, for financial reasons, rent space in industrial parks or other developments erected by larger-scale developers.

Today, before it locates, an industry may undertake exhaustive studies of contemplated sites. The design of industrial structure has contributed substantially to modern architecture and suggests the importance of the resulting prestige to the owners. Most industrial users would prefer avoiding homes they might possibly offend with noise, odor, smoke, heavy traffic, or perhaps even with late or early working hours. Industry has found complaining owners or tenants to be costly and time-consuming, and productive of a bad image with resulting injury to sales. In many conversations with officers of manufacturing companies, I have come to the conclusion that heavy industry may now be equally as anxious to avoid homeowners as homeowners are to avoid industry.

In a small community with few transportation facilities and limited amount of land, industry will tend to be confined within a few areas. Houston has a large number of transportation facilities, and, therefore, more potential sites, many of which, however, may not be acceptable because of proximity to homes or other uses. The amount of separation from other uses that an industry will want appears dependent on the character of its operation. It might be most costly for heavy industry to exist alongside a subdivision of new middle-income homes, and such industries can be expected to locate a considerable distance away. By contrast, a well-landscaped, single-story, research plant may have minimal difficulties at the same site. This kind of industry may have no more (possibly less) adverse influence on home values than apartments or commercial, or even heavy traffic streets, and might even be preferred over apartment buildings, which often are an alternative use. It may well be that in Houston there is a high correlation between the amount of harm a plant may cause to values of adjoining property and the unlikelihood of its location there. If so, this would serve to negate any injury to values resulting from any proliferation of industry.

Because operations of some plants can be harmful to others, heavy and light industry tend to locate separately. One result is the development of industrial parks in and near Houston (as has occurred in recent years throughout the country), individually catering to certain kinds of industry on the basis of specified uses or standards. These parks may command substantial land prices. Most are for light industry, but there are some very large parks for heavy industrial, such as Bayport with 8,250 acres, Jacintoport with 4,500 acres, and U.S. Steel with a potential of more than 18,000 acres. Uses within many of the parks are controlled by restrictive covenants which itemize permitted and/or prohibited uses or set forth performance standards governing use.

The FHA is generally not concerned that unrestricted land contiguous to a subdivision it is considering for approval will be used for industrial purposes, provided it is not in an area oriented for industrial development. The writer was advised in 1969 by two officials of the FHA office serving Houston[29] that in the twelve or more years in which each had been with the office, no industrial plant has ever been built adjoining a single-family subdivision accepted for home financing by their agency. Statistics submitted to me by FHA show that for the preceeding four years alone it had approved an average of over fifty subdivisions annually in Harris County, most by far in nonzoned areas.

The FHA experience can be better understood by reference to Figure 2–9, showing a location typical of many submitted for FHA subdivision approval. The major reason industry is not likely to locate next to Tract A in Figure 2–9 is the absence of any important transportation facility. Obviously, another is the proximity of a residential subdivision. But there are several other factors that tend to preclude industrial development. The development of a subdivision in an outlying area will usually make adjoining acreage more desirable for similar use and cause it to rise in value, while land for large, heavy industry usually sells for less than "similar" land priced for single-family and strip development. (Land for industry would sell for more than farm or "single-family" land not well situated.) Thus, acreage in heavy industrial parks, which contain needed utilities and adjoin railroads (and not homes) apparently costs not much, if any, more than "comparable" raw acreage adjoining residential subdivisions. Nor will the small industry be able to purchase a portion of any of the tract. An owner will not break up his tract and sell off parcels for industrial use, almost regardless of price, since such use might well prejudice sale of the balance.

The light industrial park developer and a large light industry will probably not find the price objectionable. Each might also create a buffer section "acceptable" to adjoining owners, and this buffer might even in time be used for expansion. However, areas relatively distant from downtown may be too costly for many industries because they tend to be outside of "intrastate commercial" and "switching" zones where lower truck and railroad delivery rates are established pursuant to government regulation. This might significantly impair sales of sites within an industrial park. In any event, there should be little concern on this score because of the few such single or multiple industrial parks (in relation to land supply) that have been developed to date throughout the Houston metropolitan area, suggesting that unless demand in the future changes substantially, the likelihood of one being developed adjoining a particular tract in a secondary location is most remote.

Industrial Controls

Zoning is relatively unimportant in actually eliminating odor and foreign matter from the air. It serves more to keep industry that create such problems, either from proximity to properties that could be harmed, or entirely out of the community. Many factories with undesirable emissions were erected prior to the adoption of a zoning ordinance, and by comparison modern industry is relatively clean. If the plant that created such problems predated the zoning ordinance (or comprehensive amendment thereto), it might become a nonconforming use upon its passage, but it is rarely subject to being eliminated as such, unless possibly it was in an area zoned (or rezoned) for residential use. But, even in residential areas, variations may be granted to permit the use to continue beyond the time limitations of the ordinance. Antipollution laws are the principal devices now used to combat contamination of the air, and uses permitted by zoning ordinances may be restricted under antipollution regulations. Nuisance laws can be helpful in eliminating odor, noise, and vibration from adjoining properties in both zoned and nonzoned areas. Most municipalities have nuisance ordinances enabling them to abate nuisances. The common and statutory laws of nuisance may offer relief by way of injunction or damages to those actually damaged by alleged nuisances, but such relief is generally not an absolute right of the aggrieved party, and depending upon the circumstances, he might be denied any relief.

Industrial uses are also categorized and separated by zoning ordinances into various zoning districts. The major difference compared with the treatment of other uses lies in the creation of "industrial performance standards" in the modern zoning ordinances. These enable a user to locate within any existing industrial district on the basis of the standards of the district, without the need for rezoning. By using devices to eliminate or reduce its offensive emissions, noises, and vibrations, an industry ordinarily categorized as heavy will be able to qualify for location in a light industrial zone. But the adoption of performance standards has still not eliminated the usual problems of the "zoners": determining requirements for each district, its location, the amount of land area of the city to be included within each, and, of course, accommodating the various and sundry pressure groups or special interests involved—any of which is a most difficult undertaking, and, in the aggregate, Herculean. Because the performance standards are technical, they may be difficult to interpret and enforce. Little difficulty is involved in issuing a permit for a specific use named in a district; it is much harder to ascertain, either before or after construction, whether the quantity of sound, vibration, or smoke emitted by a factory complies with the requirements of a district. The difficulties involved may allow for considerable administrative discretion and possibly political abuse. And this can be adverse to the plant owner who purchased in reliance upon the zoning. If, as it appears, industry will generally locate favorably from the standpoint of property values, there is little purpose in these standards, especially in light of remedies given by pollution and nuisance laws.

Apartments and Townhouses

Houston has experienced two apartment booms subsequent to the end of World War II. The first began in 1962 and lasted for about three years, and the second commenced in 1967 and appears to have much greater momentum. In both 1968 and 1969, permits issued for multiple-family units accounted for over 75 percent of permits issued for residential units. In 1971 and 1972, the percentage began to decline for the Houston metropolitan area as home construction increased substantially in the outlying areas, within and outside the borders of the city.

It is not unusual for areas adjoining factories, railroads, gas stations, or heavily travelled streets to be zoned to allow apartments and townhouses. Such zoning is frequently intended to serve as a buffer separating single-family dwellings from such "undesirable" and "incompatible" uses. As previously stated, many modern ordinances (as well as all the older ones) permit apartment buildings in business districts. A similar pattern of development is evident in Houston where no excuses are necessary, suggesting that these zoning decisions are acceptable in the market place.

In addition to location restrictions, the principal control exercised under zoning over multiple-family developments is through density and height requirements. In Chicago, the six apartment districts vary principally with respect to allowable density, there being no height limitations. The most restrictive category requires 2,500 square feet of land area for every unit constructed, about a net yield of 15 units to the acre, whereas the least restrictive requires only 115 square feet, or about 400 units to the acre. These figures are based on the net acreage available for construction after deducting from about 10 percent (for high rises) to 15 percent (for low rises) of the gross area for streets. Density requirements of different suburbs differ widely in the Chicago area, ranging from 10 to 40 units per acre in districts that do not allow more than four stories. In Dallas, the multi-family districts for the lower-rise buildings allow from 1,800 to 800 square feet of land per unit, about a net of perhaps from 20 to 45 units per acre. High rises may cover in excess of 250 to the acre. Some of Los Angeles low-rise districts allow about 50 to the acre, and the high-rise districts allow over 200 to the acre. (PUD requirements may also control density, some-times almost at the will of the municipality.)

In Houston, the only density control on apartments is indirect; the re-quirement that a certain portion of the parcel or tract be set aside to meet off-street parking requirements. The entire balance can be built upon, pro-vided the building lines, if any, are observed. The result is not maximum-density usage at all times. If it were, only high rises would go up. In fact, relatively few high-rise apartment buildings have been built in Houston as some of those erected have been unprofitable, owing to the competition of the lower-cost garden apartments. What it does mean in many, probably most, instances is maximum density for the more successful two- and three-story buildings.

For those who can afford lower-density construction, there are many rental developments with densities about the same or less than would have been allowed under the A-1 apartment district, the most restrictive multiple-family classification of the zoning ordinance proposed in 1962. It allowed for a lot coverage of only 40 percent, which, according to the city planning director, exceeds the coverage of many then existing and subsequent proj-ects. Competition has caused developers to maintain open space and install recreational facilities in many of the newer and larger developments. At the same time, the city does not have the power to force such open spaces on the many developers who cater to tenants who cannot afford such luxury, or possibly who prefer interior rather than exterior luxuries. The result, as will be shown subsequently, is a rather wide range of densities.

It is difficult to generalize about the apartment market in Houston, for the major factor seems to be the consumer. If a builder believes a particular building can be rented or sold at a potential profit and financing is available, it is likely to be built. A notable exception is townhouses that are for indi-vidual ownership (not for rent) and that by reason of the subdivision regulations probably cannot be built for the lesser-income portion of the private market. The subdivision regulations provide for at least 2,500 square feet of land area per unit and contain other requirements that as a whole tend to inhibit the erection of lower-cost townhouses. In general, however, what does occur in Houston contrasts sharply with what takes place in many zoned cities. Due to the scarcity of such zoning, most multi-family projects require rezoning. Although the larger cities are not neces-sarily reluctant to rezone for more intensive multiple-family use, they often will not do so, and when they do, they may encumber the rezoning with many restrictions. The exclusionary policies of many zoned suburbs toward multiple-family dwellings has received national attention within recent years (see Chapter 4).

An almost equally difficult problem is the amount of density that will be allowed. Density restrictions also serve those who seek to reduce the amount of multifamily development. It is often said by those involved in promulgating zoning restrictions that the absence of density standards would result almost inevitably in extremely dense development. The Houston experience suggests that this is not accurate. Table 2–2 shows average, minimum and maximum densities per acre of multifamily developments receiving final plat approval by the Houston Planning Commission or recorded for the period from 1959 to 1971, as calculated by the City Planning Department. The department considers these figures approximations made largely for its own use and not necessarily precise. Also, most apartment developments probably do not require plat approval and therefore are not included in these figures. In addition, a wide variety of rental projects is included and this tends to reduce the significance of the averages. There are some inherently-low–density projects, such as those containing only rental houses and townhouses (often containing less than ten units to the acre), and some of very high density, high-rise apartment buildings. For the most part, however, the figures relate to garden low-rise apartments. Notwithstanding these limitations, these statistics are revealing of much of the densities of multifamily construction, and indicate that competition and consumer demand exert highly effective controls over density.

Most multiple-family construction in Houston has taken place close to the downtown area (largely within ten miles of its center) and there has

Table 2–2

Chronological Index of Houston Private-street Plats Receiving Final Approval–Density Characteristics

| Year | No. of Plats | Number of Units, per acre | | | Total Units |
		Average	Minimum	Maximum	
1959	3	42.2	23.6	68.7	422
1960	3	29.8	17.0	38.5	239
1961	4	32.4	15.4	64.6	290
1962	22[c]	26.6	18.1	61.9	3620
1963	26	26.86	9.2	48.2	2802
1964	12	22.48	1.95	60.91	1486
1965	12	22.4	7.96	38.88	949
1966	21	21.43	3.13	38.8	3036
1967	15	21.4	3.15	33.4	2126
1968	33	26.09	3.82	49.0	7318
1969	57[a]	25.5			11716
1970	53[a]	22.0[b]			10125
1971	81[a]	21.0[b]			18993

Source: The above figures are taken from records of the Houston City Planning Department.
[a]Recorded plats.
[b]Rounded-off statistics.
[c]Includes 1 plat for convalescent home.

been relatively little in outlying areas fifteen miles or more from the downtown center. The reverse is presently true for single-family construction. Apartment construction in these outlying areas has largely been confined to the strip areas adjoining major thoroughfares. Demand for the multiple-family accommodations is not sufficiently strong in the outlying areas to warrant development of large tracts, particularly when smaller parcels are available there within the strips.

Multifamily development also follows a sectional pattern. In the 1960s most apartment buildings were constructed in the southwest section of the city. In more recent years these have been built further north. In 1969, 84 percent of platting activity within the city limits required under the private-street plat regulation (largely multifamily) concerned a section in the western half of the city; 76 percent in 1970; and 68 percent in 1971.

Perhaps the major reason for the softness of the apartment market in the more distant areas is the large supply available closer in. This suggests an interesting comparison with what might have taken place under zoning. By controlling use and density, zoning would have reduced the number of apartments constructed in the near areas and thereby might have created considerable pressures for apartment development further out. This might have resulted in more mixtures of homes and apartments in these newly developing sections than presently occurs, a somewhat strange twist to the proposition that zoning is required to separate uses.

Downtown

It is difficult to define the limits of the downtown area, or central business district (CBD), of Houston, although there is an area of tall buildings and intense auto and pedestrian traffic that delimits its core.[30] The city's planning director contends that the traditional CBD designed to serve the pre-automobile-age business, civic, and cultural needs of the region is now obsolete, particularly in a city with limited public transportation facilities, for the automobile brings within ready accessibility various downtown activities at scattered locations (even though there may be additional costs in driving and parking). The automobile has also allowed for development of many outlying shopping centers with more convenient parking facilities. As a result, the street-level area of the downtown core has, in effect, become another major shopping center.

That the downtown area is sprawling and not confined is probably attributable to the absence of zoning, but not necessarily. One might reason that zoning tends to confine the downtown by surrounding it with residential uses. However, Los Angeles and Phoenix have sprawling downtowns, and Dallas and Wichita Falls do not. Many nonsprawling downtowns developed in cities prior to zoning. Had Houston adopted zoning in 1962, the downtown area would not have been more confined; however, the 1948 ordinance would have zoned for residential purposes some areas that can be considered as part of the present downtown area. Since the city would have been much smaller, it is likely that if zoning had been adopted earlier than 1947, more of what is now regarded as the downtown area would have been classified for residential purposes. Subsequent changes in the zoning ordinance might also have restricted development within the CBD. Zoning might likewise have impeded the development of some competitive shopping facilities in other parts of the city, thereby benefitting the downtown, but at most, probably this would have had a minimal effect.

It has been said that Houston's downtown area has "sprawled and spread and left obsolescence and blight behind."[31] While this statement is presently accurate with respect to many blocks, it becomes less applicable with the passage of time as new buildings are erected to replace the "blighted" ones. At a time when downtowns are problem areas for many large cities, announcements of proposals for and completions of large office buildings and other substantial projects in the downtown area seem almost commonplace in Houston. According to members of the planning department, considerably more than several billion dollars worth of construction was under way or contemplated for the downtown area throughout 1970 and 1971.

One can readily observe frame buildings whose only future lies in demolition for new business edifices, and they are used and maintained accordingly. This condition enables many small businessmen to have (perhaps temporarily) downtown offices at low cost. Many "blighted" sites have been cleared and remain vacant or are being used as parking lots. Hence, in effect, the downtown area presently contains a substantial land reservoir for future development, probably not dissimilar, except perhaps in size, to what existed in many cities of the North in their earlier stages of growth.

The downtown area is a good example of the virtues of "disorderly" growth, as distinguished from "orderly" growth, traditionally an objective of many planners.[32] Developers have "leap frogged" over vacant land and buildings whenever the price was too "high." Some believe that planning could have prevented this and caused a consecutive "orderly" use of the land. It is difficult to conceive how such control could have been achieved with private ownership of land, but if this had occurred and as a result the downtown area had been contained, many of the sites now contemplated for development would already have substantial structures and their acquisition would probably be unfeasible. Construction within recent and future years would have been substantially deterred. Nor is it possible in a competitive society for government to establish land reservoirs without government ownership. A similar analysis is pertinent for other areas of any city, inasmuch as "this condition of scattered development may, in the long run, prove healthy and serve the city by permitting the interspersal of new uses—by providing breathing space."[33]

The largest development currently underway in the downtown area involves thirty-three square blocks containing approximately seventy-four acres purchased in 1970 by the Texas Eastern Transmission Corporation. The property purchased was in an older, deteriorating section of the downtown area, and it is alleged to have cost between $40 and $55 million. Once part of one of Houston's more elegant residential neighborhoods, the thirty-three-block area was occupied at the time of purchase by a wide assortment of commercial structures, parking lots, apartment buildings, small hotels, and houses, some of which apparently once housed some prominent families. The owner has termed its development "Houston Center—the City of the Future," and the plans are grandiose:

Houston Center represents something never attempted before. The creation of an entirely new city offering fresh approaches to work, recreation and residence. It may well be the prototype of the city of the future. . . . Initial projects will be office buildings, retail stores, hotels and motels, selected entertainment facilities and garden apartments. The type and number of tenants have been carefully planned to insure an economic mix of activities that will generate business for all. . . . An influx of office workers and shoppers by day, a host of entertainment facilities, transient visitors and apartment dwellers by night will create a round-the-clock vitality. . . .[34]

Could this development occur had Houston been zoned? One may speculate that a portion of the section in question might have been zoned for residential at an earlier period and retained that or some less restrictive residential classification. That part of it once contained lavish homes would lend support to this possibility. More certain, perhaps, is that the existence of zoning might have had a chilling effect on the accumulation of the various tracts for the development inasmuch as it is most doubtful that enormous sums will be spent for property without some reasonable certainty as to the use that can be made of that property. The absence of zoning provides that certainty. Since there was diverse ownership of the property, perhaps 150 different owners, the existence of zoning restrictions might have caused the purchaser to enter into option agreements with most of the owners of the more costly tracts pending resolution of any zoning problems. This can be a lengthy and costly road. Many owners may not give long options or they exact better terms if they do. The ability to negotiate and purchase without the risk of some adverse governmental decisions is one of the beneficial consequences of nonzoning.

Modern zoning would probably establish setback requirements for buildings in the downtown section either on a negative or incentive basis. Fortunately zoners are not the only ones so benevolently guided. The Houston Chamber of Commerce has provided information on setbacks established by some of the major buildings in the downtown area in excess of the ten feet required by the city. This is shown in Table 2–3.

Billboards

The only controls Houston exercises over billboards are those involving safety of construction and safety of the motorist: for example, prohibiting easily misunderstood words such as "stop," "look," "drive-in," "danger,"

Table 2–3
Some Voluntary Setbacks in Houston CBD

Building	Approximate Setbacks
Humble Building	Almost half a block on the north, with fountain plaza
Southwestern Bell Telephone Company	40 feet on south for landscaped area
First National Bank	30 feet on west for flagpole plaza and deeper setback section for landscaped area
Tenneco	60 feet on the east for landscaping with trees
One Shell Plaza	40 feet on both east and west sides for landscaped area
Electric Tower	30 feet on south, with bridge spanning Japanese style garden on basement level; 30 feet on east and west sides for landscaping with ornamental trees
Houston Natural Gas	20 feet on north and south for areas with planters; 15 feet on east
Esperson	13 to 14 feet on three sides
Houston Lighting and Power Electric Tower	14 feet on three sides

Source: Houston Chamber of Commerce.

and the use of moving pictures. As with other uses, the location of billboards, which have to compete with other advertising media, will be based on economic considerations, and, as a result, they will be placed only in high traffic areas for maximum exposure. They are generally absent from interior streets, and from many areas of major thoroughfares and expressways, because either there is insufficient traffic or the property is unavailable to such use. Expressways and major thoroughfares (technically referred to as "major arterials" and "collector" streets) constitute approximately 20 percent of the total lineal mileage of all public thoroughfares within the city. But, the motorist, of course, spends much more driving time on these than on the interior streets. One sign that few in Houston can fail to observe is a huge revolving illuminated oil company sign atop one of the tallest buildings in the downtown area.

Municipalities have for alleged nuisance, safety, and aesthetic reasons[35] usually controlled billboards by zoning ordinances and, at times, by separate sign ordinances. Chicago's zoning ordinance is typical of the larger cities; billboards are permitted only in commercial and industrial districts, and then within prescribed limitations. Both proponents and opponents of billboard controls have usually advanced the safety-of-the-motorist arguments in support of their respective positions. The argument to regulate or remove billboards, however, is one primarily based on aesthetics, although it has often been couched in safety or nuisance terms to obtain the approval of the judiciary troubled by the subjectivity involved in aesthetics.[36]

If zoning had been adopted in either 1948 or 1962, there would have been minimum effect on the billboards then in existence. Both ordinances would have permitted billboards in the commercial zones and, because most existing uses were "frozen," would have zoned most of the areas where they are found as commercial. As can be expected, Houston has its antibillboard and probillboard factions. The "antis" want the city, in effect, to adopt their standards of city architecture, which would involve virtually the elimination of all billboards where they are presently found. Another point of view, in terms of "aesthetics," is held by some professors (among others) in the architecture departure of Rice University. They contend that billboards add desirably to the architecture of the modern automobile city, and they approve of the existing policy of the city. Their view is generally consistent with those of architectural commentaries appearing in recent years favorable to a nongovernment-controlled urban environment and critical of the "virtues" of "garden city" and conventional planning approaches.[37] (See discussion in Chapter 7.) But there is little problem in finding support for the more traditional position on billboards.[38] What has probably deterred the city council from acting against billboards is not the aesthetic arguments, but rather the substantial investment and employment involved in the billboard industry, as well as the revenues derived by landowners. There probably is also lacking in Houston a political climate responsive to demands for the control of the use of property.

Land Values

Houston has been called a real estate broker's paradise. This writer's conversations with real estate brokers suggest that they were pleased with the low level of controls exercised by the city over real estate. But they seem oblivious to the many paradises existing in the zoned areas, where fortunes await those of great persuasion, fortitude, and stamina who can convince the city council to change the zoning on their land from less valuable to more valuable use. "When the planning commission and the zoning board flit about sprinkling little golden showers here rather than there, they make millionaires of some and social reformers of others."[39]

Nevertheless, owning land in a zoned community over a period of time can be a hazardous investment. This is not necessarily due to the possibility of its being rezoned for a less valuable use, for the courts may disapprove unless there have been substantial changes in conditions. More likely is that the community will make changes in the zoning ordinance that the courts are unlikely to upset, such as reducing height limitations or increasing the severity of density, floor-area ratio, and parking requirements, each of which has an effect on value. Concurrently, such changes may support the values of existing properties by reducing potential competition.

Use Separations

It should be apparent from the discussion to this point that the real estate market does not operate chaotically or haphazardly; it is quite rational and orderly. An illustration of this is the location of different uses. Economic forces are highly effective in causing uses to locate separately. The land use maps of medium-size Texas cities that are not zoned provide dramatic evidence for this proposition. As previously indicated, the land use maps of Pasadena, Wichita Falls, and Baytown show that industry has largely segregated itself. These maps also show that almost all commercial uses are along major thoroughfares. The land use map of the only other medium-sized Texas city that is not zoned, Laredo (population 70,000),[40] shows a similar pattern of separation between industrial, commercial, and residential uses. Regrettably, economics is also the reason why these maps, some of which are in color and larger than page size, have not been reproduced in this book.

Baytown presents a particularly interesting case. It has some of the heaviest industry in the state as well as subdivisions where homes are valued at upwards of $50,000. When one is in the midst of the industrial area, it is hard to believe that expensive, residential subdivisions exist a relatively short distance away, and a similar reaction about industry occurs in the midst of the residential subdivisions. The subdivisions have been built with due allowance for prevailing wind patterns to avoid odors and fumes from industry.

When some incredulous person attending my lectures demands to know who is *really* responsible for these separations, I have credited the Great Pumpkin (from the Peanuts cartoon strip), who is at least as accountable as anyone for the master planning that occurs within the marketplace. I hope this answer will soothe the feelings of those who believe that good can only come from some higher direction of individual enterprise.

These maps disclose exceptions to the general pattern, but probably little or no more than might occur under zoning in these cities. The land use maps of Amarillo, Lubbock, and Abilene do not suggest that zoning is more effective with respect to industrial proliferation[41] There is little difference apparent in the location of commercial uses; they usually are on the major thoroughfares. Amarillo was zoned in 1931, when it had a population of about 43,000, and its population in 1964, the date of the land use map, was about 130,000. Lubbock was zoned in 1941, when its population was about 32,000; its population in 1964 was about 135,000. Abilene had a population of about 35,000 when it was zoned in 1946; its population in 1965 was about 90,000. The substantial increases in population since the adoption of zoning indicate that it has influenced land use patterns in these cities. Because land use maps of significant size are not available or are difficult to interpret, I have not been able to examine enough of them or adequately to conclude that these zoned cities are representative. At the very least, however, they do create doubt as to whether zoning is more protective than nonzoning against the proliferation of industry. I urge readers to obtain the land use maps of the seven cities referred to, and without looking at the names of the cities, play the "does-she-or-does-she-not-have-zoning" game.

The basis for use separation in the nonzoned cities is much more dependable than the designs of Linus' Great Pumpkin. In Houston, every oil company has the choice of purchasing for gas station construction a lot on an inside or local street for a price often less than $5,000 or of purchasing a lot on a major thoroughfare one or several blocks away for from $50,000 to $100,000. Invariably, it chooses the lot on the major thoroughfare. Comparable choices are daily presented to other commercial users and apartment developers. Industrial users have other reasons that influence their location decisions. Certain locations and areas simply are economically more suitable for certain uses.

There is much reason to conclude that zoning operates to proliferate uses. Consider the situation with apartments in Houston. Approximately 68–84 percent of the land platting activity concerning apartments from 1969 to 1971 were for a certain portion of the city's western section, where there is much vacant land. This was obviously the area in demand by tenants who could afford the rent in new buildings, and the market responded accordingly. There were no zoning restrictions to curtail development there. If, for instance, zoning had been in effect and the amount of apartment construction had been reduced by, perhaps one-half, where would the tenants who were not housed in that area have found new accommodations? It is likely that apartments would have been constructed in other parts of the city where zoning was made available to satisfy at least part of this demand. The result would have been much greater proliferation of apartments and the usual controversies emanating from this kind of situation.

Similar proliferations will occur when a city has not provided sufficient amounts of certain kinds of industrial zoning. And who can conceivably predict future industrial needs and demands? The city fathers will then face the choice of allowing additional industrial development in various other sections of the city or of precluding further industrial expansion, and it is likely that the latter would usually be the choice in the cities.

These pressures explain some of the zoning controversies of more recent years. Thus, Dallas, faced with the pressures of an apartment boom, re-zoned much property to accommodate this demand, much to the displeasure of single-family property owners. So displeased were homeowner groups there with rezoning practices on apartments and commercial uses that they formed a city-wide homeowner's association, which sponsored three candidates for election to the city council in the April 1969 elections, on a platform based on planning and zoning. The same group had requested a moratorium for six months on all zoning amendments pending a re-study of the city's planning. The Dallas City Council had ten seats and all of the homeowner candidates lost, each receiving about 20 percent of the vote.

Concluding Remarks

These are some conclusions drawn from the examination of Houston's system of nonzoning, with some appropriate comparisons to zoning.

⋆1. Economic forces tend to make for a separation of uses even without zoning. Business uses will tend to locate in certain areas, residential in others, and industrial in still others. Apartments will tend to concentrate in certain areas and not in others. There is also a tendency for further separation within a category; light industrial uses do not want to adjoin heavy industrial uses, and vice-versa. Different kinds of business uses require different locations. Expensive homes will separate from less expensive ones, townhouses, duplexes, etc. It is difficult to assess the effectiveness of zoning in furthering this process. It is more successful in this respect in the "bedroom" suburbs, but much less so in the larger cities. However, pressures may develop under zoning leading to greater proliferations of uses.

2. When the economic forces do not guarantee that there will be a separation, and separation is vital to maximize values or promote tastes and desires, property owners will enter into agreements to provide such protection. The restrictive covenants covering home and industrial subdivisions are the most prominent example of this. Adjoining property owners (such as those on a strip location) can also make agreements not to sell for a use that will be injurious to one or more.

3. In the absence of zoning, municipalities will adopt specific ordinances to alleviate specific land use problems.

4. Because many of the early restrictive covenants in Houston were (a) limited in duration, or (b) legally insufficient, or (c) not enforced by owners, zoning would have kept more areas as strictly single family. The covenants created subsequent to 1950 were more durable and as a practical matter will remain in force for long periods. One reason for this is that the city since 1965 has enforced these covenants. They may be as effective as zoning in maintaining single-family homogeneity. They are usually more restrictive than zoning.

5. When covenants expire, land and properties will be used as economic pressures dictate. In time, commercial uses, apartments and possibly a few (probably light) industrial uses will develop along the major thoroughfares. Most business uses will not locate on interior (residential) streets because they require favorable traffic conditions available only on heavily travelled streets. Within recent years, the most important factor influencing diversity in non-restricted interior areas is the strong demand for multiple-family accommodations. But this demand does not extend to all sections of the city. Accordingly, some areas fronting on interior streets will remain relatively free of diverse uses after their covenants expire.

6. Because it is more valuable for these purposes, more land along major

thoroughfares is being or will be used for all varieties of commercial and multifamily purposes than would be the case under zoning.

7. A nonzoned city is a cosmopolitan collection of property uses. The standard is supply and demand, and if there is economic justification for the use, it is likely to be forthcoming. Zoning restricts the supply of some uses, and thereby prevents some demands from being satisfied. It may likewise impede innovation. In general, however, zoning in the major cities, which contain diverse life styles, probably has responded and accommodated to most consumer demands. This has not occurred usually in the more homogeneous suburbs.

✱ 8. The most measurable influence of nonzoning in Houston is its effect on multiple-family dwellings. If Houston had adopted zoning in 1962, this would probably have resulted in higher rents and a lesser number and variety of apartments, and, in consequence, some tenants would have been priced out of the new-apartment market. (See discussion in Chapter 4.)

9. The experience of the FHA suggests that the appreciation over the years in values of new and existing single-family homes has not differed in Houston from those of zoned cities.

3

Are Restrictive Covenants "Virtually Identical to Zoning Ordinances"?

This is the question I have been asked most often concerning "nonzoning," usually by someone who is prepared to argue that the answer is in the affirmative. That thesis has now appeared in the learned literature. A note in the May 1971 issue of the *Harvard Law Review* argues that not only should courts limit the zoning powers of local governments, but also advocates that comparable restraints be applied upon the enforceability of restrictive covenants.[1] Its writer takes the position that zoning and restrictive covenants have similar exclusionary effects, stating as follows:

Restrictive covenants may be virtually identical to zoning ordinances. They can affect as large an area; they bind all residents of the area; they can be altered or lifted only by the unanimous agreement of the property owners; and they are enforceable by official sanctions. Restrictive covenants covering large areas thus verge so closely on being zoning ordinances that courts should be willing to view them as state action, and apply the same standards of equal protection suggested here for zoning ordinances.[2]

The writer of the note is wrong in his basic assumptions and conclusions. Restrictive covenants are not virtually identical: It is most unlikely that they will affect as large an area or the same areas; they are binding only for periods as specified by their terms; and there is relatively little discretion given the state in their creation and enforcement. They function, for these reasons, with far less exclusionary effects than zoning. Restraints created for economic considerations necessarily operate unlike those where political considerations are dominant. Moreover, given the manner in which restrictive covenants do in fact operate, property owners should not be deprived of this freedom to protect their interests. Few restrictive covenants would be vulnerable under the equal protection test proposed by the writer of the note.

It is true that within the boundaries of a subdivision there is not much difference, in terms of exclusionary effects, between zoning and restrictive covenants. The difference arises with respect to land and property exterior to the subdivision. The rights and powers of homeowners accorded by and under restrictive covenants generally terminate at the subdivision boundary line. They seldom have any rights over any land except that in which their subdivision is located. This means they have virtually no control over vacant land once a subdivision is completed.

Zoning provides home owners with substantial powers over the use of

77

vacant land—and this is what has caused most of the problems. Through operation of the political process, they have often been able to greatly influence or even determine all land use within a locality. In many suburban and rural areas, home owners have effective control over the use of land much greater than the size of the subdivisions in which they live.

The statistics of land use for Houston reveals this contrast. Based on the fact that about 25 percent presently accommodates single family use, it can be estimated that not much more than this percentage of the land within the present boundaries has even been subject to restrictive covenants. It is likely that a portion somewhat smaller than 25 percent of the city is currently restricted inasmuch as (1) some areas were never restricted, (2) some of the covenants have expired or are no longer enforceable, and (3) no more than approximately one percent of the city's area is subject to restrictions for townhouse and industrial use.

Most important, only a small fraction of the land subject to these covenants is vacant. The vast bulk of the land so encumbered consists of vacant lots within subdivisions, present in significant amounts generally only in the newly developed subdivisions. The covenants on these lots would seem to be the most defensible of exclusionary devices inasmuch as they do in fact contribute to stability and maximization of values.

This leaves the balance of the land within the city free of local governmental or private land use controls, except for the relatively small number of regulations imposed by the city and the contractual and rental arrangements of the private market.

A similar pattern of controls exists in most of the other non-zoned cities in Texas, but the statistics obviously differ. In these cities, restrictive covenants also are largely confined to single family residential, and, therefore, the amount of land presently used for this purpose differs probably no more than several percentage points from the amount that has ever been subject to them. The amount restricted would be less in older cities with long histories of large, low-income populations, such as Laredo, Texas because of the tendency in the past not to restrict low income areas. The most recently published land-use surveys show that the following percentages of total land within these cities were used for single-family: Wichita Falls (1964), 22%; Pasadena (1966), 26%; and Baytown (1964), 8%.

It is most unlikely that restrictive covenants will cover all of the vacant land within a municipality unless development is controlled from one source, as, for example, in the new towns. In such developments, most or all land use ultimately may be controlled through restrictive covenants, either within the framework of zoning or in its absence.[3]

The objectives governing the use of covenants in these situations as in others differs from those of zoning. The developer's motivations are primarily economic and, therefore, tend to be inclusionary. To obtain maximum revenues, he will seek to develop all of the property within the town in the shortest time-span. He will designate uses for land consistent with current or expected market demands.[4] And he will make great efforts to avoid imposing restrictions that will impede sale or development of any of the land. Similar motivations do not guide local legislators in the zoning of vacant land.

The much discussed new town of Reston, Virginia, provides an interesting example of economics dominating developmental policies in the new towns. When the highly publicized and often heralded planning policies of its founder did not prove financially successful, he was removed from control and replaced by a corporation "whose spokesman says that a developer should 'listen to the market' rather than [to] the city planners and architects."[5]

Most developers in nonzoned areas will seek to maximize values by restricting only those portions of their property programmed for development, leaving the balance (if any) unrestricted and available for other uses or possible sale in the future. Although the balance of the land may have been planned for similar use, probably it will not be restricted until development plans are finalized or representations to this effect made to prospective purchasers. Frequently, some of the land is under option, and the owner would be reluctant to restrict it prior to consummation of the sale. To restrict property "prematurely" would be to deny a possible opportunity to profit from future trends in the real estate market. The landowner who engages, in effect, in exclusionary land use practices by restricting "excessive" amounts of land risks suffering the economic sanctions of the private market, a hazard never confronted by local legislators.

There are in some parts of the country large, partially developed areas which have been restricted by covenants to large lots, one or more acres in size. This appears to occur infrequently in the Houston area, where the use of covenants appears to be highly responsive to market demands. The Houston experience may be representative; there is probably a narrow market for larger lots, and this form of development may involve, on the whole, not very much land in the absence of zoning.

A note in the *Michigan Law Review* has suggested that if zoning were eliminated from suburban and rural areas zoned for large size lots (pursuant to "snob" zoning ordinances), the owners might thereafter enter into covenants to similarly restrict the area.[6] This is virtually inconceivable. While many homeowners would be so inclined, it is doubtful that very many owners of vacant tracts and acreage would forego the greater financial rewards that would or might accrue with the sale or development of property for a multitude of other uses. Many of the lots restricted for single-family development would also be smaller than they would be under zoning in order to accommodate the less-affluent portions of the home market. Chapter 15 contains some examples of what has occurred upon termination of restrictions. The situation would be comparable in the event zoning were eliminated: covenants would be imposed principally by homeowners living on residential (interior) streets.

Another question often raised concerns whether zoning or covenants is the more flexible to meet changing conditions. This is not much of a contest; it is probably as relevant in the one case as it is irrelevant in the other. Inasmuch as most new construction by far takes place on land that has always been vacant and unsubdivided, restrictive covenants do not affect most developers in the nonzoned cities unless they choose to impose them. (There may be an exception to this proposition for the new towns as previously discussed.)

Therefore, any meaningful comparison of flexibility between covenants and zoning is limited to the minority of construction that involves redevelopment of property already occupied by homes. It is only with the passage of time, as the amount of vacant land diminishes, that this question will become significant. Principally, older homes would be involved.

Reclassifying improved property may be a very complex matter. In most instances it is probably much more difficult to rezone property containing houses than unimproved property. The two major reasons for this are: (1) The proposed rezoning may become a matter of "people removal," an issue which has attained considerable importance in urban renewal and some expressway construction projects and could well block almost any change; and (2) there may be more owners adjoining or surrounding an established area than a vacant one and they have the power to force a larger than majority vote for rezoning on the part of the local legislature. This refers to the usual provision in zoning ordinances that requires a two-thirds or three-fourths vote of approval of the local legislature when 20 percent of the owners adjoining or across the street from the property under consideration protest the proposed rezoning.

Of course, zoning does not remain static; ordinances do change as a result of amendment or even court action. In the case of improved properties, however, it is doubtful in the event of any opposition by residents that local legislators (or even courts) will approve rezoning (and, therefore, possibly some "people removal") unless they strongly favor what the developer proposes to do. In all cases of rezoning, however, whatever is developed on the land that is rezoned will still have to comply with the provisions of the ordinance.

Here again restrictive covenants present different alternatives. Until the covenants expire, the developer will be unable to redevelop an area unless he buys all, or virtually all of it. However, when private restrictions on land or property in a nonzoned area expire and there is no renewal, relatively minimal local controls remain over development. In Houston, the property may thereafter be developed or redeveloped for almost any use consistent with market conditions, and there are few controls affecting density and bulk. The developer in a zoned area will still be bound by the use, density, height, and bulk restrictions pertaining to the new classification or to the requirements of and exactions under PUD, and the tendency over the years has been for these controls to become increasingly restrictive (and exclusionary), reducing the options available to a developer.

The distinction narrows in the case of covenants containing an automatic extension provision. If the majority of owners so desire, they can continue the covenants indefinitely, with perhaps some modifications over the years. And amendments may be adopted only at specified intervals. It is possible that zoning might shorten the period for restricted single-family use and that new classification might be less limited than would be the case if the majority of owners controlled this decision; however, it can also be argued that in "mature" subdivisions the majority would be as or more susceptible to economic pressures for change than would the local legislators. Substantial changes in market conditions or purchase by a developer of a number of homes or vacant lots could result in a majority agreement to rescind or amend. It would seem that the more vacant land within the subdivision, the greater the likelihood that this will occur.

Zoning is likely to be more flexible than covenants imposed in perpetuity, especially when the covenants are enforced by the municipality, as in Houston. Fortunately, the incidence of use for perpetual covenants appears to be relatively small. This is the situation in Houston and probably elsewhere. Thus, a provision for a perpetual term may not be acceptable to the FHA, and a manual of the National Association of Home Builders specifically recommends against its use.[7] Courts have traditionally disfavored long-term restraints on real property, although covenants in perpetuity are usually held to be valid. This judicial attitude, however, may cause courts to void perpetuity provisions in certain questionable situations.

Compromising the enforceability of covenants might have unfortunate consequences for many owners of property if not for the community. In the nonzoned areas, it would likely lead to some form of zoning. Many problems also would be created in the zoned areas for multiple ownership developments and for cluster-type developments. For example, townhouse and similar planned unit developments generally require the creation of restrictive covenants to allocate rights and obligations of owners whose accommodations are separated only by party walls or small open spaces and who may in common own private streets, utilities, park areas, and recreational facilities. The stability and viability of such developments depend on very detailed exposition and definition of the rights of ownership contained in their restrictive covenants.

This need not preclude rendering unenforceable those provisions of restrictive covenants that are clearly contrary to public policy, as has occurred with respect to racial restrictions.[8] Where covenants control land usage within the entire area of new towns, there may also be problems presented that are not raised in smaller subdivisions. Thus, voting arrangements established solely on the basis of property ownership may conflict with constitutional voting guarantees.[9]

Restrictive covenants partake of the law of real property and the law of contracts. Courts have no difficulty in enforcing a contractual arrangement between two or more parties. Restrictive covenants, however, may govern relationships between persons one or more of whom never formally consented to their terms. Thus, it is clear that the developer and his purchasers may, as part of their contracts of sale, agree as to future use of property.

The developer agrees that (1) he will not erect any structures other than homes on the balance of the subdivision, and (2) he will contract with all other purchasers to the same effect. The purchaser, in turn, agrees not to use the property for any purpose other than a home. The problem arises because this agreement would be practically meaningless if subsequent owners were not also subject to its terms. Unless they or their properties were likewise bound, property within the subdivision could be used for other purposes. The judiciary evolved rules to protect the actual intentions of the original purchasers and the probable intentions of most subsequent purchasers.

Consequently, when a purchaser of a home acquires title that is subject to a restrictive covenant, he assumes certain obligations and acquires certain rights relating to his property and those of other owners for a specified period of time. This need not be considered in derogation of an "open" market, nor contrary to rights of property ownership, for there are many commitments and restraints operative in any market.

Contractual arrangements necessarily limit various economic freedoms of the parties for the duration of the agreements. Obvious examples include employment contracts, franchise agreements, exclusive sales agreements, and leases. Shopping center leases control even sales procedures. They may also control the location of other businesses of their tenants within certain distances of the center. Franchise agreements limit the rights of the franchisors within certain areas as well as the sales and operating practices of the franchisees. Easements are created by contract for long-periods or in perpetuity, and sometimes implied by law. These restraints are essential to the viability of a market and generally will be upheld by courts unless they are not reasonably related to that objective. These are not inconsistent with an open market, for the market could not possibly operate without the freedom of contract.

The terms and provisions of contractual agreements vary with the requisites of individual markets and their customs and practices. As with other legal agreements, restrictive covenants will differ in terms, duration, and enforcement, depending on the maker, the parties in interest, and the particular section of the housing market involved. Covenants intended for the less wealthy will differ from those for the more wealthy; the latter can better afford strict homogeneity and greater upkeep, and usually have different tastes and attitudes. These factors will also determine the degree or extent to which covenants are enforced.

Restrictive covenants are not entered into as a result of individual negotiation and to this extent appear to differ from the more common forms of contract, such as leases, mortgages and purchase and sales agreements. However, many provisions of these other agreements are also standard and common. Also, in any one period, market conditions may be such that there is no room for negotiations. For example, leases in apartment buildings frequently are submitted to the tenant in a more or less "take it or leave it" basis. Mortgages on homes often are also executed on a similar

basis; the duration and interest rate are merely inserted, along with descriptive material, on a lengthy printed form. Contracts for homes in real
estate developments are virtually printed forms. Moreover, unlike a restrictive covenant, none of these documents is drafted primarily to protect
the interests of the consumer.

Restrictive covenants are a device of the market to maximize the value
of homes. Most American homeowners prefer to live in a homogeneous
single-family environment, and they should have the freedom to pursue
this goal, provided others are not thereby harmed. Restrictive covenants
come close to achieving this balance. On the other hand, existing zoning
laws allow almost unlimited pursuit of this objective with consequent adverse effects upon many others.

The incorporated cities and villages within and adjoining the boundaries
of Houston exemplify this contrast. In passing through some of these
municipalities, one can almost see the "invisible walls" which the suburbs
have created. But, then, it is contended, this is why so many moved there;
to raise their families and live their lives in what they believe to be the
better environment. Does this require that they be protected in their way
of life to the limits of the town's boundaries which may, of course, be
many miles from their homes? In striking contrast are some very expensive
subdivisions of Houston, such as River Oaks and Tanglewood, covering
much smaller areas, but judging from the price level of the homes, as much
or more in demand. This would suggest that the wants and desires of the
more affluent members of the population may be reasonably satisfied without the need for their controlling large areas of vacant land.

What effect can the construction of apartments many blocks away from
a subdivision have on property values within the subdivision? A high-rise
apartment building was erected across a thoroughfare from River Oaks,
probably the most affluent subdivision in Houston, where houses may sell
for hundreds of thousands of dollars. Values are probably less for the row
of homes closest to this high rise, and even possibly for the next row, than
they would be if there were other homes in its place. It is hard for me to
believe that the effect is much greater. This relatively small diminution in
values on the perimeter of the subdivision hardly justifies a grant of power
to River Oaks inhabitants to allow them to eliminate this construction. Yet
such reasoning does underlie the exclusionary policies of the suburbs.

It is also possible that values of suburban homeowners would be more
secure if they did not have zoning and had to rely instead on restrictive
covenants. (Some or many single-family subdivisions, of course, are subject
to both.) Restrictive covenants are more likely to preclude any use of
property which might be harmful to values. They allow for much greater
architectural and aesthetic controls than zoning does. Thus, under zoning,
the local zoning board may grant variations on the size of the required site
(from, say, fifty feet of frontage to twenty-five or thirty), churches and
home occupations are often permitted uses, and there is generally minimal
control over the nonconformist (allowing for, "eccentric" architecture and

the use of a "lesser" quality of materials). More control over the character of one's own neighborhood may enhance values and aesthetics to a greater extent than control over someone else's neighborhood.

Restrictive covenants can also add a constructive note in the controversy over the extent to which zoning powers should be limited. The courts are constantly faced with the problem of determining the point at which zoning restrictions become arbitrary and unreasonable and, therefore, unlawful. In many states, the decisions may vary greatly, depending upon individual fact situations, thereby creating a form of judicial havoc for both sides. I suggest that the line can be much more specifically and rationally drawn on the basis of the experience with restrictive covenants in the nonzoned cities. Homeowners there have only the power reasonably required to protect their values in accordance with evidence established in an excellent proving ground, the marketplace.

The exercise of zoning powers by existing residents at the expense of society's needs for more and better housing and better housing conditions demands reexamination of some fundamental questions underlying the basis of zoning:

1. What is the extent of protection to which property owners are entitled?
2. What powers should existing residents have to exclude other people and things from the municipality?

Empirical answers to these questions are provided in the land use experience of Houston. It shows that communities can function reasonably well and the values of homes and other real estate can be maintained and enhanced without the need to give homeowners much more protection than they are accorded by restrictive covenants. The land use powers of the homeowners, usually the most exclusionary group in the community, are limited to what seems reasonably essential to maintaining and maximizing the values of their homes. Specific ordinances concerning land use can and should be adopted only when needed to regulate specific problems of land use. (A parking ordinance would be an example of this.)

This program of controls appears to balance well the exclusionary and inclusionary housing objectives of our society. It also sets forth for courts deciding zoning controversies a realistic basis for testing the reasonableness of zoning restrictions in the usual due process or "taking" inquiry, or even for evaluating the justification presented for zoning if questions of equal protection are raised. (A more detailed discussion of the judicial aspects of zoning is contained in Chapters 12, 13, and 14.)

Part II
The Effects of Zoning

4 The Effects of Zoning on Housing

When housing is involved, a zoning controversy is not simply one of municipality versus landowner, or a case of people versus property; it is one of people versus people. It is basically a controversy between those who already live in a certain area and those who would like to live in that or an adjoining area. Zoning allows existing residents of a community to greatly influence or even determine who can and who cannot move into that community.

It likewise gives inordinate powers and privileges to existing residents over people outside the community, who would benefit from the filtering effect created by new housing, as well as those within the housing market who would benefit from a greater supply of both land and housing. Involved are restraints on mobility and opportunity and the creation of social and economic difficulties for many, particularly those of average or less incomes. One group, those who got there first, exercises considerable restraints over the production of housing beneficial to many other groups.

The consequences of zoning are quite pervasive and reflect throughout a housing market. Because a market for housing has no relationship to the boundaries of municipalities, the effects of zoning transcend borders. As the subsequent discussion will show, the erection of one housing unit in a suburb may possibly affect the tenant of a housing unit in the inner portion of a city, many miles distant. The number of units produced within a housing market will influence prices and conditions throughout that market, again without regard to local boundaries. Hence in the case of a suburb, the cumulative effects of its zoning on property exterior to that suburb are likely to be much greater than on property within it. The same can be said about zoning practices for the outlying sections of the cities, which are the areas largely subject to new development.

Consequently, zoning practices have much extraterritorial effects. It is most doubtful that with respect to new housing there is such a thing as a purely local zoning action.

In this chapter, the effects of zoning on housing will be considered. The discussion will evaluate separately (1) exclusionary effects within the municipality, (2) effects on the filtering process, and (3) price effects. The housing experience of Houston will be employed when illustrative of the operation of the housing market. Zoning has also a major influence on the extent to which property is developed, and on business and employment, all matters affecting finances of government, and likewise of great importance to owners and tenants. It also affects competition among producers and sellers. These aspects of zoning will be discussed in subsequent chapters.

87

Exclusionary Effects within the Municipality

Mary Brooks has written, "exclusionary zoning" is one of the catch phrases of the day, symbolizing the problems created by zoning which excludes low- and moderate-income housing.[1] The same theme recurs in much of the learned literature. The inference is that the balance of zoning is not exclusionary, that the other restrictions are well or better founded: in effect, that "bad" zoning is exclusionary, whereas "good" zoning is not.

The catch phrase and its underlying definition are inconsistent with the operation and effects of zoning. Exclusionary zoning is actually a redundancy. All zoning is exclusionary, and is expected to be exclusionary; that is its purpose and intent. The provisions governing almost every zoning district operate to exclude certain uses of property from certain portions of the land, and thereby in the case of housing, the people who would occupy the housing excluded.

Exclusion is accomplished in two ways: First, directly by not permitting, or prohibiting, certain construction through location, area, and density restrictions; and second, indirectly by establishing requirements which increase costs, limiting the numbers of eligible buyers.

The provisions of the ordinance may be specific in not permitting certain uses at designated locations, but the same end may also be achieved through density and bulk restrictions. Thus height limitations may exclude high rises, and coverage and setback requirements may exclude inexpensive townhouses and duplexes. Large-lot or minimum floor-area standards may exclude average- and lower-priced homes, and specified bedroom counts may exclude three-bedroom apartments in some areas and efficiency and one-bedroom apartments in others.

Zoning operates indirectly to increase costs when it enables local authorities to require additional items of construction or design as a condition for approval of a request to rezone property. Some requirements not intended to raise costs may have this effect. An example of this is presented when a zoning ordinance permits mobile home parks to be established only in industrial districts, where land is more costly than in areas zoned for homes or agriculture.

Actually any governmental regulation that imposes a cost over what would be required by competitive conditions tends to raise prices, and therefore operates to exclude buyers from the market. Sometimes zoning is simply superfluous, in the sense that it does little over and above what would occur in its absence. And it may encompass regulation whose exclusionary effects are justified. When restrictions are *clearly* essential to the maintenance of the public health, safety, and welfare, the requirements of organized society exonerates the increase in cost. This broadly encompasses the common law precept that one is free to do whatever he pleases with his property unless he causes damage thereby to that of others. The regulation of nuisances would thus be justified, as would, in my opinion, the far less clear situation of residential off-street parking.

However, the line between justifiable and unjustifiable regulations becomes muted in the zoning process. Planning rules have been established creating broad and highly subjective definitions of harmful effects. Moreover, the determination as to what should be regulated, and how and to what extent, is left frequently to the discretion of parties with a strong partisan interest in the outcome of these questions, the local residents. Through the conduct of the legislative process, they greatly influence, if not often determine, what is to be designated as "incompatible," "undesirable," and "adverse." They are able to judge in their own cause. They can be expected to and do act in what they regard as their best interests; and this has resulted in the erection of invisible but highly effective exclusionary walls throughout the country which exclude a substantial portion of the population from a substantial portion of the land.

A policy of deliberate exclusion toward multiple-family housing has almost become an accepted part of the life style of most American suburbs, especially those that were largely developed subsequent to World War II. This policy has been a topic for numerous articles and studies and has provided much litigation throughout the country.[2]

In those instances when apartments have been permitted within suburbs, they have often had to comply with rigorous "snob" standards. It is understandable that, given a choice by the zoning process as to the type of tenants they can have, the suburbanites act in what they deem to be their own best interests. They will want the "better" people to occupy expensive (highly taxed) apartment buildings; especially those that will not "overload" the schools with children and therefore allegedly raise taxes.

Because there have not been enough areas zoned for such use, probably most multiple-family projects have come about through rezoning and by way of planned unit development (PUD) provisions of a zoning ordinance, which are usually utilized for the largest developments. Hardly unexpectedly, the petitioners who proposed the more luxurious projects were the most likely to be approved, particularly if the legislative body of the community were convinced that they would attract single people or families without children.

In contrast to this trend in suburban areas, some community groups in Chicago in 1971 caused the adoption of zoning text amendments designed to exclude certain types of buildings containing largely efficiency or one-bedroom apartments, because, among other things, such apartments do not attract tenants with children. The prior zoning allowed such construction, and apparently these groups feared that the newcomers, families without children, who comprise a different social category, would change the character of *their* community. Unlike the suburbanites, these groups want apartments that will cater to large families. They succeeded in obtaining the desired legislation at a time when for a variety of reasons there was little interest or activity in the erection of these structures, and the realty interests did not formally oppose it. Subsequently, the real estate groups became concerned and succeeded in modifying the original ordinance—indicating the presence of powers which they usually do not have in the suburbs.

A survey of municipalities would undoubtedly reveal numerous other pressures for limiting occupancy within either the neighborhood or the city. The smaller and more homogeneous the community, the more likely that such pressures will result in the adoption of the desired zoning restrictions, with the result that the epitomes of such exclusivity are the bedroom suburbs. Some states have enacted legislation to give neighborhoods more power over land use within their areas, thus tending to neutralize or overcome other forces within the city that would not serve the "interests" of that community.

In the larger cities the zoning ordinances will usually have several or more multiple-family districts as well as business districts in which the erection of multiple-family dwellings are permitted. Thus, in addition to most of its business and commercial districts. Chicago has six districts, R-3 to R-8, allowing multiple-family construction; Los Angeles has nine such districts; and Dallas has four such districts. These other cities also allow apartments in commercial zones. In Chicago, which has no height limitations on apartments, the primary difference between the districts is the density requirements, allowing for from 2,500 square feet of land per unit in the R-3 district to 115 square feet of land area per unit in the R-8 district. Height limitations may also vary between districts in Los Angeles and Dallas. Again, the city is confronted with determining the "magic" numbers of the required density, height, and other restrictions for each district and its location. Which area should be high density and which area should be low density? Where should the district begin and where should it end? Whose property will get the valued R-8 and whose property will get the much less valued R-5? The stakes can be high for the landowner. If a parcel in Chicago can be rezoned from R-4 to R-5 to R-6, its yield in apartment units will possibly be doubled, and so might its value.

The creation of different apartment districts will influence considerably land development within a city, but, of course, not conclusively, since zoning cannot control demand. It would seem that the more multiple-family districts created, the greater the overall inflexibility of these provisions; changes are only possible within narrow limits. For example, no matter how persuasive he and his facts are, the owner of property in an R-4 district can ordinarily, at most, expect a rezoning for R-5 or possibly R-6, inasmuch as the city could successfully defend on the ground that a denser use would be inconsistent with the planning for the general area and would thus peril the entire plan for the city.

Exclusionary policies also impede single-family construction to the disadvantage even of middle-income groups. Zoning ordinances may establish districts with single-family lot size requirements bearing little or no relationship to market demands. Thus in very large sections of counties within the Chicago metropolitan area, a minimum of about 10,000 to 43,560 square feet (one acre) of land is required for each lot, despite the fact that frequently subdivision within incorporated municipalities nearby are zoned for about 7,500-square-foot lots. A Douglas Commission survey shows that 25 percent of metropolitan area municipalities with a population of five thousand or more permit no less than one-half acre lots. In some areas, three to five acres are required.[3] It is said that 50 percent of the vacant land zoned for residential use within fifty miles of Times Square is classified for a minimum of one-acre lots.[4] A study of eight counties in New Jersey showed that 60 percent of the vacant, residentially zoned, developable land was classified for a minimum lot size of one acre or more.[5] An additional 22 percent was zoned for a minimum of one-half to one acre.

Requiring the purchase of considerably more land than market conditions warrant usually adds cost directly to the purchase price of a home and also adds indirectly to the cost by reducing the supply of land. In recent years, cost considerations have caused builders to reduce the size of lots, a trend which appears to be at variance with what has frequently occurred under zoning. Thus in 1970, the sites under homes purchased with FHA-insured mortgages averaged only 8,851 square feet in area, down 17.5 percent from the 10,709-square-foot average for homes built in 1965.[6]

There are also zoning ordinances which create districts permitting only the erection of homes with minimum specified floor areas. This amount is often greater than would be otherwise erected in the area and larger than many existing and marketable homes. Such restrictions clearly operate to raise the prices of homes.

If going prices of open space in new houses average, say, $15 per square foot, each 100 square feet of floor space required may add about $1500 to the price of a home, quite a price to pay to satisfy local public opinion. Within recent years, builders have been reducing the size of houses as a way of reducing costs and such restrictions obviously impede these efforts.[7]

Perhaps heading the list of housing types excluded by zoning are mobile homes. They appear to have the distinction of being unwanted almost as much by the central cities as by their suburbs. Often they are not permitted within the entire jurisdiction, or if permitted, are confined to industrial districts. Sometimes they qualify only as special uses—allowing participation by the public at the hearings held on requests for approval, something highly conducive to obtaining a rejection. The executive director of the National Association of Counties describes the situation as follows:

Typically the major preoccupation of most local governments have been to find mechanisms to keep out mobile home parks. In all too many cases these parks have been located in industrial areas and in places as remote from fixed-foundation homes as the law and human ingenuity will allow.[8]

The Douglas Commission reported that a 1964 study of 237 zoning ordinances in New York state revealed that over one-half effectively excluded mobile homes, and only eleven permitted mobile home parks to locate within residentially zoned areas.[9] A study of a four-county area in northeast New Jersey disclosed that mobile homes were effectively excluded from 100 percent of all of over 500,000 acres of land suitable for development.[10]

Even when permitted, zoning requirements may be so onerous as to effectively exclude mobile homes. It is hard to conceive of a luxury mobile home intended for the wealthy, but that is apparently the only kind permitted in one New Jersey township, which requires 1,500 square feet of floor space and one acre of land for each mobile home.[11] An average mobile home in 1970 contained in excess of 700 square feet.

This policy against mobile homes is particularly objectionable at a time when much effort and money are being expended to produce subsidized housing. Mobile homes provide housing for many who would otherwise be limited to subsidized housing. They serve the needs of the group in the population that is most in need of better housing. They have grown considerably in popularity within recent years; in 1960, about 100,000 units were produced; while in 1971, this figure rose to almost 500,000 (not all of these, however, are used for housing).

As the courts become more sensitive to the housing needs of the less affluent, local government may resort to higher zoning standards as a device for excluding them—which will be burdensome and costly to monitor. Areas that are now havens for mobile homes will become much less so as these areas increase their homeowner population or adopt zoning ordinances. Florida has ranked in recent years as one of the leading states for mobile home shipments, most of which probably located in the unincorporated areas. With the passage of legislation enabling the counties in that state to adopt zoning, counties have enacted zoning restrictions that operate to exclude many mobile homes, and thus unwittingly perhaps to give existing mobile home parks a preferred status. It is difficult to envision any possible reconciliation between the interests of both existing and prospective mobile home owners and zoning.

Effects on the Filtering Process

When new homes or apartments are constructed and occupied, the families that move into them usually vacate their former residences for occupancy by others. These others, in turn, may vacate other units and the process may continue through a number of sequences. This is the filtering process induced by new construction.

This filter-down effect of new construction has been subject to controversy.[12] I have been personally "assured" that it does not really operate or that its desirability has been conclusively disproven; and in addition, that any reliance upon it to solve housing conditions is an affront to the less fortunate, who, it is contended, are entitled to new housing as a matter of right. Conversely, a rather wealthy friend paid it homage by acknowledging that he had never lived in any home that had not filtered down. As is probably the case with most lawyers, I have observed filter-down operate for those clients who enter into contracts to purchase new homes conditional on their being able to sell their old homes. Builders and realtors are accustomed to making such agreements, and sometimes even third parties are involved, adding another succession of moves.

Many questions have now been resolved as a consequence of an extensive study of the filtering process related to new construction conducted during the middle sixties by the Survey Research Center of the Institute for Social Research at the University of Michigan. The results of this study appear in a monograph published by the University in 1969, entitled *New Homes and Poor People*.[13] The study followed every movement resulting from new construction, throughout the country, when necessary. The new construction studied was a probability sample of dwellings in seventeen standard metropolitan statistical areas (SMSA's). Chains of moves came to an end when the last persons in a sequence leave no vacancy behind or if the last house or apartment in a sequence is removed from the housing stock physically or from residential use.

The turnover of housing generated by new construction apparently has accounted annually for about one-half of the moves that occur each year. According to this survey, the construction on the average of 1,000 new units, both homes and apartments, makes it possible for a total succession of about 3,500 moves to occur to different and likely better housing conditions. "If they move, they benefit."

Hence, the addition of one new housing unit to the market serves not only its intended occupants, but also several other families or individuals who are able to move as a result to other and presumably better accommodations. The exclusionary effects of zoning consequently do not terminate at the boundary line of the municipality but continue on throughout the housing market of which the city or town is part.

Some other conclusions of the survey follow:

1. The results indicate that poor people (at the time of the survey families with incomes of under $3,000) do benefit indirectly from new construction. The survey estimates that about 9.4 percent of the movers were poor. This group constituted numerically about 13 percent of all families in the metropolitan areas included within the study. (But they may have benefited more in another respect, as is discussed in Item 7.) As can be expected, the poor were under represented in proportion to their numbers in the population in moving into new homes and in the subsequent succession of moves. Thereafter, beginning with the third succession of moves, poor families were represented in approximately the same proportion which they represent of the population.

2. Families of moderate incomes (between $3,000 and $6,000 annually at the time of the survey) benefit even more. Close to 27 percent of those who moved were in this category, although this group made up about 19 percent of all families in the metropolitan area studied. Clearly under-reported were people of higher incomes. Those with incomes of $10,000 and above made up 38 percent of the population, but only 29 percent of all families in the sequence of moves.

3. The moves caused by new construction in the newly developed areas of the city extend to older areas near the center. "New construction on the periphery does have indirect consequences for crowding in the center of the city."

4. By and large, the higher the value of the new house, the longer the average

length of the chain of moves. Over the course of sequences, average value of homes fell from a median value of $25,900 for new homes to a median value of $17,300 for the sixth or later sequence. In the case of rental units, the median rent was $135.00 for new units to a median of $100.00 for the sixth or later sequence. (Forty-two percent of the chains started with a new rental unit.)

5. About one out of four sequences begun by new construction end in a demolition or other permanent withdrawal from the housing stock. This should result in improvement of the housing stock.

6. The housing market is not significantly segmented by age, stage in family cycle or social status, and therefore operates relatively free of such considerations. This suggests that the creation of any new living unit will tend to create a succession of moves. Further, any policy which increases supply will affect the prices in the market.

7. Measured strictly in the number of moves, blacks do not appear to benefit from filtering nearly as much as do whites. However, evaluated in terms of overall effects, the benefits may be more comparable. "We estimate that the proportion which Negroes represent of families in the sequence of moves . . . is about .70 [70 percent] of what would be predicted on the basis of the incomes of all families in the sequences and the proportion which Negroes form of each group in the metropolitan areas being studied." The principal reason for this appears to be that blacks occupy somewhat less than 61 percent of the new homes than might be expected on the basis of their incomes. This is not only the result of discrimination, it is also because of their low average assets, which makes difficult both down payments and the subsequent monthly payments needed in the purchase of new homes. In 1962, several years prior to the survey, the average net worth for whites was more than five times the average for blacks.

When they do move, they are more likely to move into a new apartment than into a new home; as of the date of the survey, about 57 percent of blacks who moved into a new dwelling moved into an apartment, compared to 42 percent of the whites. More beneficial to blacks proportionally is the sequence of moves initiated by new construction rather than the new construction itself.

The statistics on the sequence of moves by blacks does not appear adequately to reflect the full benefits derived by them. Thus, the numbers by themselves do not describe the extent to which crowded conditions are alleviated. Thirty-three percent of all moves by blacks leave someone still occupying the former home, compared to seventeen percent of whites. "It appears that Negroes are crowded, and when a Negro family moves into a different dwelling, often some member of the group who had been living together still occupies the original dwelling. As a result, sequences of moves involving Negroes tend to end more quickly than sequences involving only whites." It is possible to conclude that at least some of the people who will be less crowded will benefit as much as those who move. Their housing accommodations will be improved. The filtering effect may convert along the line into a thinning effect.

The considerable space I have devoted to this survey should not be interpreted by the reader as signifying full concurrence with its methodology and conclusions. Others with greater knowledge in such matters have approved its methodology.[14] Its results are consistent with what I would have anticipated on the basis of my experience in the real estate market, although I would have predicted a greater number of moves than the study shows. The exact numbers are not that important; the significance of the study lies in its analysis of the operation of the real estate market, of the direct and indirect consequences of new construction.

It is difficult to understand the philosophy of those who discredit the benefits of the filtering process. Often, they argue that our society has failed us unless we provide every family the opportunity to buy a new home or rent a new apartment. This is simply not realistic; even with all manner of government subsidies, it is not possible for enough new homes and apartments to be constructed and sold at prices that all or nearly all could afford. The objective should be to give everyone the opportunity to acquire *decent* housing, whether new or old. And that it is new need not necessarily make it better. Many older homes and apartments are obviously as comfortable and convenient as, or more than, the new ones. Many of our sophisticated architectural critics condemn much of the new and praise much of the old, and friends of mine who can well afford it, reject most new housing because of its "sterility."

Nor does *new* necessarily mean *decent* housing. Relatively new public housing and subsidized housing projects are frequently in worse repair than much older housing. These projects provide examples of four- or five-year-old apartment buildings that are in much worse condition than buildings more than ten times their age. Government sponsored or subsidized programs have shown that when new apartment buildings are built in deteriorating areas, they may deteriorate rapidly and soon be in worse condition than much older housing in other sections of the city.

There are very few in our society who are not limited in the attainment of material goods. There are a great many who cannot afford new cars, tailor-made clothes, gourmet foods, or new housing, and this is and always will be the case in every country of the world. The objective of civilized society is to allow everyone to attain these goods in decent quality and quantity. Maximum production through the market system is the key to achieving this objective in housing.

The operation of the filtering process is a most important means to better housing and better housing conditions. Removing impediments inhibiting the construction of new housing will allow the process to operate more effectively. Government policy should be directed at stimulating this process, certainly not curtailing it as inevitably occurs and will continue to occur under zoning. Not the least of the virtues of filtering is the fact that little if any federal government monies need be involved in the creation of better housing conditions. A freer market in housing thus provides great housing benefits at little cost to the taxpayer.

Effects of Zoning on Prices of Housing

Zoning influences the prices of apartments and homes principally in three ways: First, by controlling the supply of sites for various uses, it influences the price of land classified for different residential purposes. This price is ultimately reflected in the price to the consumer as one of the component costs of the house or apartment. Second, zoning also influences rents and prices when it operates directly or indirectly to reduce or enlarge the supply of multiple- or single-family accommodations. Third, it may provide for requirements that will add to the cost of the land and the cost of construction.

If zoning is not always the most critical element in determining land price as some have contended, it is certainly a most important factor. Often the price asked is contingent upon property being rezoned from a less valuable to a more valuable classification.

In the absence of zoning, supply and demand largely control the price of land that is not subject to restrictive agreements. When a zoning ordinance is imposed on the supply, new price relationships are necessarily created. The terms and provisions of the ordinance governing the use of one's land together with the amount of other tracts similarly restricted will henceforth determine values.

By imposing standards of density, bulk, and height, zoning will operate to reduce the supply of vacant land available within the community, assuming that the same uses will be permitted by the ordinance as could have been erected prior to its adoption. Usually, however, the ordinance will operate to reduce demand for land to some extent by eliminating or reducing certain kind of uses; that is, mobile home parks, townhouses, motels, gas stations, and so on. But some of this demand, such as that for townhouses will be channeled into a demand for apartments, or possibly for homes which utilize more land than townhouses. And some of the land will remain unused while the owner seeks to overturn the zoning to allow for the more valuable use.

Houston provides an analytical base for evaluating the influence of zoning on the prices for real property. That there are substantial differences with what results under zoning can be readily ascertained from a cursory investigation of land prices there. It was a somewhat surprising experience for me, accustomed as I am to steep prices for land zoned for multiple-family use, to learn that in Houston much land unrestricted as to use is more valuable for single-family than for multiple-family purposes. Many landowners and their brokers readily acknowledged to me that their land in outlying sections was "overpriced" for multiple-family use. Had "comparable" land been zoned for multiple-family in a zoned city, there is little question that much of it would have been priced much higher and completely out of reach for the single-family developer.

There is, therefore, an obviously different relationship of land prices under zoning and nonzoning. What follows is an attempt to summarize this and other differences using the specific experience of Houston as a basis for much of the subsequent analysis.

Single-Family

The reader's attention is directed to Fig. 2–9. It sets forth a hypothetical situation in an outlying section of the Houston metropolitan area. Only one of the six tracts shown has been subdivided and the question presented is how the other five tracts will be used. Other assumptions of the illustration are therein described.

Given the facts shown in Fig. 2–9, the highest price for Tracts 1 to 5 from 1968 to 1970 would be most likely to come from a developer of single-family homes, and as a result the price of each would have been based on its use for a subdivision of homes (with contiguous strip commercial and/or multiple-family development). This would be the case, notwithstanding that for the years cited Houston was at the height of its most recent apartment boom. The apartment market was generally "soft" in most areas located about fifteen to twenty miles from the downtown section. For this reason, it would generally have been too expensive for an apartment developer to purchase a large tract of land. Although he might have shared the tract with a home builder, his proposed use of a portion for multiple-family might detract from the value of the balance for homes.

Further, apartment developers are normally not interested in acquiring tracts containing about 100 acres, the size of the tracts shown in Fig. 2–9. Thus, for the period from January 1959 to September 1969, inclusive, only 8 out of a total of 208 private-street plats given final approval by Houston's planning commission (almost all of which were for multiple-family development) contained 20 or more acres, with the largest approved in 1969 having 37 acres. In 1968, 3 of the 8 were approved, but the average recorded that year was 8 acres. The average size of subdivisions recorded under the private-street plat regulation in 1969 was 7.26 acres; in 1970, 8.78 acres; and in 1971, 11.03 acres. By contrast, the average number of acres per subdivision recorded under the regular (largely single-family) subdivision requirements for each of these years was 31.80, 39.83, and 39.96, respectively.

In addition to distance from the downtown area, another important factor influencing the location of apartments is the sectional preferences of tenants able to afford new apartments. In Houston, most such tenants apparently prefer living in the western and southwestern sections of the city within about ten miles of the downtown center, and, therefore, the bulk of apartments have been built within this general area. Almost any parcel of land and many existing homes and other structures there are prime candidates as multiple-family sites. This is not true for other sections, although there is demand and apartments have been erected throughout the city.

As a result, homes as well as lots in the close-in areas where apartment demand is soft are generally too expensive to purchase as sites for multiple-family structures. This explains why interior areas of so many subdivisions whose restrictions have long expired contain few apartments or townhouses. Vacant sites in these subdivisions are likely to be used for homes (see Figs. 2–1, 2–2, and 2–3). As previously indicated, vacant lots in the Denver Harbor section, which is quite close to downtown, have been the sites for new homes in recent years, and some owners there have even demolished older homes to replace them with new ones.

Thus, the market has created its own "zoning." While apartments generally will allow for greater land cost per square foot than homes, the

combination of low apartment demand and "big" tracts has largely eliminated the apartment developer from the market for acreage in the more
outlying sections—at least until market conditions change. In the areas
closer to downtown, demand for apartments also differs substantially between different sections of the city, which in effect classifies properties for
different residential purposes. This classification process is also aided by the
fact that much of the limited demand for apartments in the outlying areas
and in soft closer sections of the city can be satisfied on the strip properties.
In areas where the demand is soft for multiple-family accommodations, only
the sites most suitable will be utilized for this purpose, and these usually
are within the strips along major thoroughfares. They are highly accessible
and provide good exposure to many prospective tenants.

In areas where the apartment demand is strongest, land generally will
be priced for apartment use, and this will virtually eliminate its use for
homes. One reason for the softness of the apartment market on the outskirts is the large supply available in the near areas. Similar reasoning would
help explain the strength of the house market in the more distant sectors.
These same factors also apply to different sections of the city. The portion
of land in the "in-between" areas will reflect the market for both single-
family and multiple-family use, with some tendency for prices to increase as
apartment demand increases, reflecting the greater price for multiple-family
land.

Some comparisons with zoning are now warranted:

1. Since substantial tracts of land would be marketplace "zoned" as single-
   family (except for the strip areas), zoning could only have reduced the
   supply of property for such purposes in the areas in question. Some of these
   tracts might have been zoned (or possibly "rezoned") for other residential
   uses and commercial and industrial uses, or even another category of single-
   family use (such as the "R-2-B" category of the proposed Houston zoning
   ordinance of 1962, which allowed both "two flats" and businesses operated
   out of the home). Some investors may purchase such properties solely to
   await future appreciation of the zoning category, and by this action will
   thereby preclude possible use of such properties for single-family structures.
   Because of the huge quantities of land available in most of these areas, such
   zoning limitations probably would have had a minimal effect on the supply
   of single-family homes for a time at least. (The 1962 proposed ordinance
   did, however, restrict large quantities of land to the "CU" category, which
   permitted a variety of uses. This may have been an instance of "overzoning.")
   A similar situation probably existed in all the near city areas of Houston for
   the period when such areas were largely vacant and subject to development
   principally for single-family use. By the time that the apartment boom
   arrived most of the areas zoned single-family would have been developed
   and those lots that were still available would be very expensive for such use.
   (Many probably would have been rezoned for more intense residential use.)
2. In most zoned cities, the supply of land for minimum-sized lots has also
   been reduced by the creation of zones restricted to large-sized lots. Dallas is
   an example of this. Its "lowest" single-family zone permits construction on

lots having a minimum of 5,000 square feet, which is similar to the minimum in Houston. But, it also has six additional single-family districts which require from 7,500 square feet to 43,560 square feet (one acre) of area per lot. Apparently the major portion of single-family zoning there requires a minimum lot size of 7,500 square feet. The larger lots will generally have to sell for more (among other reasons) because (or possibly if) they require the installation of larger quantities of street, water, and sewer improvements.

3. By zoning areas for single-family, a municipality can maintain the supply of land for such purposes over a period of time, despite economic pressures to the contrary. This will reduce prices for such land compared to what might take place in the absence of these restrictions. But there are serious limitations on the benefits derived from such policy. First, "snob zoning" practices, by raising requirements would reduce if not eliminate the benefits for the less affluent. Second, large lot zoning would reduce the supply of single family lots, adding in time to the cost of the lots. Third, the presence of apartments and townhouses in the community would serve as a competitive lever upon the cost of average and less than average new and used homes. And fourth, the gains would also be compromised by increased amounts of real estate taxes which other land uses could help defray. (This will be discussed in the next chapter.)

On balance, it is difficult to evaluate within a locality the impact of zoning in the price of single family homes and lots. In many suburbs, it appears to lower the price for the rich and raise the price for the poor. It will obviously vary with conditions of supply and demand within the community as well as with the zoning practices.

What about Houston? What effect would zoning have had there on the price of homes? Obviously, the best evidence in making this determination would be to compare Houston's experience with some "similar" zoned city. The city that would seem to be the best candidate for study is Dallas, with which Houston is most often compared, although as with all cities, there are numerous differences. But there are enough important similarities to warrant comparing and analyzing Dallas' experience in housing. Dallas adopted zoning in the early 1930's.

Houston is 50 percent greater in population than Dallas and its SMSA close to 30 percent greater. In 1970, the population according to the census, was 1,232,802 and 844,401 for the cities, and 1,985,031 and 1,555,950 for the SMSA's. Statistics related to personal income, living costs and building costs show great similarity between the two cities and their SMSA's. Tables 4–1 through 4–4 show these and other relationships; and it is apparent that both cities and their SMSA's are close in the items as designated. Dallas is slightly more affluent and its cost of living slightly higher, whereas Houston's building costs (according to two of the three comparisons set forth) may be slightly higher. The statistics contained in Table 4–1 are for the cities, and those in Table 4–4 are for areas less than the SMSA's and greater than the cities. All of the other tables concern SMSA's. The figures upon which Figure 4–1 is based are also for SMSA's except that relating to the annual number of permits for apartments in Houston.

More than three-quarters of the Houston SMSA is not zoned and over three-quarters of the Dallas SMSA is zoned. Within the last five years at least, each of the major cities have accounted for more than 80 percent of the building permits issued in the SMSA.

These census figures show the close relationships between the cities and the SMSA's:

	HOUSTON	H. SMSA	DALLAS	D. SMSA
1960 Census:				
owner occupied, median value	$10,900	$10,700	$11,300	$10,800
Contract rent median	$58	$58	$62	$60
1970 Census:				
owner occupied, median	$14,500	$14,600	$16,700	$16,800
contract rent median	$97	$95	$110	$110
1960 Census:				
Median Income-families and unrelated indivs.	$5,093	$5,310	$5,079	$5,083
families only	$5,902	$6,040	$5,976	$5,924

It might be thought that the absence of zoning would tend to deteriorate values for single-family housing or possibly create a somewhat chaotic condition in that market. As is shown in Tables 4–5, 4–6 and 4–7, this is not borne out by comparing the average price of new and existing homes insured by FHA (and the estimated prices of the underlying land sites) for the two areas in the years 1960 to 1969, inclusive. These figures show that for these years, the cost of the average house in the Houston area insured by FHA (and possibly the site thereunder) retained about the same relationship to the cost of the average one insured in the Dallas area, and that the differential generally was small.

The figures contained in Tables 4–5, 4–6 and 4–7 are taken from annual data covering all FHA sales activity within the SMSA as reported by the FHA Division of Research and Statistics. Analysis of Tables 4–5 and 4–6 shows that overall for the years in question FHA-insured new and existing homes may have effectively cost about the same in both SMSA's. Although the average prices there were greater generally for both new and existing homes, the homes in the Houston area usually had larger average areas and often contained more amenities, giving the purchaser frequently approximately the same or more value per dollar of expenditure. For example, in 1969, the average existing home sold in Houston cost $2,191 more than in Dallas. This constituted the largest percentage difference in price for any of the years shown. However, the average home contained 239 more square feet of floor area, which at a minimum price of approximately $8.00 per square foot for such space, was worth over $1,900.00. In addition, the existing homes sold in that year in Houston had more bedrooms, bathrooms, garages, and central air conditioning than did their

Dallas counterparts. These cost factors may differ in other years, and for some years the effective price in Dallas seems lower. A complete analysis of price differences would also take into consideration siding, basements, appliances and other features. I have not included these in the tables because of the absence of this information from the FHA data for most of the years in question, and because the information when available, does not suggest that it would affect the conclusion presented.

Table 4–1

Some Economic Comparisons Between the Cities of Houston and Dallas

	Houston	*Dallas*
1960 Census Report on 1959 income:		
Median income of all families and unrelated individuals	$ 5,093.00	$ 5,079.00
% of families with incomes		
under $ 3,000	18.8%	18.4%
over $10,000	17.5%	18.9%
(1) 1963 Effective Buying income per Household	$ 7,418.00	$ 7,690.00
% of households with incomes		
under $3,000.00	19.7%	19.4%
over $10,000.00	19.4%	20.8%
(1) 1967 Effective Buying Income per Household	$ 9,295.00	$ 9,355.00 ·
% of households with incomes		
under $3,000.00	19.4%	19.2%
over $10,000.00	25.7%	25.9%
(1) 1970 Effective Buying income per Household	$11,094.00	$11,528.00
% of households with incomes		
under $3,000.00	15.8%	14.9%
over $10,000.00	38.5%	39.6%
(2) 1969 Estimated Income per household	$12,079.00	$12,162.00
1970 Census (preliminary figures)		
Median income of all families and unrelated individuals	$ 8,056.00	$ 7,984.00
Average income of all families and unrelated individuals	$ 9,840.00	$10,374.00
(3) % Vacant Land of total land area (Houston '66; Dallas '64)	47.08%	47.20%
% Single family used land (Houston '66; Dallas '64)	22.82%	21.80%
Housing units per person — 1960 Census	.340	.340
Housing units per person — 1970 Census	.347	.359

(1) © *Sales Management Survey of Buying Power,* June 10, 1964, June 10, 1968, and July 10, 1971. Further reproduction is forbidden.

(2) *1969 Editor and Publisher Market Guide.*

(3) Land Use Surveys for each city — Planning Department of City for Houston, and Texas Highway Department for Dallas.

Table 4–2
Consumption Comparisons by Differing Living Standards and Family Size, Houston and Dallas SMSA's

Year and Family Size	Living Standards					
	Lower		Moderate		Higher	
	Houston	*Dallas*	*Houston*	*Dallas*	*Houston*	*Dallas*
Autumn 1966 consumption						
family of four			$6,794	$6,861		
retired couple			3,411	3,421		
Budget						
family of four			$8,387	$8,472		
retired couple			3,628	3,639		
Spring 1967 consumption						
family of four	$4,614	$4,664	$6,716	$6,751	$ 9,333	$ 9,526
retired couple	2,422	2,403	3,459	3,436	5,320	5,284
Budget						
family of four	$5,542	$5,607	$8,301	$8,345	$11,897	$12,157
retired couple	2,531	2,511	3,679	3,655	5,995	5,949
Spring 1969 consumption						
family of four	$5,000	$5,102	$7,255	$7,388	$10,062	$10,388
retired couple	2,652	2,679	3,779	3,826	5,762	5,844
Budget						
family of four	$6,110	$6,258	$9,176	$9,340	$13,161	$13,613
retired couple	2,771	2,799	4,020	4,070	6,514	6,621

Source: U.S. Department of Labor, Bureau of Labor Statistics, Bulletins 1570–1 (1966); 1570–4 (1966); 1570–5 (1969) 1570–6 (1969) and supplements.

Table 4-3

Comparison of Cash Income Breakdown Estimates Between Dallas and Houston SMSA's – 1967 and 1970

Net Cash Income ($000)	1967 Houston		1967 Dallas		1970 Houston		1970 Dallas	
	% Households	% Income	% Households	% Income	% Households	% Income	% Households	% Income
	$4,599,776		$3,793,157		$6,466,256		$5,395,867	
$0 - 2,999	19.2%	3.3%	19.1%	3.2%	15.8%	2.2%	14.8%	2.0%
$ 3,000 - 4,999	14.3%	6.8%	14.9%	7.1%	11.0%	4.3%	10.5%	4.0%
$ 5,000 - 7,999	25.8%	19.7%	26.7%	20.1%	19.9%	12.8%	20.1%	12.4%
$ 8,000 - 9,999	15.4%	16.0%	14.3%	14.8%	14.5%	12.7%	14.4%	12.1%
$10,000 - 15,000	15.1%	21.0%	14.8%	20.6%	24.1%	28.2%	24.3%	27.4%
$15,000 - 25,000	7.3%	16.0%	7.2%	15.7%	10.6%	19.6%	11.3%	20.0%
Over $25,000	2.9%	17.2%	3.2%	18.5%	4.1%	20.2%	4.6%	22.1%

Sources: © *Sales Management Survey of Buying Power*, June 10, 1968 and July 10, 1971. Further reproduction is forbidden.

Table 4-4
Comparison of Construction Costs Between Houston and Dallas

A. *Dodge Historical Local Building Cost Indexes* - taken from Dodge Building Cost Calculater and Valuation Guide published by McGraw-Hill Information Systems Company (N.Y., N.Y.) Edition 6 (April-June 1972)

Each entry indicates that city's percentage of the New York City Building costs which are the highest in the country. (New York City annually = 100). Areas involved exceed boundaries of cities but are less than boundaries of the SMSA.

	Houston	Dallas
1960 Average	82	78
1961 September	82	78
1962 September	80	78
1963 September	80	78
1964 September	79	77
1965 September	79	77
1966 September	78	77
1967 September	77	76
1968 September	78	77
1969 September	79	78
1970 September	77	75
1971 September	77	77

B. *Boeckh Building Costs Modifiers* - Computed and published periodically by Boeckh Division of the American Appraisal Company (Milwaukee, Wisconsin). The figures shown for various types of structures represent the percentage of cost for that city at mid-year to erect the structures for which building costs are set forth in Boeckh Building Valuation Manuals I and II (1967, Boeckh Division, American Appraisal Company). Figures through 1967 are shown in the said manuals. Areas involved exceed city boundaries but are within those of the SMSA.

| | Frame Residences | | Masonry Residences | | Commercial Bldgs | | | | | |
| | | | | | Wood | | Steel | | Masonry and Concrete | |
Year	Dallas	Houston	Dallas	Houston	Dallas	Houston	Dallas	Houston	Dallas	Houston
1960	.80	.82	.79	.79	.76	.77	.75	.77	.73	.75
1961	.81	.82	.80	.79	.76	.77	.75	.77	.74	.75
1962	.82	.83	.81	.80	.77	.78	.77	.79	.75	.75
1963	.83	.85	.82	.82	.78	.80	.78	.82	.76	.77
1964	.85	.87	.84	.84	.80	.82	.80	.83	.78	.79
1965	.86	.88	.86	.86	.81	.83	.81	.85	.78	.81
1966	.90	.91	.89	.90	.84	.87	.84	.88	.79	.83
1967	.95	.97	.93	.97	.88	.94	.89	.95	.83	.86
1968	.98	1.00	.97	1.00	.92	.97	.93	.98	.87	.93
1969	1.09	1.09	1.08	1.08	1.04	1.05	1.05	1.06	1.05	1.05

C. *Marshall Local Multipliers* - local multipliers to be applied to average costs for construction as determined by Marshall Valuation Service. Information received by letter dated June 27, 1971, from Frank Swift of Marshall and Swift Publication Company, Los Angeles, California, to the author. Figures are comparative for each year only. Areas in question exceed boundaries of cities, but are less than the SMSA.

| | Wood Frame | | Masonry | | Reinforced Concrete Frame | | Structural Steel Frame | |
Year	Houston	Dallas	Houston	Dallas	Houston	Dallas	Houston	Dallas
1960	1.02	1.01	1.01	1.02	1.01	1.02	1.01	1.02
1961	.97	.97	.96	.96	.97	.98	.96	.99
1962	.96	.97	.94	.95	.95	.97	.96	.99
1963	.96	.98	.94	.96	.95	.98	.96	.99
1964	.96	.97	.93	.95	.95	.96	.96	.97
1965	.94	.97	.92	.95	.93	.96	.94	.97
1966	.95	.98	.93	.97	.93	.98	.93	.98
1967	.95	.98	.93	.97	.94	.98	.94	.98
1968	.98	.99	.97	.98	.98	.99	.99	1.00
1969	.98	1.00	.97	.99	.98	.99	.99	1.00

Table 4–7 shows that the *estimated* average and median prices of sites for both new and existing homes insured by FHA were higher in the Houston area, and this also could have raised the price of its homes. There is some, perhaps much, question about the accuracy of the figures in this table, particularly when used for comparative purposes between different places. They are estimates by employees of each local office, made separately, and similar criteria as applied in practice may differ significantly between offices. The figures are presented because they are the only ones available and may provide reasonable estimates of cost changes within each city.

The square foot area per site for the four years from 1966 thru 1969 was larger in Dallas (Table 4–8), but unless the variance in the amount of area between sites is appreciable, perhaps 15% or more, prices should not be affected.

One reason that could be given for the differential in land cost, *if it actually exists,* is that land in Houston for homes might be greater in price owing to the potential that every site has for multiple-family use, which ordinarily brings a higher price. If this is the case, there should be some correlation annually between the extent of demand for apartment building sites and the price of land used for single family homes. One measurement of this demand is the number of permits for apartments issued annually in Houston (shown in Fig. 4–1). This graph also shows average prices of new and existing homes and estimated prices of land involved in FHA transactions for both cities during the same periods.

If land prices for homes were influenced by the alternative use for apartments, the price would be greater in periods of heavy demand for apartments than in periods of light demand. No such relationship is apparent, either for houses or land, for FHA insured properties. (In fact, at the height of the latest Houston apartment boom, prices for homes appeared much more favorable to the buyers in Houston than in Dallas. (Tables 4–5 and 4–6)

(That property can be utilized for a premium purpose does not necessarily mean that the price will be controlled by that particular use. Many sites are zoned to allow gas stations which carry premium prices, but have to be priced much cheaper because they are not in demand for this use. Much of Houston is "zoned" for gas stations and high-rises, but only those relatively few tracts that are sought for these purposes will be priced on this basis.)

Accordingly, the foregoing evidence indicates that the absence of zoning has not operated detrimentally to prices of the new and existing homes with which FHA is principally involved. These homes usually exist or are erected in areas with minimal demand for apartment use, and there are few diverse uses present to diminish values. However, there will be considerable effect on the price of land in sections close to the center of the city where the demand for apartments is substantial and usually much less land is available.

Table 4-5
Comparison of Annual Cost of FHA-Insured Existing Homes: Houston and Dallas SMSA's

Year	City	(1) Average Sale Price	Houston Higher $	Houston Higher %	(2) Ave. Calculated Floor Area - Sq. Ft. no. sq. ft.	Price per sq. ft.	(3) Houston Increase in sq ft	Ave. No. Bdrms	(4) Percent More than 1 bath	(5) Percent Garage	(6) Percent Car-Ports	Percent Central Air Conditioning
1960	Houston	$11,675	$ 443	3.9%	1222	$ 9.55	131	2.6	25.6%	35.8%	62.1%	–
	Dallas	11,232			1091	10.29		2.5	24.3	90.9	4.0	–
1961	Houston	12,059	585	5.0	1271	9.48	143	2.7	33.7	37.3	60.8	–
	Dallas	11,474			1128	10.17		2.6	29.5	89.3	4.9	–
1962	Houston	12,150	–216	–1.7	1267	9.58	62	2.7	33.1	76.1	19.1	–
	Dallas	12,366			1205	10.26		2.6	37.4	87.1	7.9	–
1963	Houston	12,797	273	2.1	1308	9.78	93	2.8	43.3	93.9	3.4	–
	Dallas	12,524			1215	10.30		2.7	39.0	86.7	8.5	–
1964	Houston	13,184	683	5.4	1365	$ 9.65	150	2.8	48.6	94.7	2.6	–
	Dallas	12,501			1215	10.28		2.7	40.9	88.0	7.1	–
1965	Houston	13,499	324	2.4	1405	9.60	129	2.9	52.5	93.3	3.4	17.0%
	Dallas	13,175			1276	10.32		2.8	50.1	87.7	7.8	12.5
1966	Houston	13,810	196	1.4	1417	9.74	125	2.9	55.7	96.0	2.4	33.4
	Dallas	13,614			1292	10.53		2.8	55.1	87.8	6.4	32.1
1967	Houston	15,032	830	5.8	1452	10.35	171	3.0	65.9	95.6	2.9	42.9
	Dallas	14,202			1281	11.08		2.8	54.5	87.1	7.6	35.8
1968	Houston	14,621	735	5.2	1384	10.56	165	2.9	55.7	93.5	2.9	38.3
	Dallas	13,886			1219	11.39		2.8	47.3	82.9	7.6	29.4
1969	Houston	16,799	2,191	14.9	1428	11.76	239	3.0	63.5	94.4	2.3	44.8
	Dallas	14,608			1189	12.28		2.7	40.6	79.9	8.2%	25.1

Source: U.S. Federal Housing Adm. Div. Research & Statistics, Data for States and Selected Areas on Characteristics of FHA Operations under Sec. 203 (annual, 1960–1969).

Table 4-6
Comparison of Annual Cost of FHA-Insured New Homes: Houston and Dallas SMSA's

Year	City	(1) Average Sale Price	Houston Higher $	%	(2) Ave. Calculated Floor Area - Sq. Ft. no. sq. ft.	Price per sq. ft.	(3) Houston Increase in sq ft	Ave. No. Bdrms	(4) Percent More than 1 bath	(5) Percent Garage	(6) Percent Car-Ports	Percent Central Air Conditioning
1960	Houston	$14,244	$ 410	2.9%	1216	$11.72	4	3.0	59.8%	32.3%	67.6%	—
	Dallas	13,834			1212	11.41		3.0	78.2	97.3	2.5	—
1961	Houston	14,050	739	5.5	1210	$11.61	12	3.1	67.1	34.7	65.3	—
	Dallas	13,311			1198	11.11		3.1	78.3	98.0	1.9	—
1962	Houston	14,857	1176	8.5	1291	$11.50	62	3.0	80.0	67.7	32.1	—
	Dallas	13,681			1229	11.13		3.2	85.5	97.5	1.6	—
1963	Houston	15,108	437	2.9	1339	$11.28	12	3.1	89.2	99.3	.5	—
	Dallas	14,671			1327	11.05		3.2	88.1	99.2	.5	—
1964	Houston	15,965	512	3.3	1412	$11.30	44	3.2	95.9	99.0	.3	—
	Dallas	15,453			1368	11.29		3.2	89.5	94.9	5.1	—
1965	Houston	15,921	217	1.4	1404	11.33	35	3.2	93.8	99.6	.1	16.0%
	Dallas	15,704			1369	11.47		3.1	89.6	99.0	1.0	29.9
1966	Houston	16,325	-90	-0.5	1411	11.56	65	3.2	94.6	99.2	.3	68.8
	Dallas	16,415			1346	12.19		3.2	94.8	95.3	3.8	70.2
1967	Houston	18,268	926	5.3	1461	12.50	143	3.2	99.0	98.8	1.2	96.5
	Dallas	17,342			1318	13.15		3.1	97.1	99.0	.8	83.8
1968	Houston	19,279	1354	7.5	1468	13.13	159	3.2	99.5	97.6	2.3	98.0
	Dallas	17,925			1309	13.69		3.1	97.3	99.6	.1	91.5
1969	Houston	21,794	1932	9.7	1527	14.27	208	3.2	99.2	93.9	6.0	98.0
	Dallas	19,862			1319	15.05		3.2	98.3	97.4	2.0	90.6

Source: U.S. Federal Housing Adm. Div. Research & Statistics, Data for States and Selected Areas on Characteristics of FHA Operations under Sec. 203 (annual, 1960–1969).

(1) *Sale price* is the price stated in the sale agreement, adjusted to exclude any portion of closing costs, prepayable expenses, or costs of non-real estate items excluded from the mortgage which the agreement indicates will be assumed by the seller.

(2) *Calculated floor area* is the area of spaces in the main building above basement or foundations, measured at the outside surfaces of exterior walls. Garage space, finished space in attics when less than 50% of the ground floor area and areas with ceiling heights of less than 5 feet are excluded.

(3) *Houston increase over Dallas* is a calculation of the excess of square footage in Houston homes over those in Dallas.

(4) *Baths* are defined as number of full bathrooms having a tub or shower stall, a lavatory and a water closet, plus the number of half bathrooms having a lavatory and water closet. Example: A full bath plus a half bath has been considered as two baths for the purpose of this computation.

(5) *Garage* is defined as a completely enclosed shelter for an automobile.

(6) *Carport* is a roofed automobile shelter, not completely enclosed.

Table 4–7
Comparison of Estimated Market Price of Sites for New and Existing FHA-Insured Homes: Houston and Dallas SMSA's

| | | Estimated Market Price of Site (1) | | | | | |
| | | Average (2) | | | Median | | |
Year	Site	Houston	Dallas	Hstn. % Higher	Houston	Dallas	Hstn. % Higher
1960	New	$2117	$2051	3.2%	$2152	$2084	3.2%
	Existing	2262	1845	22.6%	2275	1759	29.3%
1961	New	$2155	$2009	7.2%	$2101	$2008	4.6%
	Existing	2334	1923	21.3%	2314	1837	25.9%
1962	New	$2295	$2034	12.4%	$2267	$2026	11.8%
	Existing	2295	2096	9.4%	2305	2108	9.3%
1963	New	$2296	2113	8.6%	$2242	$2084	7.5%
	Existing	2451	2197	11.5%	2342	2202	6.3%
1964	New	$2426	2207	9.9%	$2370	$2206	7.4%
	Existing	2566	2198	16.7%	2410	2201	9.7%
1965	New	$2514	$2344	7.2%	$2398	$2290	4.7%
	Existing	2618	2349	11.4%	2480	2349	5.6%
1966	New	$2572	$2439	5.4%	$2477	$2480	0.1%
	Existing	2674	2399	11.4%	2499	2415	3.4%
1967	New	$2862	$2593	10.3%	$2713	$2633	3.0%
	Existing	2860	2643	8.2%	2752	2667	3.1%
1968	New	$2990	$2785	7.3%	$2790	$2765	0.9%
	Existing	2773	2727	1.7%	2606	2797	-6.9%
1969	New	$3407	$3184	7.0%	$3105	$3207	-3.2%
	Existing	3166	2993	5.7%	2968	3025	-1.9%

Source: U.S. Federal Housing Adm. Div. Research & Statistics, Data for States and Selected Areas of Characteristics of FHA Operations under Sec. 203 (annual, 1960–1969).

(1) Note: See text for evaluation of estimated information. *Estimated market price of site* is defined as the FHA estimated price for an equivalent site, including street improvements or utilities, rough grading, terracing, and retaining walls, if any.

(2) These figures are taken from same tables that show average sale price of homes. They may differ slightly in some years from figures shown in other tables for average price of site.

Table 4-8
Comparison of Sizes of FHA-Insured Sites for New and Existing Homes: Houston and Dallas SMSA's

Year	Site	Average Sq. Ft.			Median Sq. Ft.		
		Houston	Dallas	% Dal. Higher	Houston	Dallas	% Dal. Higher
1966	New	8275	8558	3.4%	7717	7960	3.1%
	Existing	8562	9670	12.9%	7911	8531	7.8%
1967	New	8274	9249	11.7%	7798	7937	1.7%
	Existing	9311	9992	7.3%	7919	8529	7.7%
1968	New	8204	8657	5.5%	7659	7888	2.9%
	Existing	8384	9942	18.5%	7748	8282	6.8%
1969	New	8255	8610	4.3%	7678	7841	2.1%
	Existing	8921	9790	9.7%	7899	7991	1.1%

Source: U.S. Federal Housing Adm. Div. Research & Statistics, Data for States and Selected Areas on Characteristics of FHA Operations under Sec. 203 (annual, 1966–1969).

Note: No data available for 1960 to 1965.

Table 4–9

Indexes of Comparative Costs of Consumption and Rent for a Family of Four for Various Standards of Living in Houston and Dallas SMSA's. (U.S. Urban Average Cost = 100).

| Standard | Date | Total Cost of Family Consumption | | |
		Dallas	Houston	Dallas % Higher
Moderate	Autumn 1966	94	93	1%
Lower	Spring 1967	96	95	1
Moderate	Spring 1967	93	93	0
Higher	Spring 1967	96	94	2
Lower	Spring 1969	97	95	2
Moderate	Spring 1969	95	93	2
Higher	Spring 1969	96	93	3
		Total Renter Costs*		
Moderate	Autumn 1966	99	84	18%
Lower	Spring 1967	96	86	12
Moderate	Spring 1967	100	85	18
Higher	Spring 1967	122	81	51
Lower	Spring 1969	93	87	7
Moderate	Spring 1969	98	85	15
Higher	Spring 1969	123	80	54

Source: U.S. Department of Labor, Bureau of Labor Statistics Bulletin Numbers: 1570–1 (1966); 1570–5 (1969); 1570–5 Supplement (1972).

*Average contract rent, plus the cost of required amounts of heating fuel, gas, electricity, water, specified equipment and insurance on household contents.

Multiple-Family

Houston presents an example of how also multiple-family dwellings would fare under zoning and nonzoning. Certain provisions of the zoning ordinance proposed in 1962 created maximums for height and lot coverage of apartment buildings and provided for certain front-yard requirements.

The A–1 (first apartment) and CU (community unit) district regulations provided a height limitation of three stories, a maximum lot coverage of 40 percent of the gross lot area, and a prohibition of parking in the front yard. The A–2 (apartment and office) district regulations had a similar height provision (except for main thoroughfares), certain front-yard parking requirements, and a 50 percent coverage of the gross lot area. Multiple-family dwellings were also permitted in the commercial districts, C–1 and C–2, and in the light industrial district, M–1, none of which had height maximums. The C districts had the same area-coverage limitations as did A–2, but M–1 had no such limitation.

Figure 4-1. Number of apartment permits issued in Houston; rise in home and lot prices from 1956-69 in Houston and Dallas. (1)

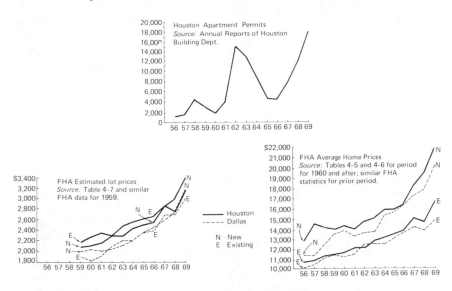

(1) This figure is partially diagramatic and representational and is not scaled nor proportioned to show numerical correlations between permits and prices. As explained in the text of this chapter, the figures on prices are limited in what they disclose about the actual prices of homes and lots. Another perspective for the relationship between apartment building activity and the prices for homes and lots for homes is afforded by the following table which compares for the period shown, annual percentage increase or decrease of (a) apartment permits in Houston, (b) average prices of FHA insured new homes in Houston and (c) estimated average lot prices of FHA insured new homes in Houston.

Year	(a) No. of Permits	Annual Percentage Increase	(b) Prices of New Homes	Annual Percentage Increase	(c) Estimated New Home Lot Prices	Annual Percentage Increase
1956	1,256		$12,797			
1957	1,785	42%	14,540	14%		
1958	4,855	172	14,109	−3		
1959	3,288	−32	13,950	−1	$2,070	
1960	1,955	−40	14,244	2	2,117	2%
1961	4,347	122	14,050	−1	2,115	0
1962	15,433	255	14,857	6	2,295	8
1963	13,578	−12	15,108	2	2,296	0
1964	9,373	−31	15,965	6	2,426	6
1965	4,974	−47	15,921	0	2,514	4
1966	4,905	−1	16,325	2	2,572	2
1967	8,272	69	18,268	12	2,862	11
1968	12,523	51	19,279	5	2,990	4
1969	18,328	46	21,794	13	3,407	14

Since the vast majority of apartment buildings are three stories or less, the passage of the ordinance would have had little effect so far as height is concerned as of this date. The land coverage and parking requirements would probably have had little effect on most projects (as we discussed in Chapter 2 in Apartments and Townhouses); nevertheless, a number of large projects mostly but not exclusively for the lesser-rent market and probably many more individual small apartment buildings would have been required to omit units or purchase additional land. Accordingly, these observations are submitted as to what might have occurred had the zoning ordinance been adopted in 1962:

1. By forbidding construction of apartments in the single-family and certain other districts, the zoning ordinance would have reduced the overall amount of land available within the city for such use. Because of the huge quantities of land that could be so utilized, both before and after adoption of the ordinance, its effect with respect to total supply would probably have been minimal. However, the more appropriate measure is the effect upon the supply of land within various areas of the city in which there is direct competition between vacant parcels. The elimination, for example, of ten thousand apartment-unit sites in an area near the center of the city would have had little effect on the price of land near the outskirts, but it might have reduced supply in the former area sufficiently to increase thereby the price per unit of apartment land. Such a higher price would come either subsequent to the adoption of the ordinance if substantial demand then existed, or, in time, if and when the demand grew. Similarly, the effect in price will become greater as the amount of vacant land in the area diminishes. (Nor could a city rezone sufficient land to keep pace with demand.) It would seem, therefore, that the adoption of zoning would in general increase the price of land per apartment site, possibly to a substantial degree in some areas of the city.

2. Such increase in land prices would have (a) caused fewer apartments to be constructed, and (b) been reflected in increased rents. One result would have been that some who could have afforded to rent new apartments prior to zoning would not have been able to do so subsequent to its adoption. This in turn would have prevented a decrease in rent in the older buildings.

3. But, it may be contended, many multiple-family projects in zoned areas are constructed on land that was originally zoned as single family. Rents should, therefore, reflect the price of single family land. This is most unlikely. The seller had the option of pricing his land in one of three ways: (a) as single-family, (b) as multiple-family contingent upon rezoning or (c) somewhere in between these two to reflect the potential of the land for multiple-family zoning. It is possible that if the developer purchased the land for less than the multiple-family price, regardless of market conditions or government formulas, he would set his rents to reflect the savings. Much more likely, however, is that the cost of land will be raised for purpose of the building venture, and profits sought on the basis of multiple-priced land. One who receives a gift of a new automobile is not likely to sell it for much, if anything, under the market price.

Nonsubsidized rents are normally based on existing market prices, regardless of the owner's costs. The market rent will reflect the going price for apartment-zoned land—for if it does not, there would be no additional value attributable to the change in zoning classification. In the case of the subsidized rental programs, HUD formulas will establish the land value —generally regardless of cost—and regulate rents in accordance with the provisions of the program involved.

Regardless of the actual purchase price of the land, the practical operation of the zoning process will tend to make the final cost effectively greater. When local legislators rezone property or authorize a planned unit development for multiple-family purposes, they are likely to exact conditions, legal or extralegal, which can be quite expensive. As will be shown more specifically in Chapter 8 they may require costly improvements to the land and alternations in construction and design which the developer would not consider necessary to market his units. The time and expense of obtaining approval also add to his cost: it may take as long as a year. Many times the requirements may be so severe that a developer could only afford to buy the land at or near single-family prices; for total cost of the land plus the cost of the proceedings and conditions required to obtain rezoning may not differ much from what his cost would have been if he had purchased the property already zoned for multiple-family purposes and priced accordingly.

4. The importance of the level of rents in a housing market can be discerned from an FHA study of Harris County. This shows that although the median income for all families after deduction from federal income tax in 1968 was $7,350, that for the renter families was $5,200. In addition, 59 percent of renter families had annual incomes (after the said deduction) below $6,000 as compared to 37 percent of all families, and 69 percent of renter families had less than $7,000 as compared to 46 percent of all families.[15] Thus, many and perhaps most tenants are at income levels where any increase in rent brought about by zoning could be quite burdensome. For a family struggling to maintain financial solvency, any increase in rent can determine the success or failure of that effort.

5. The market will accommodate to more restrictive density requirements, either by a reduction in the number of units constructed, or by the use of greater quantities of land, or by a combination of both. Any increase in the quantity of land used will cause a decrease in the total land supply of the community. About 100,000 multi-family units were constructed in Houston between 1962 and 1972, and this would have required about six square miles of land (at a density of about 25 to 30 units per acre). Even if there had been a lessening in apartment construction as a result of zoning, there still might have been as many or more acres removed from the supply of land in that part of the city—the southwest—where the bulk of apartment construction has taken place. Thus, at 20 units per acre, six square miles of land will produce about 77,000 in units.

6. A builder who owned a small parcel on which he proposed to develop, say, thirty apartments would have found upon passage of the ordinance that unless he obtained a variation from the density and parking location requirements (which would be unlikely because of the considerable change involved) only twenty to twenty-five might be built. If he still went ahead with the minimized project, he'd find the construction cost of an individual apartment would probably have increased. His unit cost would have been considerably less had the building contained 20 or 25 percent more units, as originally planned. Such increased unit costs might cause some small buildings to become economically unfeasible. Costs would also be increased

per unit if the builder purchased enough land to allow for erection of thirty apartments. Similar analysis is applicable to larger projects.

7. The arguments favoring the limitation of lot coverage and the removal of off-street parking are the obvious ones. The city was attempting to impose its "garden city" concepts on all developers and thereby limit individuality for some. For the reasons hertofore given, the cost of such aesthetics would be borne most heavily by the average- and lesser-income renters, who, if asked, would presumably be unwilling to subsidize the city's indulgence in such luxury. The results of Houston's zoning vote would certainly suggest that this would be their answer. They would also as vehemently disagree that their welfare required the proposed land coverage restrictions. It is para-doxical that the mere fear of the possibility of creating adverse housing conditions (through alleged overcrowding) should, by impeding production and thus limiting competition, contribute to the support of those already in existence.

8. Although vacant land for apartment use usually sells on a yield basis, land that already contains revenue producing structures or that is priced for other than residential uses, does not. In both the latter situations, lot coverage or density controls may add to the land cost of an apartment. Thus, rede-velopment of an area might be impeded when limitations are placed on the yield available to the potential redeveloper.

It would now seem appropriate to compare rents in Houston with those in Dallas. The only published comparison of these costs by a nationally rec-ognized agency, to my knowledge, are those contained in standard of living studies of selected SMSA's throughout the country made by the Bureau of Labor Statistics, U. S. Department of Labor. Rental costs shown in these re-ports are one of the component costs of consumption as determined by the Bureau for three standards of living for two different types of families, a four-person family and a retired couple. Indexes of the comparative costs of consumption and rent for Houston and Dallas were published for three periods, autumn 1966 and spring of 1967 and 1969, and these are shown in tables 4–9 and 4-10.(The categories given in the tables were established for purposes of the surveys and do not necessarily correspond to any other existing income classifications.)

The measurement is of renter costs for an unfurnished rental unit (house or apartment) in sound condition meeting certain specifications. The unit size for the four person family (Table 4–9) was five rooms con-taining a private bath and kitchen, and the size for the retired couple (Table 4–10) was two or three rooms with similar facilities. For the higher standard in the four person category, the dwelling unit might have more than one bath, and the unit might provide extras such as central switchboard, secretarial service, swimming pool or special recreational facilities. The cost of water, heat, light or cooking fuel was added to the contract rent in those cases where they were not included. To enable the reader to place the indexes in a monetary perspective, Table 4–11 shows the average rental costs in the Houston SMSA and the Dallas SMSA developed for each standard.

The Bureau attempted to determine what the average rents for apartments of the same specifications would be in various metropolitan areas of the country. Rents for dwellings were obtained from tenants during the regular rent surveys in Autumn 1966 and Spring 1969 for the Consumer Price Index. Costs for Spring 1967 were derived by applying price changes between Autumn 1966 and Spring 1967 reported in the Consumer Price Index to costs of the earlier period. For purposes of comparing rental costs between areas, the findings must be qualified in the following respects:

1. The quantity of data available for each standard was limited since it was taken from a sample made in that area of a broader range of rental units used in calculations for the Consumer Price Index.
2. The data apply only to those units meeting the specifications, and these units represent only a portion of all the rental units within any one area. In some areas, there may be many such units, in others, few.
3. Although the specifications are narrow, it is difficult to hold constant all quality aspects of rental housing, such as neighborhood, view and floor number.

Table 4–10

Indexes of Comparative Costs of Consumption and Rent for a Retired Couple for Various Standards of Living in Houston and Dallas SMSA's. (U.S. Urban Average Cost = 100)

Standard	Date	Total cost of Consumption		
		Dallas	Houston	Dallas % Higher
Moderate	Autumn 1966	94	94	0%
Lower	Spring 1967	94	95	-1
Moderate	Spring 1967	95	95	0
Higher	Spring 1967	99	100	-1
Lower	Spring 1969	95	94	1
Moderate	Spring 1969	96	95	1
Higher	Spring 1969	100	98	2
		Total Renter Costs*		
Moderate	Autumn 1966	86	79	9%
Lower	Spring 1967	84	83	1
Moderate	Spring 1967	88	82	7
Higher	Spring 1967	121	121	0
Lower	Spring 1969	91	81	12
Moderate	Spring 1969	97	82	18
Higher	Spring 1969	124	115	8

Source: U.S. Department of Labor, Bureau of Labor Statistics Bulletin Numbers: 1570–4 (1966); 1570–6 (1969); 1570–6 supplement (1971).

*Average contract rent, plus the cost of required amounts of heating fuel, gas, electricity, water, specified equipment and insurance on household contents.

Table 4-11

Average Annual Rental Costs for Two Family Sizes and Three Living Standards in Houston and Dallas SMSA's

Year	Lower		Moderate		Higher	
	Houston	Dallas	Houston	Dallas	Houston	Dallas
4-Member Families						
Autumn, 1966			$1,051.00	$1,243.00		
Spring, 1967	$872.00	$973.00	1,086.00	1,277.00	$1,575.00	$2,369.00
Spring, 1969	931.00	989.00	1,175.00	1,340.00	1,721.00	2,642.00
Retired Couples						
Autumn, 1966			754.00	818.00		
Spring, 1967	628.00	636.00	790.00	856.00	1,756.00	1,757.00
Spring, 1969	662.00	744.00	878.00	1,039.00	1,855.00	1,997.00

Sources: U.S. Dept. of Labor, Bureau of Labor Statistics, Bulletin Nos. 1570-1, 1570-5 and supplement; 1570-4, 1570-6 and supplement.

Table 4-12

Comparison of Consumption and Rent Indexes for Moderate Living Standard in South Region, by SMSA's and Family Size (U.S. Urban Average Cost = 100)

SMSA	Autumn–1966			Spring–1967			Spring–1969		
	Consumption	Rent	Rent Higher	Consumption	Rent	Rent Higher	Consumption	Rent	Rent Higher
Four-Person Families									
Atlanta	92	88	-4	93	88	-5	91	88	-3
Austin	89	79	-10	89	81	-8	89	80	-9
Baltimore	94	108	14	94	107	13	96	109	13
Baton Rouge	94	83	-11	93	85	-8	93	85	-8
Dallas	94	99	5	93	100	7	95	98	3
Durham	93	93	0	94	94	0	95	109	14
HOUSTON	93	84	-9	93	85	-8	93	85	-8
Nashville	95	89	-6	94	88	-6	93	89	-4
Orlando	93	97	4	92	98	6	92	104	12
Washington	101	108	7	101	107	6	102	107	5
Retired Couples									
Atlanta	93	82	-11	93	83	-10	91	86	-5
Austin	91	91	0	93	93	0	92	89	-3
Baltimore	100	103	3	98	101	3	99	99	0
Baton Rouge	90	74	-16	91	76	-15	91	74	-17
Dallas	94	86	-8	95	88	-7	96	97	1
Durham	93	89	-4	95	93	-2	95	88	-7
HOUSTON	94	79	-15	95	82	-13	95	82	-13
Nashville	96	93	-3	96	91	-5	96	94	-2
Orlando	95	111	16	95	112	17	95	109	14
Washington	105	113	8	104	112	8	104	108	4

Sources: U.S. Dept. of Labor, Bureau of Labor Statistics, Bulletin Nos. 1570–1, 1570–4, 1570–5 and supplement; 1570–1, 1570–5 and supplement; 1570–4, 1570–6 and supplement.

Consumption represents family's total cost of goods and services (as provided for in the moderate living standard devised by the Bureau of Labor Statistics).

Rent represents average contract rent plus cost of required amounts of heating fuel, gas, electricity, water, specified equipment and insurance on household contents.

Nonetheless, because the specifications were narrow and similar for all areas and data were obtained at two different time periods, the comparisons may be quite representative. The periods surveyed were at the beginning and about the peak of the late sixties' apartment booms in both cities, and the vacancy rate was relatively low. The studies show that although the total cost of consumption was slightly higher in the Dallas SMSA, the cost of rent for the units surveyed were significantly higher there than in the Houston SMSA. Variance in rents was slightly less in 1969 than it had been in 1966 and 1967 for the categories surveyed in Table 4–9 and moderately higher for those in Table 4–10. The results overall are consistent with what should be expected to occur in the absence and presence of zoning.

Table 4–12 shows indexes of the comparative costs of total consumption and rent for the moderate standard for both the four person family and retired couple in all ten cities designated by the Bureau as within the "South" region. (Only the moderate standard is shown because it is statistically more reliable than either extreme.) It presents the Houston and Dallas statistics in the context of these other cities. Houston rental costs are among the lowest and those of Dallas tend toward above-average. The only SMSA in the South region that has lower rent costs than the Houston SMSA in relation to total cost of consumption, is Baton Rouge, Louisiana, all of which is zoned. The difference in this respect between Baton Rouge and Houston is small, much smaller than that between Houston and Dallas. Baton Rouge is a relatively small SMSA; its population in 1970 was about one-seventh of the Houston SMSA. Consequently, the overall demand for land for commercial purposes would be much lower. For this and possibly other reasons, the price of land per apartment unit on the average is substantially less than in the Houston area; the variation appears much greater than that between the cost of consumption in these two areas, as shown in Table 4–12. Real estate taxes may be near several percentage points lower than those in the Houston area when measured as a percent of gross rentals. The experience of the Baton Rouge SMSA is, therefore, not inconsistent with the analysis herein presented.

Zoning is certainly not the only factor influencing the rent structure. And the zoning practices in some areas may be substantially less restrictive than those in others. Even without zoning, New York City, with its much greater population pressures and higher costs would have still higher rents than those in Dallas. There are some differences between Houston and Dallas that might account for some of the rental variations shown, but these appear to be small. For example, real estate taxes measured in percentage of gross rentals appears to be about one or two percent higher in Dallas. (This may be attributable to higher land assessments based on higher land prices, which, in turn, would be the result of zoning.) There may, of course, be special situations of which I am unaware that better explain the variations—possibly even operating to lessen them—and as already noted, there are limitations to the data obtained by the Bureau.

Notwithstanding these qualifications, a strong case seems to be established that zoning is the major factor accountable for the rent differences shown. A more precise answer to this inquiry is probably not possible without an exhaustive study of all factors that influence the cost of rents.*

Some Summary Conclusions

In many areas of Houston, developers of homes will pay more for land and acreage than will developers of apartments—a situation which rarely, if ever, occurs in zoned communities. Quite often apartment-zoned land is a relatively scarce commodity and it brings a price commensurate with such scarcity. Were zoning to be eliminated and the supply thereby substantially increased, the price of land formerly zoned for apartments would, in many areas, sharply decrease, the extent of the reduction depending on the overall supply of vacant land in the area. Supply and demand would then be controlling factors, and the more vacant land available the lower would be the price for any parcel, notwithstanding that the parcel might be used for the construction of apartments.

Illustrations of the principle involved are apparent in zoned communities. In some areas northwest of Chicago, the asking price for single-family land was in 1971 about $10,000 per acre and that for apartment land about $25,000 per acre. If a considerable amount of single-family land were rezoned for apartments, the price of apartment-zoned land would obviously approach the price of single-family land. Whether the price of single-family land would rise concurrently depends upon demand-supply factors for the area. Because of the abundant supply, many areas would no longer be in demand for multifamily. Regardless, when the supply of vacant land is large, prices would probably be determined on the basis of development for houses, and not apartments, as is the case in Houston. This is because houses, which must occupy much more land, would be the most likely use for each tract.

In areas where the supply of land is more limited and there is a strong demand for apartments, all land will be priced for use as multiple-family. The perspective home builder in these areas will pay more for his land than he would if it were zoned single-family. However, all land in areas of limited supply generally commands a substantial price, including that portion zoned single-family. It attracts only the most affluent, who, it should be remembered, constitute only a small proportion of the population. They hardly merit the special consideration of government that zoning would thus provide.

---

* Subsequent to its reports in Spring 1969, the Bureau has not published rent costs for any of the standards for the retired couple or for the moderate and higher standards for the four person family.

In Houston, it appears that financially the imposition of zoning controls would have benefitted the most affluent homeowners, and would have most adversely affected the renters. There might also have been detrimental effects on the less affluent homeowners. It seems most difficult to justify such public policy.

The comparisons made with Dallas support the preceding conclusions. Dallas, however, is a big city, much less subject to the influences of any one group in the community than the comparatively monolithic suburbs. In fact, as previously stated, many homeowners in Dallas have been extremely critical of the operation of zoning in that city (Chapter 2). If Dallas had zoning policies more satisfactory to these homeowners, it is likely that there would have been much stronger exclusionary practices with considerably greater effect on the prices of shelter. Rents would be even higher as would probably also home prices. Consequently, it should be clear that the increase in housing costs attributable to suburban zoning practices is most substantial. And, of course, this is a major objective of their exclusionary policies—to allow only persons with higher levels of income to penetrate the zoning walls. (Suburbanites should, therefore, be most pleased to read these findings.) America pays a huge price for citizen control of the land!

5 Zoning Curtails Development

With the possible exception of Beverly Hills, California, and its counterparts in affluence (if any), American towns and cities, regardless of size and location are experiencing financial difficulty. The limits of local taxation seem to have been reached almost everywhere. Bond authorization referendums for building and enlarging schools and purchasing land for parks are being defeated in greater numbers than ever before. This is no longer unusual, even in localities with long histories of invariably favoring such matters. In the past year, some communities have declared or threatened to declare school holidays due to lack of funds. Mayors individually and collectively are continually demanding federal funds for what they describe as "the major domestic crisis of our day"—the financial plight of local government. The Nixon administration has responded in part with revenue sharing proposals, but for many, these measures are inadequate. As a result of some court decisions, less reliance may be placed on local property taxes to fund education and perhaps other services, but there is still much uncertainty as to what changes will occur and when.

It is possible that in these seemingly dire circumstances, zoning could be shaped to provide for maximum tax revenues. One can readily argue that several or more commercial strips and industrial plants are an inexpensive price to pay for better schools. Such solutions are rejected by the more traditional planners, who insist that the objective of land use regulation is to foster the best pattern of urban growth and that this goal should never be "subordinated to the cure of a fiscal ailment" lest the "urban pattern suffer."[1] It is said in support of this position that:

1. The search for additional revenue has led communities to overzone for industry and commercial development. It is in large part responsible for the excessive strip commercial development that disfigures most cities.

2. The desire to avoid additional public expenditures has probably had an even greater effect on land use control decisions. This has been a primary reason for large lot zoning, for the limitation or prohibition of apartments, for the restriction or prohibition of mobile homes, and for the excessively high zoning, subdivision, and building code standards that have impeded the provision of low and moderate cost housing.[2]

Land should be used to satisfy and accommodate the needs and desires of people, and obviously the collection of municipal revenues is essential to that objective. I agree that the raising of money must not be the primary

123

goal. A community that zones for and obtains the location of certain industry may be benefitting its own taxes but hurting many people in other communities unless it also accepts its share of housing needs. By the same token communities that reject industry as well as apartments and commerce will have unusually high real estate taxes. A reasonable balance is required and this can rarely be obtained under zoning. It is much more likely to occur in the absence of zoning, for market forces will cause an optimum allocation of resources. Simply stated, development will be maximized and exclusion will be minimized.

In prior chapters, I have shown the inherent inadequacies of zoning in accommodating the demand for housing. The major detriment of exclusionary practices is sustained probably by those who do not live in the community. Zoning also operates adversely to the realization of greater municipal revenues, and in this regard it is probably most detrimental to those who do live in the community.

The statements quoted earlier in this chapter illustrate the inherent limitations of zoning in dealing with issues relating to the finances of the city. "Underzoning" or "overzoning" is a normal product of land use regulation, since it is impossible for the amalgation of planners, politicians, citizens, and courts to determine for any one or more periods the "right" amount of zoning allocations over the large territories involved. Even if correct when made, the changes in needs, fashions, and desires, as well as in demand and supply, might invalidate that decision in a relatively short time. Cities, accordingly, are betting their future tax revenues against very great odds.

The recent history of the "quick-food" franchise industry illustrate the problem. Few would have predicted their recent chronology: when they would arrive, the number that would ultimately be involved, and how many would survive competition. Yet, these franchises were several years ago a major source of demand for strip commercial property, and perhaps still are. In 1946, or 1957, or 1965, when the last comprehensive zoning amendments were adopted in Los Angeles, Chicago, and Dallas, respectively, the food franchise operation was either unknown to many or of minor significance.

The experience of the southeast side of Chicago attests to the difficulty of predicting industrial demand. Much of the land zoned industrial there in the 1957 comprehensive amendment still remains unused. What is amusing about this situation is that originally the land had been contemplated for a residential classification, but it was later changed to industrial at the behest, according to newspaper accounts, of influential landowners, who many believed were associated with local politicians. It was thought at the time that a new lake port in the area would lead to a local industrial boom, but this never materialized. Had the property been zoned for residential, in all probability it would have been largely developed by now with greater benefits for both the owners and the city.

There is little question that the fear of adverse financial consequences whether wisely or unwisely founded has been an important consideration in zoning decisions. It is difficult for a political body to ignore an opinion from almost any source that a particular zoning or rezoning will add to the tax bill. Public participation and public hearings, in particular, which often tend to encourage hysteria and irrationality will make the decision-maker much more receptive to the fear of "losses" than to the possibility of "profits." Hence, regardless of how important monies should be, the zoning process precludes intelligent and rational response to problems of municipal finances. Zoning is, therefore, a poor tool for financial planning.

Thus, despite the many condemnations of fiscal zoning in the suburbs, the suburban record in this respect appears very poor. On the whole, present policies will not augment tax revenues.

In many of the predominantly single-family school districts of Cook County, in which Chicago is located, a home must have a value of almost $70,000 to fully support the annual cost of schooling for just one grade-school student.* As a result, single-family residences are taxwise generally a losing proposition, and the development of more homes will only exacerbate the problem. Removing zoning restrictions to allow only subsidized housing is obviously also financially harmful. The solution lies in the direction of removing restrictions generally. There are some additional burdens for a municipality in servicing rental and commercial enterprises, but again the city is usually well compensated for by the real estate and other taxes these establishments pay and produce.

An example common in the suburbs northwest of Chicago offers a case in point. Because the townhouses erected there more closely resemble homes, they often will be acceptable to homeowners as the least offensive buffer use. However, they are less likely to be fiscally acceptable, since the more popular types are less expensive and, therefore, usually return a smaller amount of real estate taxes per school child than does single-family use. Garden apartments create an opposite situation: taxwise they tend to pay for the children they produce and therefore usually are profitable to the schools but are physically undesirable to many in the community. (Garden apartments there tend to have a majority of one-bedroom apartments which contain relatively few school-aged children.) The result often is that neither use will be allowed. A nonzoned community is more likely to get a combination of townhouses and apartments with possibly favorable fiscal results. And even if there are no "profits," there may not be as big a loss for the school district as would occur if the same area were restricted to single-family use.³ Moreover, more dense residential development will stimulate a greater amount of commercial and possibly industrial development, both of which are financially highly desirable.

Thus, density within an area has a substantial impact on the location of commercial facilities, whose presence in turn, should be considered as one of the financial benefits of multiple-family construction. For instance, even

* This figure takes into consideration state aid to schools. In 1969, a $70,000 house in a school district in a middle-income suburb with little industry probably had an average tax bill of about $1900 to $2100, of which about two-thirds pays for both elementary and high schools. Annual expenses per student in elementary schools was generally more than $700.

a minimum-sized supermarket will not be built within an area unless there are, it is estimated, at least 3,500–4,000 persons living within that area. This means that a development of, say, three-hundred apartment and town-house units—which may occupy one-fourth or one-fifth as much ground as homes—will produce approximately one-fourth to one-third of the estimated number of persons required to induce a supermarket to locate there. Other commercial facilities, such as a drugstore, a cleaners, repair shops, usually will be built adjoining the supermarket; they too add to tax revenues.

It is paradoxical that municipalities constantly require and demand ever greater revenues and simultaneously adopt zoning restrictions that will reduce revenues. Chicago and New York provide excellent examples of this, and, I am confident, are not unique in this respect. For example, in the spring of 1971 the city council of Chicago, in response to exclusionary pressures principally from residents in one section of the city, adopted zoning amendments reducing the percentage of efficiency (studio) units which could be constructed within an apartment building in the highest-density residential zones. (There were other provisions also highly restrictive to apartment development.) It ignored completely that in that year and for many years prior to it, efficiency apartments were not only the source of the most demand, they were, because they are occupied by very few school-age children, an excellent source of tax income.

And again in 1962, the city council had adopted another amendment considerably reducing the density for high-rise apartments (again with high expectation for few children) in commercial districts located in the downtown and near downtown areas. The following excerpts from a report to the Department of City Planning of the City of New York on April 12, 1968, by Dr. Frank S. Kristof, an economist, presently Director, division of Economics and Housing Finance of the Urban Development Corporation of New York, a state agency, detail the fiscal problems created in that city:

After six years of experience under the new Zoning Ordinance, there is little question that the effect on new private conventional construction has been disastrous as a result of the shrinkage of areas zoned at the equivalent of R9 and R10. Most present day R8 sites could have been developed under the equivalent of R10 zoning (without the plaza bonus) under the old Zoning Ordinance. The evidence is incontestable that privately financed new construction in Manhattan at R8 zoning has become virtually impossible, even on avenue frontages, given prevailing land prices and the necessity to acquire a ¾ acre site in order to develop an efficient structure in terms of both construction and operating costs.

In conclusion, there remains one final consideration. Consumers of market-rent housing in Manhattan tend to be smaller, childless households who place less than average demands upon community facilities such as schools, libraries and health centers while making higher than average contributions to the city in the form of real estate, income and sales taxes. From the city's fiscal standpoint, therefore, these households are a precious asset and any steps that can be taken to maintain or increase their number in Manhattan should be encouraged.[4]

A study of high rises in the suburbs of the Philadelphia metropolitan area in 1961 further evidenced the high tax yield of these structures. Anshel Melamed computed the tax potential of these apartment developments on a per acre basis in relation to the tax potential of other uses.[5] An ASPO report has set forth these results of the study.

The actual income from various land uses was used to show the extent to which high-rise, high-rent apartments strengthened the tax base. Property tax revenue for high-rise apartments was compared with that from a steel fabricating plant, a research laboratory, a shopping center, and a motel. From this analysis, the study showed high-rise apartments produced the second highest gross tax revenue and a per acre revenue of $7,300—more than double the next highest use.

On the expenditure side, Melamed suggested that apartments show up quite favorably in their limited requirements for public services. Of key importance, the study noted, is the small number of school-age children in such units. Interviews showed that only 7 percent of the apartments were occupied by householders with children. In none of the high-rental suburban apartment developments were there more than 10 school-age children per 100 dwelling units. This compared with an average of upwards of 50 children per 100 single-family suburban dwellings. Since school taxes represented as much as 60 percent of the total municipal levy in the suburban areas, the study concluded that the relatively low number of school-age children in apartments represented a great savings to the municipality. . . .

The second major reason why apartments produced relatively low municipal costs was that they had limited requirements for public services. The study noted that such services as police and fire protection, trash collection and disposal, highway maintenance, and lighting "are surely less costly to provide" for apartments than for other uses. . . .[6]

Nonzoning Fosters Greater Development

One way to help improve local tax revenues is to eliminate zoning. The absence of land use restrictions is financially rewarding for a community because it allows for a greater development. At the same time, the community cannot impose exclusionary burdens on nonresidents and other localities. As a negative device, zoning has curtailed development, construction activity, business, and employment, and has thereby served to reduce real estate and other tax collections. When local governments erect exclusionary walls, they not only exclude people and things, they generally also exclude tax receipts. This is an extremely high price to pay for allegedly maintaining the urban pattern which in any event as Houston demonstrates, can be preserved reasonably well in its absence. In short, the best fiscal zoning is no zoning.

The Greenway Plaza development of Houston is illustrative of the difference between development under zoning and nonzoning. This development was originally a 55-acre existing and proposed complex of high-rise and other commercial buildings contiguous on one side to a street that adjoined an expressway, on two sides to commercial uses, and on the remaining side to single-family subdivisions. The developer in 1968 offered to purchase on an all-or-nothing basis each of the 97 homes in the subdivision that bordered him on the west for cash and with permission for the owners to stay in their homes for five years, rent-free. The offer was accepted, and the developer made a similar offer the following year to each of the 140 homeowners in the subdivision adjoining to the west the one he had already acquired. This latter subdivision also adjoined on its west a smaller subdivision. This offer was accepted by all but a few of the homeowners, and the developer proceeded to consummate the purchase of all the other homes. The properties are to be used to enlarge the original development to a total of 115 acres for a major commercial complex to include high-rise office and apartment buildings, a luxury hotel, and shopping facilities.

Except for one 88-unit apartment building the only uses in both subdivisions were single-family homes, and had Houston adopted zoning in 1962, both would have been zoned single-family. A rezoning to a business district would have been required for these properties to be used as proposed. There would have been public hearings and probably opposition would have come from the neighboring homeowners. Many suggestions (and demands) for improvement and modification would have been offered, and some would have charged that only "greed" motivated the developer to the "detriment" of the "people." Questions of traffic, taxation, engineering, and virtually all items of development would have been discussed and commented on by laymen, politicians, professionals, the press, and much free advice would have been offered. It is an interesting speculation as to how it would have come out, how long the proceedings would have taken, and what changes would have been required to accommodate and appease the opposition and others, and at what cost. Would it have been possible for the two subdivisions to be purchased separately, or would the opposition within the second (and largest) subdivision have required both to be purchased at one time? If so, would this have been economically feasible? Equally important is whether all of the owners of either one or both subdivisions would have been willing to commit their properties to binding option for the entire time required, probably a year or more, to obtain a decision from the Zoning Commission and the City Council.

Had 20 percent of the property owners across the street from the property sought to be rezoned advised the council in writing of their opposition, Texas law would have required a three-quarters vote of the council, or seven affirmative votes out of a total council membership of nine to pass the zoning amendment. Even so, it is likely that any large city would have allowed for the development of a major commercial complex of the magnitude contemplated. Approval would probably have come if the politically necessary compromises had been made; however, these would have increased the cost of the development and possibly have even affected its feasibility. (These compromises presumably would not remove the dissatisfaction felt by local owners who wished to continue living in the midst of residential property.) Given all of the problems presented by zoning requirements, it is likely that the developer never would have undertaken this project were zoning in effect in Houston.

For the property to be rezoned (were zoning in effect) changes would probably have been required of the developer for planning and/or political reasons. (Perhaps, however, the developer might have beaten the game by petitioning for more than he desired and needed and then allowing the council to severely curtail what he proposed.) It is possible that were the proposed project denied, abandoned, or curtailed, zoning would have allowed the development of all or part of the project elsewhere. It is also possible that by denying or curtailing the project, zoning would have augmented the values of other properties. But for the city to be in the same position as under nonzoning, both of the foregoing possibilities would have to be realized in full. This would be most unlikely in view of the inherent nature of the legislative processes under which zoning functions. These processes must of necessity respond to many political, social, and economic pressures totally unrelated to the optimum development of property.

Consider now the difference in financial impact of the existing single-family development and of the proposed Greenway Plaza development. The developer, Century Development Corporation, advised me that in 1970 it paid real estate taxes in the amount of $86,000 on the 229 homes it owns. It also paid a smaller amount on the 88-unit apartment building it purchased. As presently contemplated by the developer the total cost of the proposed development will "amount to approximately $500 million." Even if only 20 percent of the proposed project is ultimately realized, tax obligations will substantially exceed $1 million per year.

The example of Greenway Plaza does not appear to be an isolated one. The absence of government restrictions seems to have been an important factor in the purchases for development of other improved tracts. As suggested in the Chapter 2 discussion of the downtown, this may have been an important factor in the development of projects there.

Even a seemingly innocuous restriction such as a side-yard requirement can curtail development. Some very expensive and attractive townhouses built within recent years in Houston provide an example of this. Each townhouse within a row in these developments has been individually designed and constructed on a separately owned lot. Because party walls separate the units and side yards are not provided, these structures would not comply with the side-yard requirements for individual lots contained in the zoning ordinance proposed for Houston in 1962 as well as in most zoning ordinances. Even if the property contemplated for such use was zoned for multiple-family purposes, rezoning, variances, a planned unit development, or some other special dispensation would have been required before they could have been erected. To gain approval, the developer may have had to make concessions and deals, legal and possibly extralegal, deals which likely would have altered or eliminated many of those townhouses that are now in existence. Moreover, the fact that some of these townhouses sell for amounts as high as $50,000 to over $100,000 suggests great acceptability in the marketplace. To the best of my knowledge, similar developments have not taken place in any near comparable numbers in other cities, which suggests to me that the absence of zoning has been a factor responsible for their unique development in Houston. As is apparent from the huge prices for which these townhouses sell, these townhouses have provided the city with much tax revenues.

Considered on an overall basis, there is substantial cost to a community in maintaining a zoning ordinance, for although zoning or restrictive covenants in general do maximize values of homes at least for a time within the areas covered, zoning does not similarly maximize the balance of real estate uses within a community. Rather, as previously shown, it serves to hinder the optimum allocation of resources to such purposes. Even if it is argued that with zoning the gain in values for single-family dwellings offsets the reduction in the values contributed by other uses, such an argument is inapplicable in the nonzoned communities where restrictive covenants are generally in force and are effective. Thus, were Houston to adopt zoning at the present time, it would probably have minimum effect on the amount and value of single-family construction, but probably would affect other forms of construction considerably.

The importance of examining the effect on such other construction is made clear from Houston building statistics. The total value shown on permits for single-family construction in 1968 was $68,632,711, whereas the value shown for all other nongovernmental uses (including both housing and nonhousing construction) was $220,272,827. The corresponding statistics for 1969 were $52,653,728 and $264,377,226, respectively.

Even if zoning restrictions had accounted for only a 5 percent reduction in nonhome construction in 1968, government would have lost considerable revenues. In just the one year alone, a reduction of $11 million (5 percent of $220 million) in construction would have been involved. This amount of real estate value would produce over $175,000 in *ad valorem* taxes annually for the city, county, and state (based on 1968 rates).

Nonhome construction is even more profitable for schools, since it results in considerably less children per tax dollar received than results from homes. Considering that zoning could have deterred an amount greater than 5 percent in annual construction (nonhome only), the cost of zoning to a city, measured by the amount of lost construction, is quite substantial, especially on a cumulative basis. And it is difficult to see that there can be sufficient compensation in terms of property values (including possibly even some increases in single-family construction) to the community to offset this cost. Further, the cost to the city in increased services for this additional nonhome development will generally constitute only a fraction of the taxes received.

These then are the credits that accrue in the absence of zoning. Let us now consider the problems and debits of nonzoning.

Expenditures for Improvements

One of the problems of being a nonzoned city is that it is more difficult to forecast requirements in various areas for different facilities. Thus, it would appear that in April 1969 permits for some eight to ten thousand apartments were being temporarily withheld in certain relatively close-in areas of Houston pending installation of adequate sewer facilities to serve the areas. Had zoning limited the area to single-family lots, most of the sewers would have been adequate and there would have been no such problem. Confronted with this situation, the city began to install at substantial cost the necessary sewer facilities. Builders and developers of the apartments were not required to pay for or to contribute to the cost involved. At most, they might have to bear the cost of installing a main solely intended for their developments—a main connecting to a trunk line installed by the city.

Houston was doing no more nor less than what is generally expected of a municipality, that it service all properties within its borders on a reasonably equitable basis. It was providing sewer service for sections of the city (and not specific properties) on the basis of need. Interestingly enough, the city attorney has suggested that in part the city's program of enforcing deed restrictions is predicated on the desire of the city to maintain single-family use for the areas involved. It hopes thereby to avoid the cost of increasing the size of utilities required to serve the greater concentration of people which might result from the termination of such restrictions.[7]

If there had been zoning in Houston, the nature of the problem would have been far different. Much of the property in the areas in question would have been zoned for single-family. Probably it would not have been rezoned for apartments unless there had been some certainty that the existing facilities could adequately serve the development, or that the developer would pay most or all the costs to make them adequate. Regardless of the merits of the case and the likelihood for ultimate recovery of cost, the possibility of added cost to the community (and "unearned enrichment" for the developer) would probably be sufficient to result in a denial of the petition —almost as a matter of political self-preservation on the part of the council members.

Houston may be incurring costs that would not be necessary if it were zoned, but these costs may prove to be excellent investments for the future. Thus, although the initial cost may be substantial, in the long run the citizens of Houston will profit in tax dollars from the installation of the sewers to the areas as above described.

Some simple calculations will suggest that the expenditures for the additional sewer lines which may have totalled more than a million dollars probably were well spent measured solely from the standpoint of municipal finances. Local officials estimated for me that twenty-five to thirty apartments to the acre, principally efficiencies and one-bedrooms with a sprinkling of larger units, will produce annual taxes of about $6,000 per acre. Five middle-income single-family dwellings per acre in about the same location would probably produce an annual tax bill of about $4,000. The difference in tax receipts for 350 to 400 acres containing ten thousand apartments would be in excess of 700 thousand dollars annually. Moreover, since more school-age children would probably live in the homes, single-family use would cost more to service. It might be contended that more single-family homes will as a result have to be built near the outskirts and that the city will therefore have to install utilities over greater distances. But this would also be the case if apartments were constructed elsewhere. Although a definitive answer would require a more complex analysis, it would seem that there will be gain to the city unless a large portion of such units renting for the same amounts could have been constructed in areas within the city which already contained sewers—and this is most unlikely since the areas in question were relatively close-in and the sites were optimal for multifamily use.

Future Planning

It has been argued that the adoption of zoning controls is necessary to enable the community to better plan for its schools, roads, and utilities. When areas are zoned, so the argument goes, governmental agencies will be aware as to future demands for services within such areas and make provision accordingly. The difficulty with this position is that it accords zoning a much greater role in the evaluation of future growth than is warranted. This can be demonstrated in the instance of schools.

Zoning is but one of many factors that can be utilized by the schoolboard to estimate future school enrollment within its district. Equally, if not more, important, probably individually and certainly in the aggregate, are questions relating to: (1) amount of future building activity and its character, (2) the number of children that will attend parochial or private schools, and (3) the future birthrate within the community.

In the early years of a school district, when there has been little building activity, zoning might seem of some help in predicting future development. The likelihood, however, in the more recently developed areas of the country, both zoned and nonzoned, is that most of the land within the average district will be used for single-family homes. In neither case is new school construction justified until development takes place in more substantial amounts. At the same time, the purchase of land for a future school site may be equally prudent in both situations. When the area has partially developed, as in Fig. 2–9, the character of future development will be more evident, notwithstanding the existence or nonexistence of zoning. As Houston has shown, nonzoning may be no more chaotic or haphazard than zoning. And the closer the district is to full development, the more predictable will be the future of its vacant property—bearing in mind, of course, that the character and composition of any area is always subject to change.

Thus, even if zoning were to remain completely static, its importance in determining the school population is hardly a major one. In many older sections of Chicago's southside, the population changed racially from white to black within recent years. The change also resulted in substantial increases in grade-school population due to larger families and lesser use of parochial schools. Some school districts of Skokie, Illinois, lost school population in recent years as parents continued to live in their homes subsequent to the time their children graduated from elementary schools. This occurred in school districts where for long periods there were no rezonings authorized for apartments. (In one school district, the schoolboard as a result changed its policy of opposition to apartments; its timing may, however, have been too late, since there is little land left in that district.)

Zoning, however, is not likely to remain *completely* static even in the bedroom suburbs, and considerable changes are not unlikely in the larger cities. For the schoolboard that is unsophisticated in this respect, undue regard for the continuity of existing zoning or improvident forecasting of zoning changes may lead to erroneous decisions. Obviously, there is always the question as to whether areas zoned for specific uses will ever be so developed, and to what extent and when and with what?

In those instances in the nonzoned cities where covenants terminate, the uses that enter, apartments, townhouses, and businesses, will not necessarily produce more school children, or if they do, they are also likely to provide more net tax money per child. The overall effect of covenant termination is probably not of great significance to the schools.

Comparable problems exist for those projecting future traffic patterns. It is difficult to conceive of expressways planned and installed merely on the basis of existing zoning. Expressways generally serve larger areas than do schools; consequently it may be even more hazardous to use zoning to predict future traffic needs. Predicting future development may be somewhat less important with respect to utilities, inasmuch as some sewer and water lines can be installed to approximate the time and pace of development. But the problems of overestimating and underestimating utility needs have afflicted both the nonzoned and zoned communities. In the 1960s some areas of Chicago were developed with apartment buildings of far less density than that permitted by the zoning. More intense development has occurred at the city's outskirts than might ordinarily have been anticipated. Owing to new construction or annexations, suburbs of Chicago have held referendums authorizing financing for new sewage or water plants or additions to existing ones.

Municipalities are complex entities, and this makes it difficult to isolate the financial effects of any particular use. Mobile homes may not pay as much taxes for the children they produce as do single family homes; but this does not finalize the issue. By providing living quarters for employees, mobile homes may be contributing to the development of industry and business. When a school board causes curtailment (by zoning) of residential building in its district, it may cause that much more development in an adjoining one that is not as restrictive, and thereby lose to it some businesses and possibly some industries. These decisions are much better left to the varied forces of the market place where individual speculation and conjecture are not likely to operate to the detriment of the public.

6

Zoning Reduces Competition

When zoning restrictions reduce supply, they also operate to reduce competition in the real estate market. We are highly dependent upon competition in this country. We rely upon it to protect the consumer and stimulate the introduction of new, more, and better products and services. There is no governmental agency available to accomplish these vital tasks. Nor is it possible to establish a governmental agency that could benefit the consumer and society even remotely as well.

For reasons such as these, there is a strong, antimonopoly tradition in this country, evidenced in part by the antitrust laws. These laws have made deliberate elimination of competition an unlawful act. If within a city or town, several builders were to agree to build a small number of apartment buildings and to prevent any others from being built (as has occurred in other markets), laws would quickly be adopted, if they did not already exist, to dissolve this agreement and possibly even to penalize the parties involved. This is because such an agreement would give the parties special economic powers. By restricting entry into the market, zoning accomplishes the same result. Those allowed entry would be able to charge higher prices and/or offer poorer services and/or avoid undertaking improvements and rehabilitation. The consequences should not be different: "If a legal concept produces a monopoly, the concept pragmatically is a concept favoring monopoly."[1]

Supply and competition will be greater in the absence than in the presence of restrictions limiting production. This is attributable to the profit incentives of our society, which strongly motivates many if not most people, and can be realized through the production and sale of goods and services. The existence of a market that is profitable for many or even some—not necessarily all—is usually a standing invitation for entry by others into that market. Each newcomer will increase the supply and will try to provide something better or different in the market to attract existing customers and create new customers for himself. Many entrepreneurs spend major portions of their lives creating or innovating in an effort to outdo their competitors. As this process continues, the primary beneficiary will be the consumer, who will harvest the benefits of lower prices and larger varieties and better selections. Society is thus being rendered enormously valuable services without cost.

Since no one knows the limits of the market (i.e., how many will buy and at what prices) or the total amount that will be produced, there is a tendency for each producer to produce as much as he can as a means of maximizing his profits. As the supply increases, prices will decrease with consequent detriment to the less efficient producers. This includes those who fail to satisfy the consumer at a price above cost and are forced to reduce prices below cost to obtain some return on investment. Prices will start to increase when the less efficient are forced out of the market, but the process will reverse itself when profits begin to return. Because demand, desires, and needs fluctuate and are unpredictable, there is no better means for determining the "right" amount of competition and for "regulating" it.

Consumers tend to ignore the virtues of the market processes in part, I think, because they have become so commonplace. We expect them and find much fault when something goes awry. Professor Ronald H. Coase states that one general interest which all members of society share is the maintenance of a competitive private enterprise system:

If prices exceed costs in an industry, that is, if consumers prefer that their money should be spent on its products rather than on those of some other industry, resources move out. There is a constant search on the part of producers for products which consumers prefer to those that they are now consuming, which are, of course, products in which receipts will cover costs. This applies generally and all categories of consumers benefit from its operation. It is through its working that the standard of living of the consumer has increased so greatly in recent times. Some have described its basic character as "consumer's sovereignty" —a system in which the consumer group is king.[2]

It may also be difficult to comprehend how the pursuit of one's own individual desires and rewards benefit others. Yet this is a continual process in any organized society. Individual action that results in benefits to others may be motivated by a variety of incentives; it may include "selfless" dedication to certain goals or "selfish" pursuit of the dollar. I happen to believe that the creators of the coin-operated dry-cleaning and washing machines have enormously benefitted people of lower income, probably as much or more so than a host of charitable and governmental programs. The motivation was likely profit-oriented. There are countless other examples from the local supermarts to the fast-food franchises. Professor Milton Friedman has said the following:

The great advances of civilization, whether in architecture or painting, in science or literature, in industry or agriculture, have never come from centralized government. Columbus did not set out to seek a new route to China in response to a majority directive of a parliament though he was partly financed by an absolute monarch; Newton and Leibnitz; Einstein and Bohr; Shakespeare, Milton, and Pasternak; Whitney, McCormick, Edison, and Ford; Jane Addams, Florence Nightingale, and Albert Schweitzer; no one of these opened new frontiers in human knowledge and understanding, in literature, in technical possibilities, or in the relief of human misery in response to governmental directives. Their achievements were the product of individual genius, of strongly held minority views. Government can never duplicate the variety and diversity of individual action. That is one reason for limiting its scope.[3]

In zoning, the point is that we should not exclude by law potential producers from entering the market. Whether it is the tenants of a small building in the suburbs, or the many shoppers within a city, they should not be denied the benefits of the skill, ingenuity, innovation, and energy stimulated by competition.

With this introduction, I shall proceed to a discussion of various zoning restrictions or proposed restrictions which by reducing competition in production will exacerbate the problems they are intended to alleviate. Conservationists have explained that nature is interdependent, that the destruction of some living creatures will injuriously affect many others. This principle applies to other disciplines. It is true for economic phenomena; there is no way of repealing the law of supply and demand, and it governs and affects any and all parts of a particular market. Accordingly, these are some consequences of the restrictive processes.

1. There have been many proposals throughout the country to prohibit development within specified distances from bodies of water and other scenic areas. Their purpose is certainly well motivated: to enable many citizens, not just those fortunate enough to live nearby, to enjoy nature. Also in the name of aesthetics, proposals have been made to restrict the height of buildings and to maintain low density and much open space. (Greater exposure for the bay in San Francisco, the lake in Chicago, mountains in Colorado, and rivers and streams in rural areas.)

    In communities where there is little demand for living units, such aesthetic goals can be achieved with relatively little effect upon prices and rents and living conditions. (But if the demand is small, what need is there for such restrictions?) Where the demand is substantial, however, and production is not allowed to respond, there will be undesirable consequences for many in the community as well as on community aesthetics. The obvious result will be an increase in rents either directly through the amount actually charged or indirectly through reduction of services, maintenance, capital improvements, and repairs, or most probably, through a combination of both routes. Higher rents will cause more "doubling up," increasing wear and tear on a building and increasing density within areas containing these buildings. The filtering of housing through various income levels will be curtailed. All of the foregoing will tend to create poorer housing conditions and possibly contribute to further deterioration of marginal and even older buildings and areas. The cause of aesthetics and beauty will either not be served or be compromised, and at a substantial cost to many.

2. With respect to rental accommodations, an open market will generally result in a higher vacancy rate than will a restricted market. In the absence of production limitations, builders will keep adding to the supply until profit margins begin to diminish, and will recommence building when profits rise again. This process will prevent 100 percent occupancy for much of the time.

    The absence of a vacancy rate tends to be adverse not only to would-be tenants but also to existing tenants. The landlord will then have the choice of (a) high rents and good service or (b) lower rents and poorer service and maintenance or (c) both. Notwithstanding the best of motives and good intentions, the incentives for good service, maintenance, and repair are less when there is little concern as to whether a tenant will renew his lease. The good will of an existing tenant is simply not "critical" when another is readily available as a replacement. A landlord with a lower occupancy rate has less choice; he generally will make greater efforts to satisfy and placate his tenants, each being an important source of income. Even the strictest laws governing landlord-tenant relations cannot be more effective inasmuch as, among other things, it is generally too costly or time-consuming to employ them.

Obviously vacancy rates occur under zoning, and as of 1972 there was a considerable vacancy rate in various apartment buildings in many of Chicago's suburban areas with highly restrictive zoning practices. In particular the apartments affected were those permitted, in other words, those having high rents and few bedrooms. On the other hand, many other multifamily units, such as townhouses or quadrominiums, were still in demand, for there was relatively little land zoned for their use. Consequently when they are built in these areas, they tend to be purchased rapidly. Obviously the absence of restrictions tends to exhaust demand for most parts of the multifamily market.

3. I have often attended zoning hearings and listened to residents condemn the appearance and other characteristics of the few apartment buildings in that community. They rejected zoning for new apartment buildings on the basis of their experience with existing ones. The probability is, however, that the newer buildings would be more pleasing in appearance and would also likely include some amenities not present in the existing ones. Restrictions gave the existing landlords a "free ride." The rental market operates as do other markets; each newcomer will strive to outdo his competitors in order to rent more of his apartments. Hence, newer apartment buildings for the same class of rental market in the area will tend to offer more or superior amenities or better values or most likely, both. This should, in turn, cause improvements to be made in the older buildings (or at least cause rents to be lowered, or probably both). If the newer buildings are for a different category of the market, these buildings might not have to compete directly with existing ones, but thereafter all other buildings in this category would no longer have this exemption. When the owner of an existing building creates new ones, he too will have to consider existing and potential competition.

4. When I was visiting a nonzoned Florida county in which many mobile home parks were located, I heard, not unexpectedly, criticism of conditions within these parks. Much concern was expressed for the welfare of the mobile-home owners. The solution, I was often told, was to adopt zoning restrictions giving the local government greater discretion over

location and planning (by designating mobile home parks a special use) and establishing a stringent minimum land density requirement, usually 4,000 square feet per unit.

Ordinances with such provisions have been proposed for counties in Florida. These critics, however, have never lived in mobile homes, and were in my opinion, without reflection upon their sincerity, incapable of experiencing and expressing the desires, problems, and alternatives available to those who did live in them. It would seem probable that many mobile-home owners would rather use their limited funds for items such as food, clothing, furniture, rather than for land. That decision can be made more appropriately by the owner than by a stranger who cannot possibly have the same insights into another's personal life style. Obviously greater production, not less production, of trailer sites would allow for greater range of choice.

Moreover, these restrictions will exclude many potential mobile home parks from a popular area of the country, and will, therefore, limit competition for those existing ones that are considered to be so undesirable. Yet more competition would motivate their owners to offer better values to their renters or face the possibility of increased vacancy rates and reduced rents. Instead of ameliorating bad conditions, the zoning laws will preserve and protect them. If there are health and sanitation problems, these should be the concern of the health and sanitation departments. Health and sanitation laws will of themselves constitute minimum standards for mobile homes with which few can quarrel, provided that they are, of course, related to their intended objectives.

5. A county official in a nonzoned county considering a proposed zoning ordinance once told an audience that one reason he favored adopting the ordinance was to get rid of several junkyards then located on some heavily travelled streets, which he felt defaced the local landscape. The proposed ordinance would have zoned these sites for relatively "light" (attractive) commercial uses and have made the existing use for junkyards as a nonconforming one with the requirement that they be terminated within a period of ten years. As nonconforming uses, limitations would have been placed on the right of the owner to make major repairs, alterations, and additions during this period.

I suggest that such proposals are self-defeating. By restricting the property only to certain uses as well as to bulk area, and height requirements, competition for purchase and development of these tracts was reduced to only those businesses that could qualify under these limitations. In thus limiting competition among buyers, the ordinance would probably delay purchase or development of the junk yard for other than its present use. Since going businesses were involved, the price for each tract would probably be higher than if it were vacant, which again would indicate the advisibility of removing land use restrictions, which, as a rule, tend to lower the price that a buyer otherwise would be willing to pay. Thus, there would be a much greater likelihood for the junkyards to be redeveloped for other uses without, rather than with, the adoption of these zoning restrictions. The junkyard and other "obnoxious" uses tend to disappear as the land becomes more valuable, and these uses become less economically feasible. Zoning restrictions that interfere in this process are, therefore, counterproductive.

6. A newspaper story in early 1972 revealed that McDonald's, a "fast-food" franchise company, started replacing some years ago at substantial expense its red and white tile buildings and huge arches with a brown, brick structure covered by a mansard roof and subdued arches. As of the date of the article, only about one-third of the company's 1,850 outlets remained in the old architectural style. Although the story suggests various reasons, a primary consideration was clearly founded on competitive inducements. Those who provide a more aesthetic atmosphere and better food and service (at the lowest price) are likely to profit more and remain in business longer than those who do not. Given the opportunity to patronize many restaurants, consumers will eat at those offering the best value, which includes a more pleasing environment.

If the restaurant or its food is not desirable, there is no reason to patronize it again—unless there is no other in the vicinity (probably as a result of zoning). Each individual customer, in effect, tests and evaluates the restaurant on the basis of his own standards, which in the aggregate constitute a reasonably objective measure. This may cost one the price of some bad meals, but, on the whole, it is probably much less expensive to society that is the cost of some governmental operation designed for the same purpose. Restrictions on entry of restaurants, however, will give advantage to the few who do enter, possibly necessitating greater regulation, which, in turn, might further restrict entry; and this in turn, etc. etc. . . . The process is highly self-defeating.

The last is an important point with which to close this chapter. Restrictions beget restrictions because they eliminate the most effective of restrictions: competition.

7 Publishers, Pop Architecture, and Minorities

The reason that societies with or without constitutions give free speech and press a preferred and almost sanctified status has largely to do with a marketplace: the one for ideas. Society is benefitted when all shades of opinion are allowed expression, and there is no limit upon the communication of thoughts and ideas. The marketplace is thus filled with numerous opinions, and the individual has the opportunity to select from a variety of views competing for his favor. To remove ideas from the marketplace is to deny the consumer the maximum opportunity for self-enlightenment and responsibility in a representative society. In this manner, society has the advantage of obtaining the intellectual input of a great many of its citizens, regardless of their status as part of a majority or minority on any one or more issues.

These freedoms are not unlimited or absolute; but "only the gravest abuses endangering paramount interests give occasion for permissible limitation."[1] And abuses there are! The consumer or information must basically rely upon the competency and objectivity of the dispensers of information: the communications media—who are not always competent and objective. Distortions and untruths, unfairness and prejudice, exclusion and censorship are not uncommon; in some newspapers one wonders whether they are the rule or the exception. The transgressions of the press into individual privacy and sensitive areas of crime and punishment have been recounted often and they are numerous. Much "shoddy construction" is evident in the news stories, particularly those concerning relatively complex social and scientific matters, and does not contribute to an informed public opinion.

As businessmen, the owners of newspapers seek to maximize their profits by selling the news that most people will want to buy—and much of that news has to do with matters that do not further anybody's enlightenment or education. That there is a strong profit motive operating in the selling of news and a general dissemination of information, and that millions of dollars are made in this process has not stirred many people to demand regulation of the newspapers—and for good reason. Who is to decide which news should be printed, and is it possible to do this without at the same time eliminating the maximum dissemination of ideas? Who would then protect the minority view on the countless issues confronting society? Stating the problem leads to the answer: Better suffer these "abuses" than restrict a basic element of free society, the marketplace of ideas.

141

It should by now be obvious, the foregoing is written to establish an analogy to another marketplace where input is also vitally important. Maximum competition in the land use market will allow for maximum satisfaction of both material and aesthetic needs of people. So when we allow restriction of that market, as well, we are giving power to certain individuals who will have the power of government to determine what will be produced or created and for whom—and this power must necessarily be disadvantageous to those denied the benefits of that production and creation.

This is not to say that there must be no regulation whatsoever. Another analogy is therefore presented: Publishers are restricted by libel and some other laws. Similarly, nuisance and *some* other laws are necessary to control the use of land and property. In both cases, the restrictions should be clearly warranted, beyond conjecture, to prevent harmful activity.

Any discussion of the parallels must necessarily also consider the possible detrimental effect of each activity upon the public welfare. This is fundamentally the justification for the validity of zoning. The courts uphold the constitutionality of land use regulations reasonably related to the "public health, safety, and welfare." Some may insist that the press has much less direct impact on or relationship to this sort of standard and that consequently there is no basis for similar treatment. But this is a rather dubious proposition for a representative society in which the ultimate and final decision on war and peace, prosperity and depression, and numerous other vital matters rests with an electorate dependant on speech and press for accurate and reliable information. Nor are individual victims of press misinformation and distortion likely to agree.

The comparison becomes even more balanced when we consider the example of Houston's land use experience. It shows that freedom operates well when allowed to function in the use of property.

The similarities are such, that I frequently wince at newspaper editorials decrying some proposed land usage by "profit hungry" builders and speculators" and "unscrupulous landowners," for these editorials often appear in newspapers whose publishers probably have monetary objectives similar to those they accuse. They are not publishing newspapers as a public service—and if they did, they would soon be out of business. They too are catering to the consumers in perhaps a way that often is not nearly as socially desirable as the producer of goods who satisfies the basic needs of human beings. Were one to suggest the kind of regulation readily proposed in editorials on the control of land use, the cries of "free speech" and "censorship" would unbearably scream from the headlines. Yet, I suggest that most publishers are no more or less concerned about free speech than builders are about housing. No more or less concerned about making money or profits. Nor is there any reason to believe that either is more guilty than the other of forsaking a responsibility to society. Nevertheless our society treats each institution enormously differently; little control of one and much control of the other.

Why do so many editorial writers favor zoning and severe land use controls? Why do they readily accept regulation or censorship of one market and not the other? One simple response is that they are part of the affluent group that, as zoning elections have shown, consider zoning to be in its own self-interest. This appears to be as true for rich liberals as for rich conservatives. The poorer people who vote substantially against zoning are not publishers and editorial writers. Perhaps the writers share what has come to be a common acceptance of regulation—provided it affects someone else. A similar cleavage probably exists with respect to speech and press; it is much more important for the rich, who have the time for it, than the poor, who are much more concerned about daily survival. There are also obviously considerable differences in educational levels. The position of the editorials are not contradictory when considered in terms of self-interests and personal values of the writers and publishers.

It is even more difficult to explain away these inconsistencies in the case of community aesthetics which is being subjected to ever greater control through zoning. People differ greatly in their perceptions and concepts of beauty, and this makes it most unfair and perilous to progress to allow any one person or group to impose aesthetic controls. History readily bears out that society will be enriched by being subjected to a great variety of artistic or visual experiences; modern culture is enormously indebted to creations that were highly unpopular and virtually subversive in the past.

These have become commonplace arguments in recent times, and many books have been written and museums and galleries established in support of this thesis. Unfortunately, however, relatively small minorities read these books and visit these institutions. For the masses of people, we may be creating through regulation a society in which aesthetic diversity is very limited. Many planners and zoners allege that they believe strongly in aesthetic freedom, but presumably only when it is confined to the interiors of museums and homes. Strip developments (which may contain laundramats, cleaners, drugstores, grocery stores, repair shops), gas stations, quick-food franchises, motels are routinely condemned as ugly, and were it not for the tax revenues they produce, might well be zoned out of existence in many areas. Although the poor and less mobile in the population are served well by most, if not all, of these uses, these people are not much more likely to be planners and zoners than they are to be editorial writers. "Snob zoning" creates also "snob aesthetics."

When architect Robert Venturi, in what might be referred to as a moment of "kidding on the square," announced the formation of a Society to Preserve Our Billboards, he received an irate letter from a prominent planning official that read, "You have sold out to the crassest motives of our society and betrayed your responsibility as architects."[2] Well, Venturi had not sold out; he and a number of other architects have taken a position favorable to billboards and the other conventional "uglies," that is, the commercial strips, the hamburger stands. They are part of a group dubbed as "Pop Architects," who are making an important impact on architecture. Consider some of their other heresies:[3] (1) They like the Las Vegas strip with all of its garishness, glitter, and vernacular. (2) "Main street is almost all right." Instead of getting rid of the urban sprawl that Main Street and Las Vegas represent, perhaps architects should learn to love it, or at least learn to deal with it. (3) "I'm for messy vitality over obvious unity." Diversity and complexity is more pleasing than simplicity and uniformity. (4) "We need less of a prima donna in the landscape approach." (5) Instead of elaborate architectural creations, the ordinary economic structures by the side of the road should be preferred because they respond to the needs of people in their automobiles.

The point of all this, of course, is that contributions by the Pop Architect to the culture should be welcomed, not discouraged, by our laws.[4] As in the case of speech and press, they too, should be allowed to enter the marketplace to prove or disprove themselves on a competitive basis. Nor need we fear inundation (or chaos) in a competitive situation from any one source. Every land use will find its economic level. There can be only so many gas stations and quick-food stands. Thus, they as well as billboards will be erected only where there is a high traffic count, and then only when each has successfully competed against other uses that can be established in the same space. This means, as the experience of nonzoning shows, that billboards, gas stations, and most other commercial uses will be generally absent from the residential areas and will locate only on the major thoroughfares.

There is a temptation to say that economics is not enough; there should be some additional limitations, perhaps just enough to insure that the strips along roads and highways will be more aesthetically pleasing. (Perhaps fewer food franchises and gas stations.) One might then ask: aesthetically pleasing to whom? But the bigger problem comes from entrusting this power to some person or some groups who necessarily have their own values and beliefs—and this is the reason why no one could possibly qualify for this trust in the areas of speech, press, religion. *Better* zoning is no more the answer to *no* zoning than *better* censorship is to *no* censorship. In the context of the zoning process, the controls would become irrational and counterproductive to the stated goals. David M. Gooder interprets the problem as follows:

Who will decide what may or may not be done—the layman, the expert, the politician, the mass? What protection is there against the expert, the politician, the mass? What protection is there against the ignorant, the Philistine, the pseudo expert, the devotee of a particular school or point of view, the fanatic? To whom will appeal lie from arbitrariness, favoritism, discrimination or worse? Is not governmental force or compulsion incompatible with a matter so subjective, so intangible, so fragile? Is not democracy—rule by majority vote—basically in conflict with the creative personality, with originality, with the innovator? There is danger in giving such subjective decisions the force of law.[5]

There is much anguish about equalizing our society and alleviating the economic ills of minorities; yet almost unconsciously we adopt laws to intensify these problems. Joe's Hot Dog Stand should have the same right to be along the highway as does Neiman-Marcus, provided only that he is able to provide services under the rules and standards of the marketplace. And consumers have as much right to Joe's services as to Neiman's. Some of Neiman's customers may detest the sight of Joe's place, but then his customers may feel similarly inclined about Neiman's new architecture. Some who do not shop at either enterprise will find that one or both is a welcome addition to the highway; and others for a variety of reasons would be equally happy if either or both were not present. None of these views is entitled to legal supremacy; yet under zoning those favoring Neiman's are likely to achieve preferential status.

To stay in business under the rules of the marketplace, Joe may have to satisfy in a populated area only a small fraction of that population, perhaps as little as several percent. Small groups of consumers are thus provided for and served. In large populated areas, many businessmen can profit handsomely on an even smaller volume. It is possible that few of their customers even live in the town in which the establishments are located.

Under zoning, however, to stay in business over a period of time and not hazard the hardships of being a nonconforming use, Joe's operation may have to satisfy a majority of the local governing council, who supposedly represent a majority within that municipality. (One factor certainly not likely to aid his cause is his architecture, which I suppose, would be a form of "ordinary-contemporary"). Provisions adverse to small businesses are not unusual in comprehensive amendments to a zoning ordinance. Or the matter may arise in connection with proposed amendments to business zoning regulations. Unless there are large numbers of others similarly affected, which is unlikely, Joe's opposition to new zoning provisions restricting his business will have the same degree of success as the temperance movement has upon Congress. Joe's consolation may be in that the ordinance will also remove the threat of new competition. Unfortunately, this may in time possibly result in poorer services and values for his patrons because then they will not have the protection of this competition.

In a dissenting opinion in the much cited *Stover* case (discussed in Chapter 12), Justice van Voorhis analyzed the matter in this manner:

This ordinance is unrelated to the public safety, health, morals or welfare except insofar as it compels conformity to what the neighbors like to look at. Zoning, important as it is within limits, is too rapidly becoming a legalized device to prevent property owners from doing whatever their neighbors dislike. Protection of minority rights is as essential to democracy as majority vote. In our age of conformity it is still not possible for all to be exactly alike, nor is it the instinct of our law to compel uniformity wherever diversity may offend the sensibilities of those who cast the largest numbers of votes in municipal elections. The right to be different has its place in this country. The United States has drawn strength from differences among its people in taste, experience, temperament, ideas, and ambitions as well as from differences in race, national or religious background.

Even where the use of property is bizarre, unsuitable or obstreperous it is not to be curtailed in the absence of overriding reasons of public policy. The security and repose which come from protection of the right to be different in matters of aesthetics, taste, thought, expression and within limits, in conduct are not to be cast aside without violating constitutional privileges and immunities. This is not merely a matter of legislative policy, at whatever level. In my view, this pertains to individual rights protected by the Constitution.[6]

The exclusion of commercial facilities can also result in the exclusion of some people—and this may sometimes be one objective of the restrictions. Developers of less expensive homes generally acknowledge that the proximity of commercial facilities is very helpful in the sale of homes. In a recent case in Connecticut, the supreme court in that state upheld the constitutionality of zoning regulations restricting the entire town to residential and farming uses.[7] Regulations of this nature will effectively exclude certain families that require shopping nearby.

Present pressures for lower-cost housing in the suburbs should not ignore the hardship under zoning of small businesses (which, it should be remembered, include individually owned franchises). There is a strong relationship between the two. For the suburbs to become viable for lesser-income people, who usually have limited mobility (perhaps no car, or one older one used daily by the husband) there should be a maximum amount of commercial and business facilities. As minorities, they, too, require and will be best served by an abundant and varied marketplace. For them, zoning may constitute the worst form of censorship.

Part III
Differing Solutions to Land Use Problems

8

The Current Zoning Scene

It has not been difficult, within recent years, to hear or read strong criticisms and condemnations of zoning and zoning practices. The builder or developer who condemned zoning practices that were exclusionary toward his project now finds himself in very respectable company. Several Presidential commissions,[1] some state commissions,[2] and a mounting number of academicians, writers, and planners have also come to the conclusion that zoning is exclusionary. Much space in the learned journals has been devoted to the problem, and a prestigious lawyer's organization has engaged in an extensive study and made recommendations for a general overhaul of land use control jurisdiction and procedures. Articles in some legal publications have contended that much, if not all, of local zoning is unconstitutional.[3] Moreover, legislation that would alter many existing zoning powers has been introduced in the Congress and adopted in some states.

The climate of opinion among the commentators has changed substantially in recent years. I have been somewhat surprised to learn that academicians who almost instinctively favor the state as against the individual in most economic matters are reversing this position in zoning controversies. They have learned that it is in the developer's interest to provide more housing and other necessities and conveniences, and it is frequently in the interest of the local politician and planner to frustrate these efforts.

The consensus among those who have made any in-depth studies of the subject seems to be that the record of local zoning has been largely one of failure. Nevertheless, most of these critics are urging either new and different governmental controls or just minor modifications of existing controls, and ignoring that it is governmental controls which largely account for the major problems of present land use. Many propose state and federal controls. Others want to give greater discretionary controls to local government.

In my view, most of these proposals are essentially a replay of what has occurred in zoning since its inception: more and greater controls over land use designed to cure the failures of prior controls which were likewise supposed to have cured the defects of a previous set of controls, etcetera, *ad nauseum*. The dogma persists that if zoning doesn't work, try more of it!

Some take this position because they believe that zoning laws will never be eliminated and thus efforts toward that end are futile and wasteful. Admittedly, the outlook is not favorable at present for legislative action to curtail zoning powers. There are serious difficulties involved in adopting

149

a program of less regulation in a period when the general trend is for greater economic regulation; however, if every proponent for change had been deterred by the practical obstacles confronting the adoption of his proposal, we probably would still be subject to the rule of the English monarch. A great many of our laws now fully accepted began their careers with enormous odds against their success. They never would have become law if for reasons of expediency, other proposals had been advocated instead. This country is an enormous and unlimited marketplace for ideas, and our history shows that there are few restraints upon acceptability.

Admittedly, there is a lot of "bread" in zoning for politicians, planners, and lawyers, all groups highly influential in the passage of legislation. In addition, a most influential group in the population, the affluent home-owners, are also strong supporters. That public opinion as a whole, however, may not be favorably disposed toward zoning is suggested by the record of voting in Texas and elsewhere. And, after all, majority opinion should control in this country.

Legislative surprises do occur. Some years ago in 1967 I attended a meeting of builders, local legislators, and planners. Opinion on that occasion seemed unanimous that the states would never interfere with local building codes. Yet since then twenty states have enacted legislation allowing the preemption of local codes for industrialized housing. "No fault" insurance, too, presents a most interesting example of legislators adopting something seemingly contrary to their own interests. I refer to the fact that many legislators are lawyers who will sustain personal monetary losses under "no-fault" insurance. Yet, some states have adopted some version of "no-fault," and it is being seriously considered in many others.

Zoning does involve restrictions upon individual rights of person and property, and these are matters for the judiciary. The outlook is not dim that the courts may reduce substantially many or most zoning powers of the municipalities, particularly with respect to housing. Forty-five years have elapsed since the Supreme Court originally validated the constitutionality of local zoning, and much has changed in society, including the meaning and scope of the due process and equal protection guarantees of the fourteenth amendment of the U.S. Constitution. Equally important, we now also understand much better the ramifications of the zoning process and its relation to the general welfare. A much different approach might now be forthcoming from federal and state courts.

In this and the two subsequent chapters, I shall analyze and evaluate some of the leading proposals for changes in existing land use laws. Before going into these, it is necessary to understand what is presently occurring under local zoning practices, which over the years have changed considerably. The judiciary vis-à-vis zoning will be discussed in chapter 10 and part IV.

Powers of the Suburbs

The vast majority of zoning controversies relate to the use of vacant land, which still remains abundant only in the newer cities—having fallen sharply in the older cities—and in the suburban and rural areas. For instance, the fraction of land vacant in Washington, D.C., dropped from 22 percent in 1928 to 4 percent in 1955, and Detroit was 22 percent vacant in 1943, but only 8 percent in 1954.[4] Land in Los Angeles, considered one of the newer cities, was 31 percent vacant in 1960, but it had been 64 percent vacant in 1940.[5] Houston as of 1966 and Dallas as of 1964 were each about 40 percent vacant. Notice that the gap between old and new cities may be closing rather rapidly, so much so that the turn-of-the-century figures will probably show a substantial reduction.

Vacant land is still plentiful, however, in the areas not many miles removed from central cities, and this is where much of future construction will have to occur. Open areas exist outside of older cities even in the most populous sections of the country. Thus, settlements along the highly populous Boston-Washington corridor are mostly thin strips along major roads and railroads; off the beaten path, woods and farms predominate.[6]

These suburban and rural areas have been growing more in population than the cities they ring. In the metropolitan areas designated as SMSA's by the Census Bureau, the percentage of the population within the areas outside of the central cities has been increasing since 1920. These areas became greater in population than the central cities in the mid-1960s. It is estimated that during the 1970s they will contain 50 percent more people than the central cities.[7]

Consequently, because they have much vacant land and are and will continue to be populous, the suburbs can exercise through their zoning powers enormous influence on life styles within this country. Although he may serve a small community, the impact of a local village politician should not be minimized. He and his counterparts tend to think and act alike when it comes to land use policies and in the aggregate are a major force in American life. They will have great influence in determining how or where a substantial portion of the population will live.

Over the years their role in the control of land use has become much greater. This trend has been particularly evident in the more affluent suburbs that developed subsequent to World War II. The political history of many of these suburbs in the Chicago metropolitan area probably illustrates what has occurred nationwide. When these communities were sparsely settled, there was frequently little concern about land use controls, or, for that matter, about most aspects of local government. Zoning matters might have been conducted on a relatively informal basis with little participation on the part of the residents. In many instances, favorable zoning could be obtained through friendship or possibly more material means. Often land-owners were very influential in political matters; and the tenor of government was highly favorable to all forms of property development.

As more homes were built, the new homeowners took a much more active interest in local government and particularly in zoning. They insisted upon living in an environment that differed from whence they came. They formed political parties which promised maximum zoning control to exclude industry, apartments, motels, gas stations, trailers. They ultimately wrested control of local government from the incumbents and thereby obtained dominance over land use. A major objective of these homeowner groups is to completely control land use within the community, and they have been most successful in accomplishing this. The suburbanite's wish had been achieved and he humbly gave prayer: "We thank thee, God, that thy Grace has brought us this lovely place. And now, Dear God, we humbly pray Thou will'st all others, keep away."[8]

There is little or no graft in these homeowner-controlled governments, and the favors that are dispensed are restricted to the party faithful. Integrity has a curious meaning, however. It usually means the use of all of the community's resources to maintain strict control of the land, regardless of the merits of a landowner's position under the law. Court processes are used as a device to prevent or stall undesired changes in land use. Appeals to higher courts are part of the arsenal used to impede development, and sometimes even after decisions are issued in the highest courts, efforts will be made to circumvent these decisions.

Such tactics are hardly consistent with the requirements and practices of an orderly society. If businessmen were to use the tactics favored in zoning matters by some of the bedroom suburbs, and perhaps by some larger cities as well, commerce as we know it might well cease to exist. Bills, claims, or contractual obligations would not be paid or honored without a decision from a lower or an appellate court. Such municipal policies preclude changes as required by law, and will deny many of their rights under law. They merit no less excoriation than corrupt practices.

While zoning has become more strict in the central cities, it has not been accomplished with the same degree of severity as within these suburbs. As previously indicated, there is no predominant life style in the cities which zoning can serve except perhaps that of a dominant political machine. Nevertheless, there has also been a great tendency toward stricter control of land uses in the city.

Zoning Powers Sprawl and Proliferate

From its inception, the direction of zoning has clearly been one way: greater and more minute control over property use. The drafters of the early zoning ordinances would hardly recognize the ordinances of today. What was once largely an effort to separate uses, and in particular to keep the single-family district pure, has escalated into a detailed account of what can and cannot be done on any parcel of ground. Interpretation and enforcement has become much more strict. Perhaps of most importance, the discretionary powers of local government over land use have proliferated and sprawled extensively. The doctrine of *laissez faire* seems to apply only to the passage of laws controlling the use of land.

The early arguments for zoning were all related to the needs of centers of population.[9] The objective was to protect existing neighborhoods from the onslaught of diverse uses that would deteriorate property values. Some of its early proponents even assumed that areas containing much vacant land could not be zoned.[10] As a result, much of the early zoning regulations did not provide the great flexibility required for the growth of cities. As zoning was originally envisioned, the local authorities were to adopt detailed regulations that would allow or cause development to occur automatically, and without the need to exercise official discretion, except to grant relief in relatively few instances. Once the property had been zoned, the owner was to be able to make use of it as a matter of right, generally without any special permission. Equally important, the regulations were required to be uniform for each class of building throughout an individual district; the goal was that "all properties situated alike would be treated alike."[11] The legislative discretion was again to be limited; if necessary a new district would have to be created for a particular set of uses.

The judiciary also tended to confine the discretion of the local legislature. Most courts limited the powers of amendment of the local legislature to reclassifying property from one zoning district to another. Conditions could not be exacted that were more restrictive than the provisions of the new classification. For example, if the property were reclassified to a certain commercial district, the council could not by agreement with the owner limit the use of the property to any one or more of the permitted uses; the owner was entitled to all uses set forth in that district. In a leading case, the Baltimore city council passed an ordinance rezoning the petitioner's property to a commercial classification on condition that he enter into an agreement with the city that the property would only be used as a funeral home, which was one of the uses permitted in that district. The supreme court of the state ruled that the council did not have the power to make this contract with the owner.[12] This kind of agreement has been referred to as "contract zoning," and its legality continues to be questionable.

Bassett, considered by many as one of the fathers of zoning, was quite emphatic in denouncing contract zoning in his book published in 1940:

Contracts have no place in a zoning plan. Zoning, if accomplished at all, must be accomplished under the police power. It is a form of regulation for community welfare. Contracts between property owners or between a municipality and a property owner should not enter into the enforcement of zoning regulations.

Sometimes local legislatures state they will make certain zoning changes if property owners file agreements either with one another or with the city. This is wrong, unnecessary, and unfair. The local legislative body is taking advantage of its superior position whenever it tries to force a property owner to enter into a contract in order to have a permit to which he is entitled, or before zoning regulations are made which are justified by well-settled principles. There is no consideration for such a bargain because the municipality cannot receive a consideration for taking steps in legislation. Its legislation is not and ought not to be for sale.[13]

Regardless of its legality, however, such arrangements are not uncommon today. They are often essential to resolving local disputes and are accordingly acceptable to the builders, who would not otherwise be able to proceed. Faced with opposition from local residents or in the council, a developer may have to give some form of consideration to the city itself—if not to the council members—to obtain the requested rezoning. Contributions to a school or park district, acceptance of use, height or density limitations less than that provided for the district, or setting aside land for a buffer zone are not uncommon. Yet, not long ago, this sort of bargaining was criticized as inappropriate and undignified to the legislative process:

Many planning commission hearings have taken on the character of an Oriental bazaar where applicants wheel and deal with the commission on conditions and restrictions to be imposed on zoning. Some hearings are more like the ancient circuses in the coliseum of Rome in the days of Nero, except that the Christians then got a better deal from the lions than some applicants do from the planning commission. Now instead of thumbs down or up, the planning commissioner asks for a show of hands.[14]

PUDs and Special Uses

What once appeared undesirable and strange has now become routine. The most notable and important development in local zoning within recent years has been the introduction of certain discretionary devices for land use control, the most prominent of which are the "special use" or "special exception," the "planned unit development" (PUD), and the "floating zone." As a result of the introduction of these new devices, bargaining between government and property owners is now a valid and accepted zoning practice—at least when conducted pursuant to such provisions. These forms of contract zoning have been ratified by legislatures and enthusiastically adopted by municipalities.

For readers unfamiliar with these devices, they may be simply defined as follows: *Special use* or *special exception* is a designated use which will be permitted in a specified district or districts at the approval of the local legislature, or a zoning commission or board given this power. A *planned unit development* (PUD) allows the developer of property to arrange with flexibility his buildings and streets without being bound by many specifics of the zoning ordinance if the project has the approval of the local legislature or a designated commission or board. A *floating zone* is a use that is designated in the text of an ordinance and that can be authorized by the local authorities in all or part of the municipality.

Each of these requires notice, publication, public hearings, and the other procedural formalities required to rezone property. They are what the Douglas Commission aptly calls, "wait and see techniques," giving the local legislature the power to avoid advance commitments on the use of land. Thus, David Heeter states the philosophical basis for "wait and see techniques" as follows:

. . . the point is simply that guiding the use of land requires many complex and subtle judgments, many of which cannot be easily translated into prestated criteria and which may not become evident until a specific development proposal is submitted.[15]

Municipalities with large supplies of vacant land will invariably use the PUD provisions to authorize almost any multifamily, commercial, and industrial development for significant amounts of acreage. Probably the bulk of the larger apartment and townhouse developments built within recent years has been approved as planned unit developments. In practice, the special use and floating zones devices allow the city or town similar controls over land uses involving usually one principal building.

As should be evident to the reader by now, these devices have at least one feature in common: they give the municipality greater authority than ever over what is erected within its borders. If the city fathers are unhappy with what is proposed under any of these provisions, it is unlikely that it will be built unless so ordered by a court. This form of relief is virtually impossible in those states in which the courts generally uphold zoning. In the other states, the courts are not as a practical matter readily usable by many property owners, including even the biggest ones. The delay involved can be most costly to a developer. It is therefore not surprising that PUD provisions are almost certain to be adopted once the authorities understand their operation. As the subsequent discussion will show, all these devices give the city control over almost all aspects of a particular land use except that out of which they can be talked or bargained. The locality as a result is now in a position to control elements of construction, architecture, and planning concepts over which it would have no power if the property were already zoned for the use intended.

PUD has many advantages to the builder over conventional zoning and the National Association of Home Builders has endeavored to persuade municipalities to adopt it—which is one battle the builders are certain to win. PUD allows much greater flexibility for the developer; he need not be confined to the rigidities of rectangular or grid-iron zoning. Under PUD the developer may cluster his units, mix different types of units, create private instead of public streets, develop public and private recreation areas, and possibly increase density. Lesser amounts of pavement, curb, sewer and water lines may be necessary and this can result in monetary savings. There is considerably more freedom for the architect and land planner. The complications arise, of course, because all this flexibility and freedom is still subject to the will of the local authorities.

Results of PUD

A developer will suffer much more than the local authorities if the proposed project is never built. On the other hand, a legislator's political fortunes possibly may be endangered if the project is built. Developers have had to rely on the personal conscience and ethics of local officials, and unfortunately these do not always favor their or the consumer's cause. In the absence of these personal attributes, political considerations or graft may dictate the decision, and, perhaps contrary to what the civic textbooks say, the latter is much more likely to attain more housing. By contrast the public politics of the situation tends to favor exclusion rather than inclusion.

The bargaining powers certainly are not equal. The resulting imbalance operates adversely to the housing consumer for two reasons: (1) the city fathers (or those given the power of approval) will invariably attempt to upgrade the development, which will increase its cost and thereby raise rents or prices, and (2) some or all of their conceptual and aesthetic judgments will have to be complied with, and they are not usually attuned to the demands and desires of the marketplace. Public hearings are involved, which also give a voice to local residents—and they are equally unqualified and unconcerned about the market.

Under PUD, local politicians are now deciding about details of development never contemplated as part of the zoning function. They are usually no more qualified to do this than they are to control details of practice of doctors, lawyers, or engineers. Furthermore, when they engage in battle on unknown terrain, they are at a handicap. A developer may deliberately omit certain items to enable the local authorities to "score" by including them. He may seek much more than he hopes to attain—again for bargaining purposes. Or he may reduce certain unseen or overlooked elements to compensate for the increased costs.

The following excerpt from the minutes of the land use committee of Board of Trustees of the Village of Addison, Illinois, of May 25, 1971, illustrates the extent of controls being exercised under PUD:

File #69–23–973, Mill Meadow Lot 103 Planned Development. Referred to Committee for consideration of amenities for small children as requested by Trustee Naumann:

a. Fenced-in play area for pre-school children. Mr. Cargill, Washer and Johnston were agreed that a protected play area should be provided, probably best accommodated in the swimming pool area.

b. Bicycle rack. The committee agreed that the bicycle rack was not a desirable addition, 2 to 1.

c. Cleanup sink in dry area of recreation building.

d. Storage facilities for recreational equipment. The Committee unanimously agreed that a cleanup sink and storage facilities for recreational equipment should be provided.

e. The additional equipment of ping-pong table, pool table and other game tables was approved as a requirement by a vote of 2–1. The addition of a shuffleboard was approved by Mr. Johnston and disapproved by Mr. Cargill and Mr. Washer.

f. The Committee unanimously recommended the addition of landscaping to the rear of buildings which back up on the front of other buildings.

g. The Committee unanimously recommended that fountains and similar aesthetic features not be required.

h. Although the applicant has provided written agreement to make all units conform to the size required in the ordinance, the committee unanimously agreed that it should be further agreed that there will be no architectural changes to accommodate the increase in unit size.

These and prior requirements will make the apartments more desirable. But they will also cost more to build, and this will create problems for the builders and for those seeking rental housing. Apartment buildings do get built with many amenities not required by government in both zoned and nonzoned areas. The decision as to what should be included as part of the building is invariably a difficult one for a builder due to the financial limitations of any project, a situation which anyone who has ever built a home should understand. He must determine the quality of the refrigerators, air-conditioning, stoves, windows, light fixtures, and dozens of other items. He cannot possibly install the best of each, and must forego the installation of many amenities. This would be necessary even if he were erecting a super-luxury building. The decision as to what is installed and what is omitted will be based on an evaluation of the rental market; he will do those things within the limits of his budget that will cause his apartments to rent better. While certainly not free from error, the builder should be in a much better position to make these judgments than those considerably less expert, without any personal stake in the outcome and often more concerned with pleasing people who will never live in the building. Furthermore, many of these decisions may be made in conjunction with a mortgage company and with the aid of highly experienced professionals.

Existing homeowners seem almost always to want new housing to be about as or more costly than their own housing—a basic reason for zoning! —and PUD will help them attain that goal. The "quality" of the development is frequently an essential consideration. The developer may be requested to represent the income of the prospective renters or buyers, and changes may be required to produce a product more likely to attract the more affluent. In most instances the builder who seeks to satisfy existing demand of the lesser- or average-income market for apartments or townhouses will be forced to upgrade or abandon his project. PUD has thus been used by municipalities to foster luxury apartments and higher rents, an understandable objective but hardly one best suited to the needs of the housing market. This will mean that it will become more difficult than ever for the private housing market to satisfy the housing needs of that large group who are not poor enough to qualify for subsidized housing nor rich enough to afford luxury housing.

The widespread adoption of "wait and see" techniques acknowledges the failure of traditional zoning concepts. The zoners have learned that it is simply not feasible to encumber the future of the land. There is no way to predict the future and exceedingly difficult to evaluate the present. Although these techniques have eliminated, to some extent, the problem of the future, they have created equally or more difficult problems by injecting local government directly into land use and development decisions.

Future Local Controls

It has been suggested that to prevent local decision-makers from abusing their discretion, specific criteria be established to limit their area of discretion. They would be allowed to control topographical factors but would have minimum authority to regulate matters of construction, design, and aesthetics. The short answer to this is that similar legal restraints on contract zoning have generally proven unworkable. Developers are prepared to make numerous concessions to obtain approval of their projects, and the local authorities will not allow the projects to proceed unless certain concessions are made. In practice, therefore, such limitations are likely to be ignored.

Increasing reliance on "wait and see" techniques can be expected. By zoning large areas solely for low-density residential and agriculture, municipalities would be leaving in abeyance decisions on apartments and commercial and industrial uses until actual requests for these uses would be received. Decisions could then be made as to the desirability of the proposed uses only when the developer presented his plans. This would enable maximum control to be exercised by the forces in the community that have used this power most undesirably in the past. Problems might also be created on the judicial front. Courts may measure the amount of zoning that allows for apartments and townhouses, and may overturn ordinances that have not provided sufficiently to serve the housing needs of families of lower-middle or average income.[16]

Many additional land use techniques have been proposed to supplement "wait and see."[17] The proposals vary from procedural reform to substantial substantive change that would make the government an owner of some or much of the land instead of its regulator. Some, such as the (ALI) proposal for a single administrative agency to be delegated all the functions having to do with development and use of land, will certainly eliminate some problems and can hardly do any harm (except possibly by converting petty corruption into large-scale corruption). The same is not true for other proposals which would lodge even greater powers in the hands of the same group that has proven themselves so unqualified for this authority. This includes giving the municipality power to make compensatory payments in order to maintain legally doubtful restrictive regulations on property, and to purchase and sell or lease land in accordance with local land use objectives. There are also proposals for transferring to federal and state agencies some powers presently exercised at the local level, and these will be discussed in the next chapter.

The proposals for major reforms at the local level are analogous to buying expensive new tires for a racing car instead of replacing its faulty engine. The objectives and motivations at the local levels of government are inconsistent with the needs and requirements of society, and any meaningful reform requires removal of their zoning powers.

Urban problems abound, and so does the nostalgic feeling that if we or the prior generation had been wiser, they would not exist. But, as Edward

C. Banfield points out, the forces of "logic and wisdom" must operate within those conditions imposed on society by the nature and imperatives of society:

Consider the case of New York City. The state legislative committee of 1857 . . . confidently asserted that "wise and simple laws," if only they had been adopted in time, would have checked or prevented the evils it deplored. With such laws, it said, "the city of New York would now exhibit more gratifying bills of health, more general social comfort and prosperity and less, far less expenditure for the support of pauperism and the punishment of crime." It blamed the authorities of an earlier time for not having passed the necessary laws; those authorities, it said, "were unmindful of the future public good, precisely as we, in our day and generation, are pertinaciously regardless of our posterity's welfare."

Perhaps the authorities were unmindful of the future public good. Whether they were or were not does not matter much; they could not, in any case, have changed the imperatives of population growth, transportation technology, and income level, and it is these factors that account not only for their failure to change the patterns of growth but also for the failure of authorities in later times as well, including, of course, the committee of 1857 itself.

What, one wonders, are the wise and simple laws that would have saved the situation if only they had been made soon enough? The idea of controlling land use by a zoning ordinance is a recent one, but suppose that when Manhattan was first settled an ordinance had limited the spread of warehouses, factories and other objectionable land uses. If such an ordinance had been made and enforced, the old Knickerbocker mansions would still be standing—but there would be no city. Nor, if all towns had made and enforced such ordinances, would there be cities anywhere.[18]

9

Federal and State Zoning Solutions

Considerable pressures exist presently for the states and federal government to remove and retain much local zoning powers. These pressures emanate in the main from two diametrically opposite positions. On the one side, many environmentalists and conservationists contend that local zoning alone is not, and cannot be, sufficiently exclusionary. They generally desire strong national and state land use controls to preserve and protect the environment. Many civil rights advocates, "egalitarians," and developers, on the other side, insist that local zoning has been much too exclusionary. They favor the adoption of state or even federal powers capable of over-ruling local zoning decisions that operate to exclude housing.

The former group argues that not enough of the land has been removed from development, whereas the letter contends that too much land has been removed from needed development. Although each may support rhetorically the generalized objectives of the other, in specific cases, the respective positions often appear irreconcilable. Developments considered favorably by one group may be virtually anathema to the other. Local conservation groups for alleged ecological reasons have opposed multiple-family developments and even relatively dense single-family projects. (Some have sought to stop all growth.) One group opts for limited- and low-density development; whereas the other wants to eliminate most controls that prevent high-density development. The conflict of values already has sur-faced in some zoning litigation, where the courts have had to select between the virtues of ecology and development as respectively propounded by their idealogues. The prospects are that this conflict will continue in the courts for some time to come, and may significantly affect zoning law.

Each of these groups believes that federal and state agencies will be more favorably disposed toward its position than local government has been or will be. Presumably also, each believes that it will be able to exert more influence at the higher levels. Both groups have considerable support in public opinion, and largely as a result, exert much political influence. Neither is exempt, however, from the pendulum of public opinion, whose swings may make long hard fought victories transient ones.

Each group will thus be presenting an enigma to state and federal governments approximating that given Solomon—except that there is and can be no Solomon. Officials will have to pick and choose between their respective demands, which one can be confident will always be vigorously and persistently advanced. And, because rights and wrongs in planning are largely subjective considerations, pressures having political consequences can be the decisive factor.

161

There will obviously be much conflict and competition to achieve objectives and goals. One might ask, therefore, what reason is there for either group to believe that in the long run a different level of government will be more amenable to its desires and demands. It seems just as likely (other things remaining about the same) that overall one or the other position will sustain loss in comparison with what presently exists. But even if a stand-off ensues, and things remain approximately the same, both sides will actually have lost. The involvement of more levels of government will result in a greater bureaucracy that will siphon its share off the top without advantage to any but itself.

National Land Use Legislation

The Nixon administration bill, introduced in 1971 to establish a national land use policy (S. 992), epitomizes the dilemma. It seeks to accommodate and balance the conflicting forces. But even though its terms and provisions are necessarily general and even quite vague and not much more than legal platitudes, it has already been deemed inadequate by the protagonists. The National Urban Coalition contends that the bill is too ecologically oriented and not egalitarian enough, and the Sierra Club, National Wildlife Organization, and Izaak Walton League say it is not sufficiently ecologically directed.[1] The bill is also resisted by two other diametrically opposed groups: those who favor more federal controls over land use and those who reject federal and state controls and seek to retain local controls. In short, if enacted, these many diverse interests will require a constant flow of Solomon-like decisions in its administration.*

The Nixon legislation provides $100 million over five years to states for preparing and implementing land use programs. The amount granted would constitute no more than 50 percent of the cost. The Department of the Interior would administer the grants and determine whether a state had established a land use program adequate for the protection of areas of critical environmental concern. All such grants would have to be approved by the Secretary of Housing and Urban Development, who is charged with accepting that portion of the state's program concerning growth and development. In brief, Interior is charged with concern for the environment and HUD for housing. Thus, two cabinet departments, having and representing vastly different orientations, would somehow administer jointly the federal program. It would be a strange partnership!

There is to be a full, detailed, periodic federal review of the laws and "methods" adopted by the states in response to the proposed national policy. As part of its land use program, a state is required to regulate the use of land designated to have state or regional impact. Federal review of the

* The Senate Committee on Interior and Insular Affairs by a majority vote on June 5, 1972, recommended enactment of a modified version of the administration bill. The discussion in this chapter remains relevant to the issues presented by the recommended legislation.

kind of development which actually is allowed in a given area is to be limited (ostensibly) to instances where a state is substantially disregarding its own land use program in protecting critical areas of national concern.

Added to the bill in early 1972 was a provision for penalizing states that do not qualify for the planning grants by the middle of 1975. Federal funds for airport development, highway construction, and recreational facilities would thereafter be cut for the delinquent states by an amount of 7 percent per year for the subsequent three years, or a total of 21 percent for states that have not complied by that time.

While the administration vigorously denies any desire to impose federal land use controls, it is difficult to understand how this can be avoided, given its power of the purse. Substantial monetary penalties can be exacted if the federal officials determine that the state has not met and followed the requirements of the statute in establishing and proceeding with its land use program. Although the stated intent is to subject to federal approval only the provisions of the state's land use program, not its decisions on the actual use of the land (except as previously indicated), this distinction is, as a practical matter, without a difference. The requirements set forth for a state program embody most of the prevailing popular platitudes on land use control and allow for a multiplicity of interpretations. Directly or indirectly, it would not be difficult to cause a state to adopt specific policies or programs. Indeed, it might even be hard to avoid doing so.

The administration bill would thus embark this country on a new and much different phase of land use control. Every level of government will be given one or more vague and indefinite shares of the zoning pie, and so will many significant political forces. Land use will be regulated from Washington, the state capital, and the locality! There will be even fewer crumbs remaining for those with the most expertise, the builders and developers. The administration's legislation is, and any other legislation on land use would have to be, a compromise effort to accommodate politically powerful forces. This is normal to the legislative processes of representative government, and usually most appropriate to it. However, experience has clearly shown that this process is highly inappropriate and self-defeating in determining the most desirable use of land, for this has no relationship to the priorities of political power and politics.

Given the more important role of the Secretary of the Interior, and the fact that most states are suburban-rural dominated, the direction of the controls is more likely to promote for the immediate future, at least, exclusion rather than inclusion—but of course, not necessarily. (If public opinion tires of ecology, the environmentalists might rue the day they even thought of seeking federal involvement.) The greatest danger is that the legislation in the name of helping the environment will seriously injure it. If it causes much land to be removed from production, the most acute environmental problems of the day, those having to do with housing and living conditions, will be intensified and not reduced.

What would take place on national and state levels would be analogous to what has been occurring at the local levels; those with the most political persuasiveness would be most likely to greatly influence or even determine the use of land. I summarized the local process in the conclusion of the talk I presented in Washington, D.C., and submit that it is descriptive of land use control decisions at all levels of government:

Zoning is determined through the political processes of government. It gives control over the use of land to a strange combination of politicians, planners, owners, courts, citizens, do-gooders, do-badders, etc., etc. As a result, a host of factors and forces are controlling land uses that have virtually no relationship to maximizing production, satisfying consumer demand, maintaining property rights and values, or planning soundly.

Other criticisms apply to zoning on a state or national scale as they do on the local level. The notion that land use within an entire state can be successfully planned should be one repugnant to the intelligence. Hundreds of thousands of square miles are involved, and a state agency is bound to have less knowledge and information about individual parcels than one at the local level, which, as we have seen, has itself very little. Countless decisions would be made without adequate information. Just evaluating potential uses and demands for a fraction of a mile within a metropolitan area may cost thousands of dollars and many hours, and might still leave many uncertainties. In Chicago, it frequently costs a minimum of several thousand dollars to purchase an economic feasibility study for a particular private project from companies that engage in real estate surveys. And there is uncertainty on the part of many investors as to the importance of such reports. Why should not a comparable effort at least be required of government before it imposes restrictions over private property? Or why should less be required before government interferes in the consumer market? Inasmuch as this is not possible or practical, planning, or whatever goes by that name, will be done on a most cursory basis. Land use will continue to be controlled pursuant to the opinions or guesses of those who happen to be given certain positions at certain times, and on the many pressures exerted on them. The problems with zoning that occur in the big cities (see Chapter 1) will be intensified.

Hawaii is the only state that has zoning on a state level and its experience bears this out. A statute authorizing the division of the state into three districts, "Conservation," "agriculture," and "urban," was first passed in 1961. An additional category, "rural," was added in 1963. The primary purpose of the Hawaiian legislation was to protect land used for agricultural purposes from being subjected to urban development, on the theory that the maintenance of substantial agricultural lands was vital to the Hawaiian economy. (Tourism, incidentally, has now replaced agriculture as the state's major source of income.) Under the statute in question, counties are permitted to pass local zoning ordinances only for those areas zoned by the state as "urban."

I was in Hawaii in February 1970, when legislative hearings were in progress concerning proposed amendments to the statute. It appeared that conservationists' testimony generally tended to take a friendly view of the law and an unfriendly view of the commissioners administering it. Some developers seemed to praise the commission as striking a reasonable balance. The planners appeared to be unhappy. Newspaper stories reported that an executive officer of the commission had "in effect alleged that the commissioners were running a land-zoning give-away":

One of his allegations was that the commissioners seldom failed to approve at least a portion of the land-owner's request.
Some commissioners argued that often the portion was very small.[2]

According to a report of the executive staff, the commissioners had during the perod from June 15, 1962, to January 26, 1970, rezoned 30,409 acres for urban use out of 98,526 acres that had been requested for urbanization. Of the 165 petitions on which it had taken action, it denied in full, 27, of which most pertained to small acreages.[3] The implication was that developers can obtain about what they want by petitioning for excessive amounts and thus allowing the commission to deny portions of the request. Despite this, however, the likelihood is that not enough land has been zoned for housing purposes, and this policy has materially contributed to high land and housing costs on the islands.[4] The arguments for and against growth, conservation, height, density, and use, and the pushing, pulling, and shoving consistent therewith, have certainly not disappeared in Hawaii; on the contrary, they can only multiply when zoning controls are exercised on two governmental levels.

Whether wise or unwise, regulation necessarily precludes development, some portion of which obviously would be of truly undesirable character. The problem arises because the experience of zoning clearly shows that much more desirable development will also be forbidden. We can now look back at the rhetoric of the zoning proponents of the twenties, and smile as we read about all the benefits they promised and advances they predicted upon the advent of zoning. One can become quite nostalgic reading the current rhetoric, such as that of William D. Ruckelshaus, administrator of the Environmental Protection Agency, advocating the administration's bill in a speech to the National Association of Home Builders in January 1972:

What is the best use of the land? How dense should human settlements be? What is the optimum mix of housing, transportation, recreation and commercial facilities? What should go where?
Are certain areas already saturated, so loaded with industry and commerce and transport activity as to constitute ecological disaster zones? Should population be dispersed or should some areas be kept forever wild or undeveloped? Are these problems insoluble in a finite world or will they succumb to systems analysis, urban design and long-range planning?
The trouble is that all these actions occur in a vacuum. There' isn't even a rough over-all blueprint, let alone a master plan for land use in this country. I think we need a more far-sighted attitude.

It appears to me (notwithstanding some of the preceding quoted comments) that the authors of this proposed legislation do not seek to create a vast national presence in the determination of land use. The Nixon administration has made considerable efforts to relinquish some federal powers to the states, and this legislation is supposedly intended as a means of assuring the retention of land use powers at the local and state levels. For this to occur would require enormous restraint at the federal level, a most unlikely happening.

Furthermore, once the national presence has been established, it will be near impossible to keep that presence from multiplying. A subsequent administration may not have similar ideology. More important is what is likely to occur to legislation involving economic restrictions—a slight opening in the door never remains just that. This legislation would obviously not cause the landscape and buildings to become more beautiful or cause environmental and urban housing problems to dissipate. Few, if any of the benefits that better planning and more regulation are supposed to bring about will actually occur. And if some do occur to any significant extent, it will be at the expense of equally or more important considerations. The expectations created by the rhetoric will remain just expectations.

The usual pattern emerges anew. The existing legislation will be condemned as inadequate, and new and more restrictive legislation will be sought and probably obtained. A greater federal role will continue to evolve as each new legislative version fails again to meet the expectations of the rhetoric. The same people will find that the landscape and the buildings are still not beautiful and that housing problems still remain. The chronology of local zoning will be repeated; the failure of existing land use controls leads down the Parkinsonian path to more, or more severe, controls, not less, or less-stringent, ones.

The administration bill embodies a concept that has received considerable recognition and approval, that local government should have no control over land use decisions that are not local in character. This concensus dissipates, however, over the question as to who should have these powers. The administration and many others say they want to transfer these powers to the state. Their approach is deceptively simple; the state should be given powers over land use of regional or state concern and local government should retain powers of local concern. Carried to its logical conclusion, however, this division would eliminate most local powers. Most land use decisions involve housing and all housing decisions have more than just local impact. The territories of local government have no relationship to and usually constitute only fractions within the perimeter of a housing market. The consequences of every sale or rental of housing does not terminate at the boundary line, but affects or filters down into many other localities within that housing market and sometimes even outside of it. For example, as was previously shown in the discussion of the filtering effect, zoning controls over housing by a suburb may affect housing within the inner city, and although separated by dozens of miles and perhaps several other municipalities, both areas are parts of the same housing market.

Boundary lines of local governments are so arbitrary or fortuitous that it is difficult to isolate land use decisions that are of purely local concern. Even small commercial developments may cater much more to distant rather than local customers. Where then should the line be drawn? Since gas stations sell most of their products to passing motorists, are the motorists or are local residents most affected by the exclusion of the service stations? The same argument can be made about the fast-food franchises. A factory that wants to locate in one municipality may employ workers living in other municipalities. It might, therefore, have some adverse effects on homes adjoining its proposed site, but it would and should, at least, augment property interests in other towns. The elimination of commercial facilities has exclusionary effects. The extent and availability of shopping centers and other shopping facilities are important considerations in the purchase of homes by people of less affluence. The absence of local shopping facilities will likely deter many people from moving into the community.

ALIs Model Land Development Code

The most important documents to date dealing with this and the many other quandaries of land use are the tentative drafts of the Model Land Development Code of the American Law Institute (ALI), which has become the basis for some of the important provisions in the administration's land use bill. The drafts provide for the establishment of state agencies to regulate land uses that the code designates as having state or regional impact. Matters of state concern thus become only those defined as such, a solution which for its purposes at least effectively eliminates problems having to do with logic and logical conclusions. However, if and when logic prevails, the conceptual basis for the code could result in the elimination of most local controls.

The code being prepared by the ALI is a revision of the Standard State Enabling Act and Standard City Enabling Act, which were drafted under the aegis of the U.S. Department of Commerce in the late 1920s and were adopted with, at most, minor modifications by the states. The ALI is a highly prestigious, nonprofit law reform agency which has developed model-state statutes covering different subject matter. Its efforts to propose a Model Land Development Code, which commenced in 1965, are being funded by a grant from the Ford Foundation, and they are being directed by Professor Allison Dunham of the University of Chicago Law School, who has been designated as Reporter. Present plans call for a final draft in the spring of 1974.

Presumably, lawyers should confine themselves to the law, which admittedly is not that simple in the drafting of land use controls; however, the ALI has gone much further: It has in its drafts made many policy decisions having important economic, social, and political implications. It appears that the lawyers have also become social scientists, political scientists, and economists. The drafts propose a reorganization of certain land use powers among different levels of government, a basically political decision, and make significant determinations concerning allocation of the land for conservation and development; and this involves economic and social issues. The lawyer is deciding how and when and for what purpose his client should spend his money.

Many problems will necessarily be produced when new sets of arbitrary distinctions for land use controls are created. A large number of new rules, differences, and distinctions will be superimposed on a large number of existing rules, differences, and distinctions. This explanation has been given by the chairman of the advisory committee on the code:

A key element of the entire system is the principle that the state would be allowed to become involved only in the "big cases." Probably 90% of the local land development decisions have no real state or regional impact. It is important to keep the state out of those 90%, not only to preserve community control, but to prevent the state agency from being bogged down in paperwork over a multitude of unimportant decisions.

The problem of defining the "big cases"—the cases of state or regional impact —is thus crucial to the entire system. In establishing rules to govern development, the ALI Model starts with three basic principles:
  (1) Some development has state or regional impact because of its location.
  (2) Some development has state or regional impact because of its type.
  (3) Some development has state or regional impact because of its magnitude.
Based on these three principles we have set up three categories of development that is subject to state review.

The first such category is development in districts of critical state concern. The State Land Planning Agency is authorized to define the boundaries of such districts, which may include "an area significantly affected by, or having a significant effect upon, an existing or proposed major public facility or other area of major public investment."

The term "major public facility" is defined to include highway interchanges, airports and other facilities servicing a state or region. Districts of critical state concern may also include "an area containing or having a significant impact upon historical, natural or environmental resources of regional or statewide importance."

Finally, Districts of Critical State Concern may also be designated for the sites of new communities shown on the State Land Development Plan.

The second category of case that is appealable to the state agency under proposed Tentative draft #3 is "development of state or regional benefit." This includes development which serves important state or regional needs but may have some adverse impact on the immediate area:

  "(1) Development by a governmental agency other than the local government that created the Land Development Agency or another agency created solely by that local government;
  "(2) Development which will be used for charitable purposes, including religious or educational purposes, and which serves or is intended to serve a substantial number of persons who do not reside within the boundaries of the local government creating the Land Development Agency;

"(3) Development by a public utility which is or will be employed to a substantial degree to provide services in an area beyond the territorial jurisdiction of the local government creating the Land Development Agency; and

"(4) Development by any person receiving state or federal aid designed to facilitate a type of development specified by the State Land Planning Agency by rule."

In each of these cases the developer is given the right of appeal to the state board if the local decision is unfavorable. The Massachusetts zoning appeals law offers perhaps the closest analogy under existing law.

The third category of development in which the state has an interest is development which has a statewide impact because of its size. The proposed Code authorizes the State Land Planning Agency to establish for each broad category of development limits of magnitude which, if exceeded, allow the local decision to be appealed to the state board, either by the developer, by intervenors or by the State Land Planning Agency. Thus the Agency might, for example, provide that residential developments of 100 or more units or commercial developments of more than 50,000 square feet of floor area might constitute large scale development. These limits would undoubtedly be higher within incorporated municipalities than in unsettled areas.[5]

The model code is not intended to be uniform legislation, and has been written in a manner that permits it to be used in "bits and pieces" in accordance with local conditions and experiences. This would allow modifications for local purposes, which seems commendable enough on its surface, but would also permit changes that would alter the careful balance the draftsmen have sought to achieve on many issues. Many able minds have been part of the ALI endeavors these many years and it can be presumed that great efforts were made to compromise differences by adding or subtracting provisions to provide a balance acceptable to the draftsmen. This would apply in particular to the pressing issues of ecology and housing and those having to do with the limitations of state and local controls. Yet simple legislative changes concerning these matters can cause the final product to be much more unevenly weighted and quite dissimilar in content and effect.

Because (1) most state legislatures are suburban-rural–dominated and (2) the present climate of public opinion is favorable to the conservationists, the legislation that would presently emerge in most states would probably tilt in a strong ecological direction. It is possible that the "bits and pieces" of the proposed code may be used as proposed or broadened in scope to designate many areas of the state as having significant impact upon "natural or environmental resources of regional or state-wide importance." This could result in the removal of much land potentially suitable for production. One is reminded of a bill that passed the Illinois House of Representatives in 1971 which might have curtailed all new construction within one and a half miles of Lake Michigan, Chicago's eastern border. Even Chicago's downtown area was affected. Its principal sponsor was quoted in the newspapers as being uncertain as to the precise impact of the legislation, leaving the question for ultimate resolution by the courts. Another bill (the Scenic Rivers bill) that also passed the Illinois House stipulated that any change in the use of land within certain distances of many rivers and streams must be sanctioned by the Illinois Department of Conservation. Neither bill was approved by the State Senate, but both did receive the support of the governor of the state.

Statutory provisions of this character might be the legislative price that would have to be paid by developer interests for "bits and pieces" satisfactory to them, although it is difficult to comprehend a sufficient *quid pro quo*. Hence housing interests might have no more success on the state level throughout the nation than they have had on the local level, and they might even lose in the process. The problem of exclusion will be no closer to, and possibly even further from, solution.

A prophetic view of the ALI code's probable future was recently seen in Florida. In its Environmental Land and Water Management Act of 1972, the legislature in that state used bits of "bits and pieces" from the drafts of the code, although the chief sponsor of the bill was quoted as stating, "Florida is the first state to adopt the American Law Institute's recommended approach" with respect to land use and development of state or regional concern.[6] It established state control in two categories: (1) areas of critical state concern, and (2) developments of regional impact. The second category would have to be the one principally applicable to the problems caused by local exclusionary practices. It is questionable whether it can be used for this purpose as presently drafted. A development of regional impact has been defined as:

. . . any development which, because of its character, magnitude or location, would have a *substantial* effect upon the health, safety, or welfare of citizens of *more than one county*. (Italics added)

Normal construction of this language would seem to restrict its applicability to *huge* developments, and then probably only because of substantial environmental impact. These are limited in number, even in Florida. It appears doubtful that it would operate to benefit even a relatively large proposed development that had been denied favorable zoning at the local level. On the other hand, a "huge" development given local approval would still face the hurdle of obtaining approval of a state commission.

The Florida experience suggests that the ALI code may be used as more as a glossary or compendium of provisions than as a code. The passage of national land use legislation might, however, remove some of these prerogatives from the states.

The importance of the right given certain developers under the drafts of the code to appeal to state agencies will vary with the jurisdiction, depending upon the activity of the courts in zoning matters. Developers of "large" subsidized and unsubsidized projects are, as a practical matter, the only ones given the right to appeal an adverse ruling of a local agency. In those states where the judiciary appears invariably to uphold the municipality, any additional appeal rights for property owners will be advantageous. Yet, even in these states, a developer of subsidized housing probably has the best opportunity to obtain relief either in local or, if necessary, federal courts, and, therefore, the right of appeal may be of limited significance in these cases.

In states more favorable to developers, there could be even less benefit—and the effect might be adverse—if the judiciary recedes as a result from intervention in the zoning process. In these states, developers who need it least are provided the most help. Subsidized projects have the best likelihood for success in the courts, and the biggest developers are the ones most able to seek judicial relief. It is true that there will be less difficulty and expense in appealing a local decision to a state agency created for this purpose (provided the calendar does not get clogged), but if the locality appeals to the courts the decision of the agency, the prospect for delay and procrastination will be no different than it is presently.

The proposed code may turn out most counterproductive on the judicial level. Its objective in part is to cast zoning matters into administrative proceedings with court relief limited to instances of severest abuse (which many lawyers argue is already the law). However, the results may be quite different. It may actually produce litigation that is not desirable while discouraging litigation that is desirable. The line between state and local powers in any given situation would have to meet statutory and constitutional standards, and this could create an entirely new but highly prolific category of litigation. New and uncontested categories can be, of course, productive sources of litigation. The question as to what real estate activity is or is not subject to state regulation might have to be tested in the courts. (For example, what projects come within the definition of "magnitude," and is the definition reasonable or arbitrary?) A municipality may seek court reversal of a ruling by the state agency in a matter which it contends should still be locally determined, or it may otherwise contest in the courts the decision of a state agency.

At present, the most favorable forum for alleviating the problems and tyrannies of local zoning are the courts. It has taken almost half a century for some courts to understand the constitutional infringements and unreasonableness of zoning. It may take almost that long before they reach the same level of wisdom regarding state-oriented zoning. In some important recent decisions, discussed in Chapter 13, courts have overruled municipalities on matters which the courts considered as having regional land use consequences. These courts might well conclude that the solution for such problems had been undertaken by the state through its reorganization of the zoning process and that it should be left largely with the state. They would be more reluctant to undertake any consideration of zoning questions, even of a constitutional nature, and any trend in these and other states toward greater judicial restraint on zoning might be brought to a complete halt. This will be most harmful to the builder or developer who does not qualify for state review under the proposed code. And the power of the municipality would be increased to this extent, perhaps offsetting any loss of power to the state under other provisions. Other efforts of the code to lessen court involvement in zoning might likewise have this effect.

There may also be a result not fully anticipated by the proponents of state zoning control, and it has to do with graft and personal influence. Graft and corruption have always been factors in local zoning, but the problem is far from universal and there are many municipalities where corruption is nonexistent, such as in the bulk of affluent post World War II suburbs. What will happen if one or two state agencies acquire great power over land use? At the time of this writing, incidents have occurred involving state officials that do not inspire confidence in the state as a repository of important powers: In my home state of Illinois, the former governor was then under criminal indictment for acts committed while in office; I was speaking before a national convention in Texas where the Speaker of the House of Representatives was under indictment (and subsequently convicted); and in the neighboring state of Louisiana, the attorney general had been convicted and sentenced. Stories of malfeasance and misfeasance in state office are almost routine items in the Chicago press.

Corruption in itself is bad, but it also causes severe distortions in the decision-making process. Once it infects a state agency, many decisions of that agency will be made to compensate for those issued as a result of corruption. Similar results would follow if the board is subject to special influences. Those who do not corrupt and are without influence would suffer detriment regardless of the merits of their case. Enormous distortions could occur on a statewide basis.

Powers once granted to government are rarely relinguished. Extreme caution obviously is warranted before zoning powers, which concern great personal and property values, are granted the higher levels of government.

10 Current Efforts against "Exclusionary" Zoning

The primary push currently for changes in local zoning has an egalitarian-civil rights orientation. It is contended that zoning has been one of the means used to exclude people of lesser incomes from the suburbs and suburban type areas of the cities. The objective would be to provide sites for public housing for the poor and some form of public-private housing for the not-so-poor, whose incomes are too low to purchase private housing available in the area. In other respects, the zoning powers of the municipalities would remain relatively undisturbed—and exclusionary.

Further impetus to these efforts was given by reports from the 1970 census, showing increasing concentration of blacks in the center cities and whites in the suburbs. The figures show small increases between 1960 and 1970 in the percentage of black population in one-half of the suburban areas adjoining the nation's twenty-six largest cities, about 2 to 3 percent at most. In the other half, the percentage of blacks decreased or remained about the same. Much higher increases in the percentage of black population were recorded for all of these cities during the same period (see Table 10–1). For the nation's ten largest cities, the percentages of black population in 1960 and 1970 are as follows:[1]

It is contended that even if these figures reflect a certain amount of free choice, the voluntary element of these decisions is becoming more difficult

Table 10–1

Black Population in the 10 Largest U.S. Cities, 1960 and 1970, in Percentages

	1960	1970
New York	14.4%	21.2%
Chicago	22.9	32.7
Los Angeles	13.5	17.9
Philadelphia	26.4	33.6
Detroit	28.9	43.7
Houston	22.9	25.7
Baltimore	34.7	46.4
Dallas	19.0	24.9
Washington	53.9	71.1
Cleveland	28.6	38.3

Source: National Journal, 27 November 1971, p. 2341. © 1971 National Journal.

173

because there has been a substantial movement of employment activities to the suburbs and outlying areas. Between 1960 and 1967 for example, 62 percent of all industrial buildings and 52 percent of all commercial buildings were constructed outside the central cities of metropolitan areas. More than 50 percent of all the new employment created in the 1960s in the large SMSA's were recruited to work outside of central cities.[2] What was once a problem of workers living too close to the factory has become one of living too far. But apparently not far enough to deter the migration of industry.

Poorer people, it is said, are also being denied the better educational facilities and better and healthier environment of the suburbs. This is detrimental to them as well as to society, which will be benefitted if individual potential is maximized. Some contend that stratification in low-income areas produces social and cultural isolation, which prevents or impedes individual development. The argument is further made that the benefits and liabilities of modern life should be allocated more evenly between cities and suburbs. One of the ways to accomplish this would be to cause increased dispersal of all segments of the population throughout a metropolitan area.

The issue has become most fashionable and popular, and the attack is quite widespread, even among those who helped foster exclusionary policies in the name of planning before they fully realized the consequences of their actions. For some, it appears to be an effort to reorganize the current structure of American society;[3] and for others, a nominal attempt at some social engineering.

Direct efforts through political or legislative processes to provide for public or subsidized housing in the suburbs have been carried on at the state, regional, and local levels. The courts have also factored significantly in these endeavors. Some of the more important developments will be discussed in this chapter.

State Legislation

It has been suggested that state enabling legislation be amended to require that all communities make provision for zoning of land to allow for low- and moderate-income development. Some of the Douglas Commission recommendations can be interpreted to this effect.[4] As of the present time, Massachusetts appears to be the only state to have taken this proposal seriously. It enacted in 1969, a so-called "antisnob" zoning law, which enables an appeal to be taken to a state board, the Housing Appeals Committee, from a local decision denying zoning for the construction of subsidized housing in municipalities that have not achieved prescribed quotas of low- and moderate-income housing. It applies only to federal or state subsidized housing and does not affect low-cost unsubsidized housing such as mobile homes. The statutory formula for determining whether a municipality has not met its quota of low income housing is (1) less than 10% of the housing units in the town consists of low or moderate income housing or is located on sites aggregating less than 1½% of the total land area (excluding publicly owned land); and (2) the approval of such construction would not result in building on more than 0.3% of the land area or ten acres, whichever is larger, in any one calendar year. At the time the legislation was enacted, only one small municipality in the state was capable of meeting the prescribed quota. It and about 99% of the land area of every other locality are thus exempt—at least annually—from the provisions of this law.

In the thirty months subsequent to its effective date, fourteen appeals were taken under the provisions of this statute, involving in excess of 3,000 units, and two decisions, both favorable to the proposed developers were entered. One was for the construction of 88 units for elderly housing and the other for 60 units of family housing.[5] (The 1970 census shows Massachusetts as having a population of about 5.7 million, and it has about 350 cities and towns.) Both municipalities have appealed the decisions to the Supreme Judicial Court of the State contesting the Act's constitutionality, and an opinion is expected in late 1972. Even if the constitutionality of the statute is upheld, the municipalities can be expected to seek judicial relief on other issues in future cases. In the two cases decided, the decisions were entered ten and fifteen months respectively, after the original applications for rezoning were made.

The costs of litigation might be excessive for sponsors who, to qualify for the benefits of the statute, can only be nonprofit or limited profit corporations, or a public agency—although possibly on occasion there might be a pooling of resources. However, the legislation may cause some localities to view applications from these groups more favorably. Similar legislation has been introduced in a number of other states and some of the proposed ALI model land development code is fashioned on this statute.

Regional Efforts

The most notable achievement for regional dispersement of subsidized housing has been the "Dayton plan." Adopted in September 1970, after extensive educational and public relations efforts, it calls for a specified distribution of about fourteen thousand units of low- and moderate-income housing and public housing over a four-year period throughout a five county region of which Dayton, Ohio, is the principal city. As part of the plan, the Miami Valley Regional Planning Commission (MVRPC) divided the entire region into fifty-three "planning units," and a quota of low- and moderate-income units were assigned to each unit on the basis of a complex but then politically acceptable formula. (MVRPC was formed in 1969 and is the planning agency designed by the federal government as the regional clearing house for coordinating federal expenditures in the area.) The planning units may consist of one or more separate local governments; only Dayton contains more than one planning unit (specifically, twenty-one of the fifty-three).[6]

The Miami valley region in southwest Ohio has a population of about 900,000. Three of its counties are predominantly rural in character and the other two are largely urbanized and contain the Dayton metropolitan area. The city of Dayton has a population of slightly under 250,000, more than one-quarter of the entire regional population. About 11–14 percent of the area's total population is black. Blacks constitute about a third of Dayton's population and are primarily concentrated on the city's west side.

Executives of MVRPC have given the following as partial explanation for the approval of the plan:

For still others, the motivation was highly pragmatic. Moderate income housing construction was already beginning to occur in a few suburban areas, and the decision makers there viewed the Dispersal Plan as a safeguard against their areas being deluged with such housing. Their concern was whether the quota system could be enforced to the degree that upper limits could be set in order to avoid saturation. Officials of several areas said that they were perfectly willing to accept their share of the housing, but they would not take it all and they wanted to make sure that other areas would take a share also. Thus, a good bit of interjurisdictional pressure developed over acceptance of the plan, and by and large probably contributed to the adoption of it.[7]

The decision as to whether zoning will be granted for a proposed project remains with the local government; no preemptive powers have been conferred on any agency. Local approval is also required for federal rent supplement projects. It is, therefore, possible that zoning and other local requisites may prevent or delay a quota from being fulfilled. (MVRPC in conjunction with HUD is apparently willing to exercise some financial muscle to enforce implementation of the plan.) Another difficulty of any quota arrived at by planning or political processes is that it may not be consistent with the preferences of private (or even public) developers of subsidized housing. Most communities are not likely to authorize more than their quotas, and developers who request more units than assigned will probably be rejected. And, of course, quotas do not build housing. The plan may not result, consequently, in as many units as would be erected in its absence although there may be greater dispersal, which raises the question as to which is more desirable. What is also possible and would be most regrettable is that once a community has adopted its quota under the plan, it may adopt as well a closed attitude on other housing.

The status of the program from January 1970, which the MVRPC executive director states is the starting date for crediting units, to April 1972, bears out some of these concerns.[8]

1. Outside of Dayton, 806 units were completed or then under construction; within Dayton the number was 1,769. As of April 1972, a "total of 3,362

have been filed with the FHA and HUD and are in some stage of processing."
The target figure for the area outside of Dayton is about 12,300 units; for
that within Dayton, it is 1,700. (A locality however may consent to more
than its quota.)

2. The figure of 806 includes 364 out of the entire commitment of 414 units
   made by Madison Township, the only suburban area with its assigned
   quota already filled, since the balance is in the processing stage.
3. Because the quota was filled, MVRPC rejected three separate requests to
   build additional units of subsidized housing in Madison Township.
4. Some communities have refused to grant proposed projects the required
   zoning or approval for rent-supplement projects.
5. The rural county of Darke quit the plan, but this will not affect the membership of its incorporated municipalities. It is said to be reconsidering its
   action "because they desire open space funds and . . . this lack of membership
   affects their priority." Five localities had given the required year's notice of
   intent to withdraw, leaving approximately 92 percent of the total population
   still represented in the plan. Some others were considering leaving the plan,
   also.

Understandably, the Dayton plan has been enthusiastically heralded and
approved, and recommended for other areas by HUD officials. It removes
a major obstacle to the dispersal objectives of the subsidy program: the
opposition of the rural and suburban communities. Legislation had been
introduced in the Congress, using the Dayton plan as a model, but was
defeated in committee in April 1972. As of Spring 1972, none of the other
435 planning units in the country had achieved a similar program.

The Local Scene

The board of supervisors of Fairfax County, Virginia, adopted a zoning
ordinance in 1971 which requires that builders of multifamily housing
projects of more than fifty units and less than six stories must set aside
6 percent of the units for low-income families and 9 percent for moderate-
income families. If land costs exceed HUD maximums, the developer is
nevertheless required to apply for subsidy housing and receives no special
consideration. He is, however, given a density bonus of one unit for every
two subsidized units. The developer is required, prior to rezoning or site
plan approval if already zoned, to make submissions for approval to the
local housing authorities and/or HUD. If approval is not granted within a
specified time, these requirements would be eliminated. The developer also
has the option to finance these units from his own funds.

On November 11, 1971, the Circuit Court of Fairfax County, Virginia,
entered a declaratory judgment invalidating this ordinance with respect to
conventional (permitted-use) zoning.[9] In a brief order without an opinion,
the court voided the ordinance as unlawful under the statutes of the state.
The court stated that the ordinance exceeded the authority delegated to
the county board of supervisors by the Virginia statutes; it provided for the

unlawful delegation of authority to the Fairfax County Redevelopment and Housing Authority and to HUD; it constituted "an unlawful delegation of legislative authority in that it fails to describe adequate standards to guide" those charged with administration of the ordinance; and it was "arbitrary and capricious" and "vague and indefinite." The court found it unnecessary to reach the constitutional issues. Other suits were pending concerning PUD and other provisions of the ordinance.

This does not appear to be a strange or unusual decision. It has been reported that the attitude of local zoning lawyers was that the ordinance was bad and unworkable and that no Fairfax lawyer could be obtained to defend it when it was challenged.[10] Builders and developers in general refused to participate in the deliberations concerning the measure.

A reading of some of the transcript and commentaries of some of the participants reveals testimony and pleadings customary in citizen control of the land—only this time the people who usually decry exclusion were the exclusionists. They sought and obtained controls to exclude any garden apartment building that did not conform to the criteria they deemed desirable. But, say these exclusionists, we are seeking to provide new housing in the county for people who need it most— less affluent persons who work in the area—which admittedly is a persuasive argument. But hardly more so than that of the suburbanite who pleads protection for his substantial investment of person and property in a home and community.

The ordinance is no stronger in economics than in law. It is more restrictive than its predecessor, and consequently, it will be more difficult than before to erect garden apartments in Fairfax County. It reduces the number of potential developers to only those who believe they can (or who are willing to) successfully operate the type of accommodations required. HUD requirements may add to costs and result in future limitations on income for the subsidized units; both may deter some builders and make potential developments unfeasible. There will be less production and less competition, both of which are highly important to the housing consumer, rich or poor. The success of the ordinance would depend on the response of the federal government, according to one of its supporters, the *Washington Post*[11]—and this is quite a speculation to which to subject most multifamily construction in the county. In addition, there is much vacant land in Fairfax County not zoned for apartment use, and the usual problems involved in zoning it for this use will be intensified if local residents exert greater opposition because of the requirements for occupancy by low- and moderate-income families.

If development is deterred by this ordinance, it is the poor and near poor in the general area who will suffer as much as any other group, for they will be denied the benefits of the filtering process. When expensive apartments are built, lower-income consumers move progressively into housing left behind by the more affluent. Mobility in the housing market is favorable to all classes and consumers, and legislation which impedes—

or in this case possibly terminates—this process can hardly be considered beneficial to poorer people.

One result of the ordinance is that, according to the *Wall Street Journal,* "The Board of Supervisors revised the local building codes to permit a great deal more construction flexibility, a move that is estimated to reduce the cost of a housing unit by $3,000 to $4,000."[12] This is all to the good, and, I might suggest, if coupled with the repeal of local zoning, would have been vastly more effective for "people, jobs, and housing," the alleged beneficiaries of the ordinance that was adopted.

Court Actions

In general, the rule still appears to be that a municipality may refuse to rezone property for a subsidized project if its refusal is consistent with the usual tests for the validity of zoning required by that jurisdiction. As a practical matter, however, this rule has to be qualified in two respects:

1. There are factors' involved in these cases which may dispose judges to act differently than they usually do in zoning matters. "Housing for the poor" has been elevated in many quarters as a major concern of American society, and the municipality, therefore, in practice may be held to much stricter standards.
2. If the action of the municipality appears to have been racially motivated, it will be overruled. Again because of the social implications of the issue, a community may have its zoning restrictions invalidated by a court disposed to broad interpretation of this rule.

The zoning cases constitute one portion of the larger question confronting the courts on the scope of the equal protection clause of the Fourteenth Amendment, whether its prohibitions are to be confined to racial discrimination or to be expanded to cover some economic discriminations. It is fully accepted that any willful scheme for racial discrimination is illegal, but it is not clear as to what beyond motive and intent constitutes racial discrimination for purposes of equal protection. In some areas of the law—such as concerns the poll tax, the right of appeal by an indigent criminal defendant, and residency requirements for public welfare—opinions of the Supreme Court have, or can be interpreted as having applied equal protection to remove *de facto* classifications that were created by the law and that operated to the serious detriment of the poor.[13]

In cases involving the use of the land, the Supreme Court seems, for the present at least, to have limited the equal protection clause to racially motivated discrimination. Two relatively recent cases appear to have defined the outer limits within which questions relating to subsidized housing will probably be decided in the years ahead. These cases are *James* v. *Valtierra,* decided by the U.S. Supreme Court in 1971,[14] and *Kennedy Park Homes Association, Inc.* v. *City of Lackawanna,* decided by the Second Circuit

Court of Appeals in 1970[15] and in which the U.S. Supreme Court denied *certiorari* in 1971, leaving that decision as final.[16] The major difference between the two cases lies in the distinction referred to; in *Lackawanna,* the court found evidence of a racially discriminatory purpose; for *Valtierra,* no similar intent was determined.

In *Lackawanna,* the circuit court held illegal zoning and other local regulations adopted to prevent the erection of a low-income interracial housing project in an all-white neighborhood. After the sponsors announced the project, the city rezoned the proposed site for parks and open space, and a moratorium was imposed on new subdivisions on the grounds that the sewer capacity was inadequate and that drastic measures were required to preserve scarce land for park and recreation purposes. The ordinances were rescinded after the suit was filed but the mayor, nevertheless, refused to approve the sewer application. The court determined that these municipal practices were subterfuges to camouflage a pattern of racially motivated discrimination.

Valtierra was a five to three decision and principally involved an article of the California Constitution that required approval by local referendum of any low-rent housing project "developed, constructed, or acquired by any state public body." Although there are many actions requiring a referendum in California, no similar requirement exists with respect to any other housing assisted financially by the state or national government. None of the opinions entered in the case (including that of the minority on the Supreme Court) found that the article was intended to discriminate on the basis of race. The question presented was whether the classification created by this article constituted unlawful discrimination under the equal protection clause. Justice Black, for the majority, replied that it did not, asserting his great faith in the democratic virtues of a referendum, particularly when this device is used widely and not restricted to certain situations. The majority did not accept the conclusions of the special three-judge federal district court, which had ruled the article invalid:

Although Article XXXIV does not specifically require a referendum for low income projects which will be predominantly occupied by Negroes or other minority groups, the equal protection clause is violated if a "special burden" is placed on those groups by operation of the challenged provision, if the reality is that the law's impact falls on the minority,[17]

or of the minority that:

It is far too late in the day to contend that the Fourteenth Amendment prohibits only racial discrimination; and, to me, singling out the poor to bear a burden not placed on any other class of citizens tramples the values that the Fourteenth Amendment was designed to protect.[18]

Only future court decisions will present legally meaningful interpretations of this decision, but any interpretation will have to take into account that the decision was predicated in large measure upon the considerable employment of the referendum in California, indicating that it was not an unusual burden placed solely on would-be occupants of low-rent housing projects. States which do not have a similar history may not fare as well if they now adopt such provisions. (*Valtierra* has, however, been interpreted popularly as allowing cities with or without a referendum to halt subsidized housing.)[19] At the same time, however, the decision evidences reluctance of the majority to expand the scope of the equal protection clause in a case involving land use. The majority clearly rejected the interpretations of the clause given in the lower court and in the minority opinions.

The Nixon administration has taken the position that only exclusion on a racial basis is contrary to federal law and has supported this posture with court action.[20] In 1971, pursuant to this policy, the government filed suit against the city of Black Jack, Missouri, in the federal court in that area.[21] The complaint alleges that when a nonprofit corporation proposed a subsidized multifamily housing project on land zoned for that use in what was then an unincorporated section of St. Louis County, the residents of the all-white area created and incorporated Black Jack as a city to prevent the project. Shortly after Black Jack became a municipal corporation, the city council adopted a zoning ordinance which prohibited any new multiple-family use within the city. The suit contends that this action violated the Constitution and the Civil Rights Act of 1968, and requests an order restraining the city from any interference in the development of the project.

The prior discussion has been concerned with judicial decisions that remove locally imposed barriers to housing, and this is the role courts generally assume in the land use cases. Some other decisions of recent date have departed from this role, and they also merit attention. These are cases in which the courts have taken the heretofore unusual step of ordering governments to disperse integrated housing into white areas. They are in effect doing what no one else is supposed to do: controlling the use of land on the basis of race. Thus, federal courts have ordered that public housing be dispersed out of the black-populated areas of Atlanta into the surrounding Fulton County suburbs,[22] and from the black areas of Chicago into the white sections.[23] The federal court in Atlanta went so far as to order city and county agencies to prepare for the entire metropolitan area a housing plan which the court would evaluate as to whether it was "in full compliance with the national policy of balanced and dispersed public housing." This order was affirmed by the United States Court of Appeals for the Fifth Circuit.[24] The case of *Shannon* v. *HUD*,[25] which concerned a project in Philadelphia, can be interpreted as precluding construction of subsidized housing in many areas of the inner city whose effect would be to preserve housing segregation.

The difficulty of this and the other rulings is that courts do not build housing. In the Chicago case, the court as a penalty ordered the withholding by HUD of a considerable amount of model city funds from the city pending compliance with its order for scattered public housing. Although a higher court reversed this order, the city appeared willing to accept this punishment at least for a substantial period. Due to this attitude, some black civic leaders in Chicago urged that the court vacate its order to allow construction of public housing to proceed in the black areas.

It would seem, therefore, that this kind of judicial action is not likely to produce much public and subsidized housing in the suburban areas—and may even reduce in the aggregate the amount of both kinds of housing.

The Results

Accordingly, viewed from the perspective of its proponents, efforts on both legislative and judicial fronts to establish public and subsidized housing in suburbia have not been very fruitful. But the book is far from closed. More states and localities may adopt (or be required by national legislation to adopt) legislation toward this end in the years ahead, and land use law may be stretched somehow to force unwilling communities to accept these projects. The federal government may use the "carrot and stick" approach much more forcibly than it has to date. Municipalities may be paid to enable these projects to develop, or they and the states may have federal funds cut off if sufficient efforts in this direction do not occur. It has been suggested that bonuses be given reluctant suburbs to accept poor families and help cover the resulting burden on public facilities and services. Some have urged legislation that would enable the federal government to preempt local zoning for the development of subsidized projects. Legislation to this effect was introduced in Congress in recent years and defeated in committee.

In my view, however, little will be accomplished by all these proposals in light of the necessary housing needs of the country, and what is accomplished can be considered as almost in the nature of "tokenism," notwithstanding that some individuals would most certainly benefit from that "tokenism." Moreover, these endeavors may be counterproductive to the goals of better housing. Among other things, they may give suburbs in which token projects locate the excuses or pretexts to create greater exclusionary barriers with respect to all other housing.

As a practical matter, the most these endeavors can hope to obtain for a large suburban area are probably no more than several moderate- and low-income developments, totalling perhaps from one hundred to possibly three or four hundred apartments. If however, the zoning powers of the municipalities were to be generally curtailed, many more times that number of multiple- and single-family units would be established for the same area. Although most of these units would be for an average- or higher-income market, the substantial increase in production and availability will have a much more favorable impact on almost all levels of the housing market, including those for moderate and low income and located outside the suburban area.

**The Problems of Subsidized Housing
in Suburbia**

The Power of the Purse

Consider the many problems involved in building new housing in suburbia
for the low- and moderate-income families. *First*, these projects invariably
require government participation, either as owner or subsidizer, because
of the substantial cost of both land and construction. There are obviously
difficulties in obtaining substantial appropriations for this purpose. Such a
program has natural enemies: taxpayers, suburban homeowners, and nonresident middle-income groups for whom housing opportunities in the
suburbs might be further reduced. Recently added to this list are officials
of urban areas who seek subsidized projects to help rebuild their cities and
provide employment and business opportunities.[26] But even assuming
money is available, government agencies are not likely to make or be
allowed to make disbursements indiscriminately without regard to the
political consequences, regardless of the administration in power and its
objectives in this respect. Many of the target areas of suburbia would be
able to avoid such housing on the ground that property values would be
seriously jeopardized.

The HUD position on the location of interest subsidy housing projects
provides an example of what to expect. It has apparently agreed in principle not to approve such projects against the wishes of the local government
or agencies thereof. Thus, it has entered into an informal agreement with
Houston to this effect. State agencies will probably react similarly. The
record of the Urban Development Corporation of New York, a state agency
and not bound by local zoning ordinances, suggests that if its policy is any
different, it nevertheless must move very circumspectly. If it attempted to proceed with any substantial quantity of low-cost housing in the suburban areas,
the agency probably would face political extinction. A comparable agency
in Illinois is also proceeding in a very cautious and virtually invisible
manner.

The House Banking and Currency Committee in April 1972 voted down
a section of the pending housing bill that would have created agencies to
plan the location of low- and moderate-income housing in major metropolitan areas of the country. The reason given for this action was fear by
the House Democrats that the measure would offend their suburban constituents, although the measure would not have preempted local land use
controls.[27]

Lower-Income Families in the Suburbs

Second is the question of how attractive are the suburbs for those of lesser
incomes. Certainly the schools are often better, the environment cleaner

and newer, the crime rate much lower, and some places of employment closer. But there are also some strong negative factors. Commercial facilities there are oriented to the consumer taste preferences and credit practices of a higher-income level. The absence of public transportation and the ownership of probably one older automobile will reduce considerably the mobility of a lesser-income family. (A survey of six Houston apartment projects, subsidized under the Federal 221(d)(3) program, with a total of over twenty-two hundred units, of which the majority are two and three-bedroom apartments, showed that fewer than 0.5 off-street parking spaces were utilized per apartment.)[28] Housing is, of course, highly sensitive to the racial frictions of our society, and it may be very difficult to maintain integrated developments. New kinds of ghettos may be created without the conveniences, familiarities, and amenities of the old ones. Real or imagined hostility of suburbanites can produce discomforts for a family. Given the choice, many may prefer the older sections of the city despite the schools and the two-hour drive to and from work.

There is evidence in the Chicago area and elsewhere suggesting that black families of lower-income levels are not about to flock to the suburbs. This despite the fact that surveys show that the overwhelming majority of black families want an opportunity to live in racially mixed neighborhoods.[29] These factors should be considered in this regard:

1. Officials of tenant relocation services in Chicago have described situations in which many poor black families living in substandard housing conditions have rejected new accommodations in white areas. The process has been termed playing "slum dwelling hopscotch," that is, moving from one substandard dwelling to another in order to stay in one's own neighborhood. The data is based largely on the experience of low-income families; but some of moderate income are also included.[30]

    Nor is this an isolated situation:

    > Research into the relocation of people displaced by urban renewal has demonstrated the critical importance of neighborhood location to many low-income families. For many, the choice of neighborhood is even more important than the condition of the house.[31]

2. Informal discussions with both builders and FHA officials in the Chicago area reveal that exceedingly few black families have occupied in predominantly white suburban and county areas houses constructed under Section 235 subsidized home ownership program for families of moderate income. Projects built in black or "changing" neighborhoods of the city and suburbs were occupied by black families. The U.S. Civil Rights Commission has concluded similarly:

    > Most new 235 units are being located in suburban areas and are being purchased largely by white buyers, while most existing units are being located in inner-city ghetto areas or "changing" neighborhoods and are being purchased largely by minority buyers. In those cases where minority

235 buyers are purchasing new suburban housing, it is usually located in subdivisions reserved exclusively for them.[32]

3. At a higher-income level, builders of FHA-insured townhouses in suburban areas of Chicago within fifteen or twenty minutes' driving time from industrial concentrations advise me that not much more than 1 or 2 percent of their purchasers, prospects, and "lookers" are black. These units sold in 1971 and 1972 at prices as low as $18,000 or $20,000, which was then at the lowest end of the private new housing market in the Chicago area.
4. Stoughton, Massachusetts, is a largely white suburb south of Boston, along highway 138 which is an extension of Blue Hill Avenue, a main street of the Boston slums. It is about 20 to 30 minutes driving time away. Interfaith Housing Corporation, a nonprofit sponsor, erected in that town Presidential Courts, a section 236 subsidized housing project consisting of 104 units. Occupancy was completed in early 1971. Although many of the residents of the town believed that blacks from the nearby slums would rush to occupy the development, this has not been the case. Of 217 applications, only 13 came from Boston. In the first 96 units occupied, there were thirteen black families, about one-half from Boston. Officials of Interfaith are quoted as saying that there is no concerted push by central city blacks of Boston to move into the suburbs and presents its Stoughton development as proof.[33] This organization also sponsored a 160 unit development in Framingham, which is a little further from Boston, and its experience there was similar. The latter project was fully occupied in Spring of 1972.

The Scarcity of Sponsors and Managers

Third, there may be much difficulty in obtaining good sponsorship and management. Because there are substantial questions of how financially feasible the subsidized rental projects are, experienced real estate developers may not be very plentiful to sponsor the projects. To accept the required profit limitations and suffer the agonies involved in obtaining HUD approval, the rewards should be relatively certain. As it is, the number of sophisticated real estate operators willing to sponsor rental subsidy projects may have been reduced considerably by many adverse experiences. See Table 10–2 comparing financial failures of subsidized and non-subsidized housing.

It was reported at the end of 1971 that a considerable number of offerings of limited partnerships in syndicates to invest in federally subsidized housing were being sold by security houses.[34] These efforts may have been promoted by HUD to acquire more and better sponsorship. This article points out the many risks undertaken by these investors, and the likelihood that the market for these offerings would quickly dissipate if some bad deals begin to surface.

Nonprofit groups have generally faced considerable difficulties in operating subsidized projects, and because of this experience and the limited

Table 10-2
Mortgage Defaults and Foreclosures on Subsidized and Nonsubsidized Housing

Multifamily Project Mortgages Privately Held in Default, February 29, 1972

Program	Total Mortgages (finally endorsed)	Mortgages in Default (finally endorsed)	Default Rate
236	563	30	5.3%
221 (d) (3) BMIR	1,229	127	10.3%
221 (d) (3) MIR with Rent Supplements	520	40	7.7%
Other Subsidized	381	41	10.8%
Subsidized	2,693	238	8.8%
Nonsubsidized	7,340	78	1.1%
Total (Multifamily Only)	10,033	316	3.1%

Mortgages Owned/Held by HUD, February 29, 1972

Program	Total Mortgages (finally endorsed)	In Default	In Foreclosure	Foreclosed (in HUD inventory)
236	563	15 (2.7%)	7 (1.2%)	3 (0.5%)
221 (d) (3) BMIR	1,229	45 (3.7%)	39 (3.2%)	21 (1.7%)
221 (d) (3) MIR with Rent Supplements	520	18 (3.5%)	7 (1.3%)	2 (0.4%)
Other Subsidized	381	7 (1.8%)	7 (1.8%)	1 (0.3%)
Subsidized	2,693	85 (3.2%)	60 (2.2%)	27 (1.0%)
Nonsubsidized	7,340	131 (1.8%)	37 (0.5%)	155 (2.1%)
Total (Multifamily Only)	10,033	216 (2.2%)	97 (1.0%)	182 (1.8%)

Source: Data supplied by Charles J. Orlebeke, Deputy Under Secretary, Department of Housing and Urban Development, Washington, D.C.

Note: 236 Program was authorized in 1968 Housing Act. 221 (d) (3) BMIR began in 1961 and 221 (d) (3) MIR with rent supplements, in 1965. The unsubsidized FHA program began in 1934. The default rate for all mortgages in force, including those not finally endorsed, is lower. Projects are "in default" if the mortgagor fails to make any required payment or fails to perform any other covenant of the mortgage. After a thirty day grace period, the mortgagee is required to notify HUD within an additional thirty days of the default. Payment of principal and interest may be deferred or the mortgagee may elect to assign the mortgage to HUD, or he may elect to foreclose.

number of such groups, particularly in the suburbs, they cannot be expected to sponsor very many projects.

Therefore, it may be that for a substantial amount of "successful" subsidized housing to be erected in the suburbs, financial inducements for investors would have to be appreciably increased, or direct sponsorship would have to be undertaken by the federal government. Neither is a choice many are presently prepared to accept.

Equally important, multiple-family developments for low- and moderate-income families require for success experienced, capable management. "Historically, low- and moderate-income housing requires great maintenance and management expertise. It is not unusual for a poorly managed project to completely fall apart after five years."[35] This writer indicates there was a dearth of talent in the field for these projects. The problem can be acute for a token suburban project. Unlike a tenant in private housing, the tenant of such a project may not be able to move elsewhere at the end of a rental period, for there may be no satisfactory "elsewheres." He would have to give up his subsidy if he leaves, and may want to continue living in the area because of the proximity to his employment. Problems of this character have led to bitter disputes between public housing tenants and management.[36]

To provide and train managers, President Nixon, by Executive Order issued in 1972, has created a National Center for Housing Management. HUD has also provided for greater monetary compensation for management services in the subsidized programs. Whether these efforts can produce the special talents required remains an open question.

The Experience of Subsidized Housing

Fourth, the future of all subsidized housing is subject to much question as a result of recent experience. The Housing and Urban Development Act of 1968 states that the goal of decent housing could "be substantially achieved within the next decade by the construction or rehabilitation of 26 million housing units—6 million of these for low and moderate income families." In terms of quantity, the goals for low and moderate income families seem to be on schedule as of the middle of 1972; there is much question that this intent has been accomplished in terms of quality.[37] Moreover, the governmental cost to date for constructing these units has far exceeded the grossest of predictions.[38] A significant number of projects have failed financially (see Table 10–2), and worst of all, some of these developments constructed to eliminate the slums have themselves become slums.[39]

The vast majority of the units constructed have been in or near the inner city areas, and that is also where the more significant failures have recurred. There have been considerable problems in the suburban projects also. The record is hardly one to inspire confidence in the salvation powers of government.

From conversations with government officials and builders of subsidized housing, one readily concludes that subsidy programs face serious dilemmas. If they are strictly administered and investors held to close scrutiny, production will be severely curtailed. On the other hand, relatively lax procedures will allow for much greater production and much of it will be financially troublesome and deemed physically undesirable. The news media and the public have demanded superior quality despite the limited cost allowances, further complicating administration of the programs.

HUD in 1972 began an experiment to test the housing allowance concept, which would give certain amounts of cash or housing vouchers to lower- and moderate-income families and allow them to select existing housing of their own choosing. Only a portion of the rent will be paid for by the government.[40] The experiment as programmed in mid-1972 will be carried out with variations in at least five cities and probably in time in another six. The plan might in time replace some or possibly most of the subsidy programs and thereby reduce pressures for zoning for subsidy project sites in suburbia or elsewhere.

"A Necessary Rethinking"

President Nixon has said that "a necessary rethinking" was in order on national and local housing policies. I trust that such rethinking will reveal the obvious absurdities of present policies. National goals of stimulating more housing are being frustrated by the local goals of limiting housing. It should by now be apparent that spending ever greater sums at the federal level can have no more than token effects at best, and cannot overcome the consequences of zoning and other local exclusionary practices.

Worse yet, given present zoning practices, the location of subsidized housing in the suburbs may well be counterproductive to the goal of creating more housing opportunities. I know of several suburbs that have or are contemplating "token size" subsidized developments, and may use them as a pretext or perhaps justification to maintain even bigger exclusionary walls toward everyone else. Some municipal attorneys are already advising their clients that the best way to avoid judicial interference in their zoning practices is to provide for some small subsidized project—and for the present they may well be correct. There is also a lesson in this for federal and state agencies that want to force subsidized projects on municipalities. Unless the balance of zoning powers are also reduced, the net benefit to the housing stock may be little more than zero.

The foregoing discussion, which has been largely concerned with the dispersal objectives of housing policy, should also raise some other serious questions as to the effects of the subsidy programs on the housing stock and living conditions. This country has until recently relied largely on the filtering process to produce better housing for the less affluent in the population. As we have seen, the construction of one new home or apartment in a suburban area may produce more desirable housing (or deemed to be so by the movers) for about two to three other families who do not move into that unit—and about one-third of all those who do move as a result of the new construction may be in the low- and moderate-income categories. (This figure would include both white and black families although not to the same extent. See discussion in Chapter 4.) There is also a filtering effect of subsidized construction, but it has to be more limited in the number of moves. Families frequently move from minimal or blighted conditions, or from a shared dwelling, and on the average probably no more than a fraction of one move in addition to theirs can be anticipated. The precise numbers can only be estimated; generally there will be considerably less moves produced by subsidized housing.

Thus, even assuming the subsidy programs operate efficiently and well, there are questions raised as to whether the construction of a subsidized or a conventional unit serves better families of low and moderate incomes. The "in between" group—those who cannot afford new housing and cannot qualify for subsidized housing—are obviously more favorably provided for through conventional production. However, there are other aspects to this inquiry. The subsidy programs may curtail some conventional construction, and may not provide housing of the same quality as would have been provided through the normal operation of the filtering process. Because rental and purchase terms are subsidized, these units usually have a great competitive advantage over conventional housing that may be superior in quality.

It appears that about 20 to 25% of residential starts for the years 1970 and 1971 were for subsidized and public housing, which seems to accord with the schedule sought by Congress in 1968; six million out of twenty-six million units constructed or rehabilitated were to be for low and moderate income housing. This huge portion of residential construction adds appreciably to the demands for labor, materials and financing in the construction industry, and this is bound to increase the cost of these items, and thereby the cost of homes and apartments produced by the balance of the industry.[41] (This effect will vary with the amount of non-residential construction.) A probable result of these increased costs is a reduction in the production of conventional housing.

The experience to date with respect to the quality of the housing produced is pertinent in evaluating the consequences of the program although improvements can be anticipated in the future as a result of tightened governmental procedures. Exceedingly poor living conditions have resulted already in some apartment projects, despite the fact the subsidy programs have not been in existence very long.[42] The HUD Office of Audit in 1971 found deficiencies in 173 (25.7%) of 672 new houses inspected in a random statistical audit sample of the 235-program (single family ownership), one-half of which were not in inner city areas.[43] One hundred houses showed evidence of poor workmanship or of materials that were inadequate or did not meet the minimum property standards of the FHA; in seventy-three other houses, more significant deficiencies were noted affecting the "safety, health or livability of these properties." Significant deficiencies were found in 260 (42.7%) of 609 used houses inspected.

Consequently, if the primary object of current housing policy is to create better housing and housing conditions for families of average and lesser incomes, the best route still appears to be through the filtering effect of new conventional construction. The lesson should be clear: programs and policies that inhibit maximum production of conventional housing are counterproductive to the national goals.

The housing voucher system may remove many of the problems of subsidized housing and give the family greater choice in housing. Its effects, however, will also be circumscribed by prevailing zoning practices which create higher rents and prices. Equally important, the market should be highly competitive to enable the allowances to be used to best advantage, again requiring removal of local restraints on production.

One additional observation should be made in this chapter, and it is about average-income families, who are frequently ignored in "learned" discussions of housing. The combination of prevailing subsidy programs and zoning practices raises rents and prices. It may also allow for some subsidized projects in the suburbs. The result of all of this would be an odd one. Some suburban areas may become havens for only the rich and the poor. It may be that for one of average income to be able to move into these suburbs, he may either have to strike it rich or incur financial catastrophe.

11

The Last Forty Acres under Zoning and Nonzoning

Is nonzoning feasible and desirable for all communities including those where land is scarce? The question is often asked by those who are willing to concede that Houston's system has been reasonably successful but doubt its applicability where there is less vacant land. They are concerned that nonzoning will be unable to maintain use separations and compatibility of land uses. They suggest that as the demand for the remaining parcels increases with greater scarcity of supply, there is likely to be more mixing and less separation of uses. This is probably correct, but it is also true for zoned areas. Intense pressures for land use will also inevitably be successful to some degree in the zoned communities, and there, likewise, pressures for various uses will become more intense for individual parcels as the vacant land is consumed. This is especially true in those areas where despite the demand prior zoning restrictions have limited certain types of development and which have consequently remained relatively free of such developments. The existence of a strict exclusionary policy in early years may make it most difficult to maintain in later years. The situations are thus analogous in the zoned and nonzoned cities; as the amount of vacant land decreases in both, there will be much greater pressure for the mixture of uses.

With this introduction, let us consider how development will occur on the last forty acres that still remain in a community where all other land has been fully developed. Our purpose is to compare how these last acres will be developed under zoning and nonzoning. This is perhaps the ultimate test of the virtues of the two systems.

The decision as to how this last tract of vacant land will be used in a zoned area will be made through the political processes of local government. The city council or other governing board will zone or rezone the property after hearing from all the interested parties, their lawyers, planners, engineers, and other representatives. Included are the owners, adjoining owners, local residents, homeowners' groups, civic groups, political organizations. It should include, but never does, the individual who will live in the proposed project, or will otherwise be benefitted by it. Prof. Norman Karlin points out that an organization representing the inner city should be part of every zoning hearing in the suburbs. The difficulty is that, even should this occur, such organizations would lack political power in the community considering the request.

The first step in the consideration of a zoning petition is to request the locality's planning department to prepare and present its opinion on the proposal. Planners have no fixed style but probably can be expected to

191

evaluate the proposal from at least three different aspects. First, as to its compatibility in relation to an existing city or master plan, and existing developments; second, as to the adequacy of utilities and other physical facilities to support the development; and third, as to the desirability and suitability of the proposed development. In more instances than not, the recommendations of the planners will either be rejected or be used as a pretext for action by the legislators rather than as a basis for it. The planners' recommendations may also have other significance; they may influence the granting of loans by the federal government for the project, and to some extent may even influence public opinion.

Although they present much opportunity for extensive discussion and conversation, questions of compatibility between what exists and what is proposed relate essentially to the power which existing homeowners or tenants should have to exclude other people and things. I have heretofore discussed this in great detail. There is not much more light to be shed on the matter, notwithstanding the voluminous planning criteria available on the subject.

Nor can expertise be expected with any more finality in the other areas of concern. With respect to the adequacy of utilities, this is not a question of the allowable use of land. That property can be used in a particular manner does not automatically entitle one to develop it for this purpose. That property is zoned single-family does not mandate the city to install sewer and water services whenever and wherever someone wants to build a house. Likewise, if there are no water, sewer, or storm water facilities capable of serving an apartment building, a building permit should be withheld until such time as the capacity becomes adequate. This situation has occurred in Houston, and in many areas where land is already zoned for the use intended. The owner should have the same opportunity as other owners to obtain services, but no more. (He should also be entitled to install his own system if it meets reasonable standards.) These are matters of regulation of municipal services and not of use regulation. (The adequacy of utilities will, of course, influence the decision of the owner as to whether he should proceed with one use or await improvements that will allow a different use.)

When housing is involved (and particularly when the developer seeks to exceed density limitations), planners may evaluate the desirability of the proposed housing for the people who will inhabit it. This involves questions of density, open space, school conditions, transportation, and even noise and odor. In proposing the project, the developer and his lender attest to their belief that there is a market for the housing at the prices designated. The planners, however, in effect will give their opinion whether the potential consumer should be allowed to have that housing. While it may not be difficult to compare various characteristics of housing to some established or prepared standards, when private, unsubsidized housing is involved, it is impossible to make such a determination for the benefit of the likely inhabitants. (In the case of subsidized housing, the government is virtually the sponsor and builder, and should accept the planning responsibilities of this role. It is doing so—and this may account for many of the problems of subsidized housing.)

Most people do not have a choice of obtaining optimum conditions; they must instead select the best for themselves from that available, and this selection involves highly personal and private decisions. Millions of people live in accommodations not ideal by many standards and would like to improve their surroundings in at least some if not most respects. Countless numbers have voluntarily selected to pay relatively high rents to live in accommodations that many others find objectionable. An obvious example is presented by the many apartment buildings contiguous to railroad tracks, expressways, industrial developments, gas stations, and below or close to airplane flight paths. Tenants have chosen to live in these buildings and accept the noise, dirt, and other unpleasantnesses rather than live in other buildings that they apparently consider as having greater disadvantages. Perhaps the buildings they have selected are located closer to their work, near better transportation, or offer cheaper rents, or better facilities. Trailer living may seem repugnant and even dangerous to some, but not to those who moved from a tenement. One of the principal justifications for subsidized housing with its many limitations in quality is that families are as a result living in better housing than they formerly occupied. The reasons vary but are consistent in at least one respect: if people move, they probably benefit.

Purchasers of homes usually require mortgage financing, and this provides them with the services of one who is not only an expert but also a potential investor in the property. In the process of shopping for a mortgage, the purchaser will obtain much knowledge about the property and the market, sufficient probably to offset the possible oversell of the real estate broker.

I recall a high density townhouse development in a suburb northwest of Chicago; which invariably brings criticism from planners because of its density and limited parking facilities. I happen to know one family that lives there. They moved from an old three-story walk-up in an older neighborhood in Chicago, and their townhouse is a vast improvement over their former apartment. A proposal by the planning director of Houston in 1966 which was supported by the local Home Builders Association, provides another case in point. He unsuccessfully requested the city council to amend the building code to ban the development of single-family rental projects that allowed for exceedingly high densities of as much as sixteen or more detached units per acre. Had this proposal been adopted some of these developments, due to increased costs, would never have been built, and others would have many less units. These projects were developed in marginal housing areas and have been most successful. Probably the biggest loss would have been sustained by those who would have had to continue living in less desirable quarters.

Housing accommodations that may appear undesirable to many city planners in terms of density and aesthetics may satisfy the needs of many tenants. The market itself provides certain safeguards: (1) financing cannot be obtained unless the lender considers the units acceptable to the market for most of the mortgage term which is rarely less than 20 years, and almost all builders require financing, and (2) the rental market itself is a control, for the original owner or his buyer will have to rent the apartments at a profit in competition with other units. Nor does the absence of density controls mean that all parcels will be subjected to maximum density. Densities differ substantially in Houston (see Table 2–2). Competition can lead to much open space and recreational facilities. Why should governmental restrictions narrow the area of choice and thereby deny to many the opportunity for housing improvement?

Density controls have been greatly abused by the municipalities that use them as a device for restricting multifamily development. Densities of 10 to 15 units per acre for apartments and much less for townhouses are not uncommon in the Chicago metropolitan area and serve solely exclusionary purposes; and they greatly waste land. These abuses have been so common that they would seem to be sufficient reason to deprive municipalities of this power.

The planning department may also decide that despite the willingness of the developer and his mortgage company, to invest substantial sums, the proposed development should not be authorized because the market is or will become glutted. Since it can be assumed that the planners are not privy to any special secrets or data, their evaluation of the market can hardly be superior to those willing to risk their funds. (The investors may, in fact, have made feasibility studies upon which their plans were formulated.) Their recommendations, therefore, will not operate to aid the developer. By limiting competition, they most certainly are not benefitting consumers. Unfortunately, the principal beneficiaries will be those least deserving from the standpoint of a consumer oriented society, the least efficient producers and sellers. One additional group might also sustain loss, landlords of existing buildings in which stores or apartments are vacated. This is one of the risks of property ownership. Moreover, other or new landlords will in turn benefit.

There might also be considerations of municipal "welfare." The added competition might cause some to terminate their business operation and vacate or abandon the existing premises. Abandoned gas stations are frequently a topic of concern at zoning hearings, although the problems they allegedly present (vandalism and immoral behavior) are more appropriate for the police department. The expense of policing abandoned and vacated properties would certainly appear to be much less than the taxes derived by the locality as a result of its policy allowing such developments.

Planners have frequently argued against large-scale subdivision approval, alleging that failure would saddle the community with considerable problems. Thus, with respect to proposed developments on the Island of Hawaii,[1] and in the Adirondacks section of New York State,[2] planners have contended that the developers would be forced to sell lots and not provide housing.

The contention that any proposed development is a speculation is likely to be correct. There are many uncertainties in the business world, regardless of who the entrepreneur is. Most, if not virtually all, American cities began as land speculations. The government financed new towns are land speculations in the sense that no-one can foretell how successful they will be. The only certainty about them is that they are usually endowed with sufficient funds to bail out the developer. Who would have predicted that the land speculation that began in Texas in 1836 would many years later become the major city of Houston? The same question can be asked regarding hundreds of American cities.

It is difficult to evaluate with precision market conditions pertinent to a proposed development. Future economic and population trends, the impact of which are exceedingly difficult to pinpoint for any one area, may glut or unglut a market, and this is a risk that should be borne by entrepreneurs rather than consumers.

Few developments would be allowed to proceed if success had to be guaranteed. Nor is it likely that planners' recommendations for modifications will make the project more successful. On the contrary their "normal" tendency would be to restrict the development and make it more exclusionary, and this will operate against its success.

Planners are supposed to be restrictive to justify their keep; yet they confront serious difficulties in performing well this assignment. Not many planners have ever been part of the construction industry. Even if they had been, they would not be in a position to comprehend the needs and desires of consumers in the way of the builder or developer who is in daily contact. Their information about prices, materials, innovations and trends must necessarily come from secondary or more remote sources. Furthermore, the problems of feasibility and consumer acceptability is one of market economics, rather than of city planning, and these are often "incompatible" disciplines—as the experience of Reston has demonstrated (see Chapter III). It is pertinent to note that perhaps the most spectacular failures in housing within recent decades have occurred in subsidized and public housing projects, which supposedly are carefully evaluated and scrutinized by experts in the federal government.

Although the planners' input is of some significance, the actual decision on the zoning proposal will depend on who or what are best able to influence or pressure or even pay for the vote of the local legislators. There are almost innumerable possibilities on the factors that lead to a decision, and these are some of the most noteworthy:

1. In the "virtuous" suburbs and cities, the single most important factor appears to be the amount and character of the opposition. The larger the crowd at the hearing, the less likely the results will favor the petitioner. The exception to this proposition is that small, politically influential groups can frequently be highly effective. Sometimes, a large opposition neutralizes and offsets the *usual* influences in the "not so virtuous" communities.

2. Probably ranking second in importance in these communities is the existing use of the adjoining property. This is not inconsistent with the first factor, for the use being made of the adjoining property will determine generally the number and potency of the objectors. Most objections are made by homeowners, a much smaller number by tenants (New York City is an exception in this respect), and few if any by investors in real estate. If single-family does not adjoin the site of the proposed rezoning, there generally will be no crowd and consequently possibly little concern for adjoining property.

3. Zoning procedures are particularly susceptible to graft. This is because (a) the distinctions between zoning districts are often very fine and (b) it is possible to disguise most any decision on the basis of some "pure" planning principles. It is most distressing to speculate how many major developments may have come about only as a result of the payment of graft or fees to certain parties. (Can one justify an institution where consumer demand can frequently only be satisfied by resorting to illegal or morally and socially questionable tactics?)

   Dennis O'Harrow, known to many as "Mr. Planner," now deceased and formerly executive director of the American Society of Planning Officials, once said at an annual convention of the society that in too many instances zoning has failed because it has become a "marketable commodity." He quoted a planning official who assured him that "you can buy with money any kind of zoning you want in half the communities of the United States."[3] There is, of course, no way of investigating or validating this allegation, but that it was cited by one of the most knowledgeable persons in the country on zoning makes it difficult to dismiss.

   A local investor in real estate suggested that the most appropriate title for this book would be *Goodbye Graft.*

   (Another problem created by graft is that its discovery frequently leads to greater restrictions and regulations. And this cure can be worse for housing and development than the disease.)

4. In many communities, petitions for high density development are doomed to failure because the legislators in power committed themselves against zoning for townhouses and apartments when they ran for election. They may also have committed themselves on other specific land uses. I recall elections in Skokie and Mt. Prospect, suburbs of Chicago, where some of the issues revolve about certain rezonings approved by the incumbents. When the incumbents were defeated, the new legislators promptly moved to overrule prior zoning decisions. Several aldermen in Chicago have campaigned on platforms opposed to certain types of apartment buildings. In 1969, two new members of the Broad of Commissioners of Plymouth, Pennsylvania, were elected on the basis of opposition to high-rise apartments. They formed a majority which rezoned certain land back to residential classification. This action was subsequently voided by a court.[4]

5. Local government is supposed to be highly responsive to its citizens, and sometimes it happens that it is much too responsive. The village hall is usually highly accessible in the suburbs, and this enables some persons with the time and inclination to make virtually a career of local government, even if they have never been elected to office or have been rejected for office. One can campaign for certain candidates in local elections, and if successful will thereby achieve a certain rapport with elected officials. And of course, a board member may be a neighbor or a friend of a friend. The views of individuals who have little knowledge of land planning or building may be given great deference in the public hearings even though their claim to expertise may be founded only on friendship with someone in authority. The developer and his architect and planner are placed in the uncomfortable and difficult position of having to explain technical decisions to a hostile few knowing that only too often ignorance may prevail.

6. It is surprising how many times local legislators are unable to vote their own views, even in situations when local opposition is not very large. Local trustees have on occasion told me privately that they favored a particular petition for reclassification but could not vote for it because "certain people" in the community were opposed. The "certain people" may include politicians or leaders of local homeowners' groups. In several instances, the opposition of only a handful of neighbors, apparently persistently and skillfully deployed, was sufficient to elicit this response, although a substantial housing development was proposed.

7. A position on the planning or zoning commission is frequently reserved for the party faithful and rarely goes to anyone friendly to the political or ideological opposition. A petitioner friendly to the opposition or considered so may encounter considerable difficulties.

8. In the suburbs, the ambitious politician would be well advised to condemn loudly any proposed changes in zoning for other than single-family use. This position often brings forth much favorable newspaper publicity and can be helpful in seeking higher office. Exclusionary policies tend to be politically profitable. There is certainly little political mileage to be had in favoring the request of an absentee landowner.

9. There are notable exceptions to some of the foregoing. Obviously, some local legislators make great efforts to carry out their duties without fear or favoritism. They study matters carefully and endeavor to vote for what they consider the best interests of the locality. They have thereby consigned themselves to a much more difficult task than that undertaken by their less scrupulous brethren. How is one to decide between the demands of one's constituents, the nonresident landowners, and the unstated desires of those who would like to move in? What is "compatible," "desirable," and "adverse"? How many are capable of or have the time for analyzing carefully the recommenda-

tions of the planners, the legal situation, or the effect of reclassification upon the finances of the city? It is no wonder that some local legislators have, as privately confided to me, wished to shed this responsibility, for they feel they cannot exercise it in good conscience.

Many local legislators have selected local political life with its small rewards because they have failed to attain success elsewhere. Regrettably, they too often try to even the score by voting against the success of others, that is, by rejecting various requests of developers. I was once told privately by a trustee of an affluent village that I had made "enough" on certain property and implied that he was not going to vote in a manner that would make it possible for me to make more money. (This attitude is not uncommon among many government officials.) Many reformers, even in the affluent areas, tend to be antibusiness and routinely vote against developers' proposals which usually would result in more housing opportunities for many of the people they allegedly seek to benefit.

10. The politically expedient course to follow in situations where competing forces are balanced is compromise. It is also one means for avoiding a lawsuit by a developer and possibly defeat in the courts. True compromise in many situations means that one-half of a project that is proposed for development will not be developed in one or more respects, seemingly an enormous price for society to pay for the sake of political expediency.

11. Sometimes the reason for granting zoning has nothing to do with the facts of a case (and may *not* be prompted by corruption). In Illinois and some other states, annexation of property to a municipality usually requires the consent of the owners. Communities may seek annexation for a variety of motives, such as increasing its area, enlarging the tax base, preventing other municipalities from expanding, eliminating a county's control over land, and sometimes simply for reasons of prestige (a form of local "imperialism"). To encourage annexation, highly exclusionary communities have granted property owners zoning which they otherwise would contest fiercely. Probably a considerable amount of multifamily zoning in the suburbs of Chicago is attributable to this situation.

12. The statistics do show that most petitioners achieve success for what they ask (see Chapter 1). There is, however, a correlation between the kind of requests contained in petitions and the likelihood of success. Thus, virtually no one seeks rezoning for a mobile home park in suburbia. Few attempt high rises. Statistics also do not differentiate between major and minor matters.

In their study of the Lexington-Fayette County Board of Adjustment, Dukeminier and Stapleton have suggested situations when petitioners are likely to succeed regardless of the law:[5]

a. When the petitioner is experienced and/or prominent.

b. When it can be claimed that without the variance, the business-man would be placed at a competitive disadvantage.

c. When there are non-conforming uses present in the neighbor-hood.

d. When the requested departure from the zoning ordinance is in-substantial.

e. In the absence of neighborhood opposition.

f. When the petitioner is persistent. (The board heard fourteen petitions on a rehearing or second application, and reversed itself in ten. The evidence in most of these reversals was substantially the same as given on first hearing.)

g. When board members regard themselves less like impartial offi-cials enforcing an impartial law, than co-businessmen, sympathetic to the needs and concerns of the individual citizen.

Thus, controlling decisions as to the use of land are factors and forces which have virtually no relationship to any sort of objective or rational standards for the use of land. That there may be an enormous demand for multiple-family dwellings in the community is likely to be a less important factor than the opposition to such use by some homeowners. And it is equally possible in certain areas that a developer may be allowed a certain use for no other reason than that he has "paid off" or "employed" the "right" people. These results are inevitable as long as the political process controls the use of land.

By contrast, a land use decision where there is no zoning will be more rational. The property is likely to be used in accordance with the demands of the market, which means that directly or indirectly it will be used to satisfy the predominant consumer demand. The more a developer or his successor in ownership succeeds in supplying consumers' demands, the greater his profits are likely to be.

The process by which a builder decides how to develop certain property is usually reasonably well considered. It has to be. He must risk his or his investors' capital, and since financing is almost always required, his decision will have to find concurrence in the financial community (from a mortgage banker, insurance company, or savings and loan association). The object will be to maximize one's return on investment, and this can only be done if what is developed finds sufficient consumer acceptance. Once the product is created, it will be utilized, and this of course is always to the benefit of consumers. But developers face failure unless their products are accepted by consumers at a price or rent that will be sufficient to return a profit or at least cover costs of production.

These efforts by the private sector to determine the best use of the land should not be minimized. Entrepreneurs may spend enormous amounts of time and effort researching, studying, devising, consulting, and creating ventures that will find acceptance in the marketplace. They should be reasonably expert at their trade.

It is true that often the quality and aesthetics of their products are rejected by the so-called "taste-makers," but this is inevitable since they are building usually for a market whose capacities and tastes are totally different from and largely incomprehensible to these critics. They must build with inexpensive materials and avoid costly "aesthetics" when the market is incapable of accepting costly accommodations. Most people can only afford Chevrolets, not Mercedes. Of what value is it to build an apartment that will have to rent for $500 a month if no one is available to rent it? To meet the standards of these critics would probably assure some form of financial distress or bankruptcy, for these standards generally are not consistent with the basic need to achieve maximum consumer acceptance. The critics' tastes can be satisfied when and only when they are representative of the people for whom the product is being created. Furthermore, the market-place does not ignore the taste-makers, since they too are potential consumers. In fact, most segments of society are provided for by the market because individually each presents an opportunity for success and profit to an entrepreneur

These following are additional benefits (which have been previously discussed) when site selection is carried out largely through market processes with minimal control by the state:

1. Property values will tend to be maximized for the site in question.
2. More accommodations and more things will be provided for more people.
3. Business and community finances will be benefitted.
4. A location consistent with maximizing profits is also likely to be consistent with the maintenance of neighboring property values.

Fortunately, neither under zoning nor nonzoning can the world consist of a solid mass of homes. At some point, there must be a different use. As we have previously indicated, when there is much land, most use problems under both zoning and nonzoning will be solved in a manner consistent with maximizing use separations. When land becomes scarce, the desire for use separation must necessarily yield to more important needs of society.

Yet in these circumstances the market will still operate to protect values of adjoining property. The Houston solution for compatability is to allow for reasonable certainty in this respect through use of restrictive covenants within the subdivision but to remove some of this assurance at the perimeter. It is a market solution which offers reasonable prospects for growth and stability. The line is relatively clear and not subject to political tampering.

All this is certainly not to suggest that the results are always orderly, logical, and rational—far from it. But the measure is zoning, not perfection. I submit to the reader, accordingly, that in the absence of zoning, the land is much more likely to be used productively and not wasted for the sake of planners' speculations and political expediencies. This assures the highest and best use for that very precious resource.

**Part IV
The Courts**

12 The Supreme Court and Zoning

The United States Supreme Court has issued only three opinions adjudicating local zoning, all between the years 1926 and 1928. It has subsequently remained silent on the question, dismissing appeals or denying *certiorari* on all cases brought to it involving local zoning issues. During this period, there has been an enormous emphasis on and concern for the constitutional guarantees relating to the rights and interests of the individual, and one might expect zoning issues to be carefully scrutinized in these terms. But the underlying social and economic issues involved in zoning apparently had no more penetrated the court's thinking than they have until recently other intellectual sectors of society.

The constitutionality of local zoning was upheld by a six to three majority of the Supreme Court in 1926, in *Euclid* v. *Ambler Realty Company*.[1] The justices declared that a municipality could regulate the use of land by way of a zoning ordinance provided the controls over the property bore a substantial relationship to the health, safety, and welfare of the community, which is to say, to its police power. The zoning ordinance was to be given a presumption of validity, and whether the test of validity had been met would have to be determined on a case by case basis:

The ordinance now under review, and all similar laws and regulations, must find their justification in some aspect of the police power, asserted for the public welfare. The line which in this field separates the legitimate from the illegitimate assumption of power is not capable of precise delimitation. It varies with circumstances and conditions. A regulatory zoning ordinance which, would be clearly valid as applied to the great city, might be clearly invalid as applied to rural communities. . . . Thus the question whether the power exists to forbid the erection of a building of a particular kind or for a particular use, like the question whether a particular thing is a nuisance, is to be determined, not by an abstract consideration of the building or of the thing considered apart, but by considering it in connection with the circumstances and the locality.

Moreover, a judicial inquiry on zoning was not necessarily to be confined solely to the municipality, as the court stated in one of the most quoted sentences of the opinion:

It is not meant by this, however, to exclude the possibility of cases where the general public interest would so far outweigh the interest of the municipality that the municipality would not be allowed to stand in the way.

203

In the next two years, the Court proved in two cases precisely what it had said: The measure it had established "is not capable of precise determination." The following year, the court in *Zahn* upheld a zoning ordinance, emphasizing terminology that has been used many times thereafter to validate highly restrictive land use controls:[2]

"The common council of the city, upon these and other facts, concluded that the public welfare would be promoted . . . and it is impossible for us to say that their conclusions in that respect was clearly arbitrary and unreasonable. . . . In such circumstances, the settled rule of this court is that it will not substitute its judgment for that of the legislative body charged with the primary duty and responsibility of determining the question."

This was strong language for a court which was later to invalidate considerable enactments of the New Deal period. In the following term, however, the Court seemed to speak more representatively and provided some equal time for the position of the property owner. In *Nectow*,[3] it sided with the master in the lower court and overruled the Massachusetts Supreme Court, nullifying that portion of an ordinance which zoned the plaintiff's property as residential. It warned municipalities that their zoning powers were not unlimited, that their zoning laws had to comply with the "substantial relationship" test.

The zoning battle in *Euclid* was won in the Supreme Court, but time has shown that in the contest for judicial wisdom, the honors belong to the district court, which had been overruled. District Judge Westenhaver understood rather clearly the dangers inherent in not strictly limiting the police power. His opinion has in time become one of the more perceptive critiques of what the Supreme Court said and accomplished as is apparent from the following:[4]

1. On the use of the Police Power:
If police power meant what is claimed, all private property is now held subject to temporary and passing phases of public opinion, dominant for a day, in legislative or municipal assemblies,

and quoting Justice Holmes:

"The protection of private property in the Fifth Amendment presupposes that it is wanted for public use, but provides that it shall not be taken for such use without compensation. A similar asumption is made in the decisions upon the Fourteenth Amendment. (Cases cited.) When this seemingly absolute protection is found to be qualified by the police power, the natural tendency of human nature is to extend the qualification more and more until at last private property disappears. But that cannot be accomplished in this way under the Constitution of the United States. . . . In general it is not plain that a man's misfortunes or necessities will justify his shifting the damages to his neighbor's shoulders. (Cases cited.) We are in danger of forgetting that a strong public desire to improve the public condition is not enough to warrant achieving the desire by a shorter cut than the constitutional way of paying for the change."

2. On failure to compensate for loss of property values:

It is futile suggestion that plaintiff's present and obvious loss from being deprived of the normal and legitimate use of its property would be compensated indirectly by benefits accruing to that land from the restrictions imposed by the ordinance on other land. It is equally futile to suppose that other property in the village will reap the benefit of the damage to plaintiff's property and that of others similarly situated. The only reasonable probability is that the property values taken from plaintiff and other owners similarly situated will simply disappear, or at best be transferred to other unrestricted sections of the Cleveland industrial area, or at the worst, to some other and far distant industrial area. So far as plaintiff is concerned, it is a pure loss.

3. On exclusion:

The plain truth is that the true object of the ordinance in question is to place all the property in an undeveloped area of 16 square miles in a strait-jacket. The purpose to be accomplished is really to regulate the mode of living of persons who may hereafter inhabit it. In the last analysis, the result to be accomplished is to classify the population and segregate them according to their income or situation in life.

Justice Sutherland, the writer of the *Euclid* decision, did not reply directly to these conclusions. A note in the *Yale Law Journal* contends the Court's majority believed that a zoning ordinance did not operate to exclude uses but instead channeled or sorted them within the locality.[5] It suggests that the Court looked upon zoning as a process for distributing uses within a community, not excluding them, and, therefore, had little effect exterior to its boundaries. When this was not the case, and there were effects of more than purely local nature, the Court, as previously quoted, delared that the judicial inquiry could be extended beyond the borders of the municipality.

By this decision, the Court had made zoning largely a matter of local administration with relatively little likelihood of judicial interference. Analogous to the rules subsequently evolved for administrative regulation, local zoning decisions would stand unless they were clearly irrational or arbitrary. The Court would no longer in this area protect the individual against the Leviathan except in instances of grave abuse.[6] The three cases had, however, established sufficient doctrine to justify either the most or the least restrictive zoning postures of the state courts. In either case, the Court had substantially circumscribed the right to property.

The subsequent history of the Supreme Court in zoning rests largely on its refusal to consider these cases. Viewed in the current context, it is apparent that many highly significant issues were presented to challenge the zoning concept. There is little reason to believe that had the Court considered these cases, it would have reversed or even modified its position on zoning in the intervening years. There are two cases concerning some issues involved in zoning which suggest that the Court might instead have strengthened local zoning powers.

The case of *Berman* v. *Parker*[7] had nothing to do with zoning, but the opinion—expressing a unanimous decision—by Justice Douglas has had a significant influence on some zoning issues. In that case, the owner of a building that was in sound condition contested condemnation proceedings which had been commenced as part of a Washington, D. C., urban renewal program for a largely blighted area in which his building was located. The issue presented was whether the police power authorized condemnation to clear an area of all buildings including those in good condition. Did the proposed condemnation of the sound building have a reasonable relationship to the public health, safety, and welfare?

Justice Douglas, who is not noted for his hesitancy in striking down legislative decisions, suddenly found that the police powers were virtually unbounded:

Public safety, public health, morality, peace and quiet, law and order—these are some of the more conspicuous examples of the traditional application of the police power to municipal affairs. Yet they merely illustrate the scope of the power and do not delimit it. . . . Miserable and disreputable housing conditions may also suffocate the spirit by reducing the people who live there to the status of cattle. They may indeed make living an almost insufferable burden. They may also be an ugly sore, a blight on the community which robs it of charm, which makes it a place from which men turn. . . .

The concept of the public welfare is broad and inclusive. . . . The values it represents are spiritual as well as physical, aesthetic as well as monetary. It is within the power of the legislature to determine that the community shall be beautiful as well as healthy, spacious as well as clean, well-balanced as well as carefully controlled. . . . If those who govern the District of Columbia decide that the nation's capitol should be beautiful as well as sanitary, there is nothing in the Fifth Amendment that stands in the way.[8]

These remarks have been called upon repeatedly by the judiciary to support zoning exclusions,[9] covering a wide spectrum from various forms of housing to motels to even clotheslines. They have been mischievous even for civil liberties, considered one of the Justice's strong points. In the New York case of *People* v. *Stover*,[10] the defendants had hung rags and old clothes on lines strung across their own front and side yards as a form of "peaceful protest" against the high taxes of the city of Rye. The city retaliated by adopting a zoning ordinance restricting the erection and maintenance of clotheslines in front and side yards. The highest New York court, in a six to one decision, upheld the ordinance, and, in a portion of its opinion, dutifully invoked Justice Douglas's flowing prose. This case presented an opportunity to examine the limitations of the zoning power when confronted with important constitutional considerations of speech, property rights, and aesthetics, but the U.S. Supreme Court dismissed the appeal for "want of a substantial federal question."

Another case showing the Supreme Court's strong support of local land use powers was *Goldblatt* v. *Town of Hempstead*.[11] There an ordinance adopted in 1958 prohibited any excavation below the local water table. Involved in the case was a site in which sand-and-gravel mining operations had been conducted since 1927 and which had been partially excavated to a depth of twenty-five feet, far below the water table. The site had become a twenty-acre lake together with eighteen adjoining acres that were used in the processing operations for the mining. The scenario was typical suburbia: a community had developed around the site and had wanted an "adverse" use terminated. The owner contended that the ordinance confiscated the entire mining utility of his property for which he had received no compensation. The court upheld the ordinance on the same basis that zoning ordinances are upheld: The owner had not met the burden of proving the state's action was unreasonable. Recognizing the difficulties of the town's case, the Court observed that the police power will be upheld if any state of facts either known or which could be reasonably assumed affords support for it.

It is just as well that the Supreme Court did not entertain zoning litigation in prior years; the results would probably not have been favorable to zoning's critics. But the situation may now be much different. In more recent years, scores of articles highly critical of zoning practices have appeared in the law reviews and other periodicals. Critics of zoning who were once ignored or condemned to intellectual purgatory have been rescued and are now reasonably respectable. Zoning's defenders are becoming scarcer and scarcer and may have replaced their antagonists in those dungeons. These are election results that high court judges do not and cannot readily ignore.

13

The Recent Cases: A Tale of Two States (and Perhaps Others)

The state of New Jersey received considerable notoriety in the 1950s and 1960s—and it had nothing to do with the annual beauty contest in Atlantic City. In 1952 and again in 1962, the Supreme Court of New Jersey issued two opinions on zoning which caused considerable controversy. Both cases brought into prominence the exclusionary nature of zoning, and for many made that state into a citadel of "exclusionary" zoning. Recent cases suggest that this judicial period has terminated for that state and that New Jersey may have redeemed its zoning image. It is quite possible that the sharp change in zoning approach that has occurred there will be followed elsewhere in the country.

Pennsylvania is another state that has also changed in recent years its judicial attitude on zoning. It had never achieved the reputation of New Jersey since its zoning decisions were for many years in the "mainstream." The recent position of its supreme court has made a considerable impact in the literature, if not yet on other courts. The issue may still not have been finalized, inasmuch as these decisions were made by a 4–3 majority of the court. For the time being, however, they stand as the strongest judicial voice against the exclusionary powers of zoning.

In *Lionshead Lake, Inc.* v. *Township of Wayne*,[1] the New Jersey Supreme Court upheld a zoning ordinance which created minimum floor areas for single-family residences. A minimum size of 768 square feet for a one-story building was prescribed, whereas that for a two-story dwelling with attached garage was 1,000 square feet, and without attached garage, 1,200 square feet. The case raised a virtual storm of comment: Somehow zoning was not supposed to discriminate against those of lesser means! But there was no question as to the effect of the zoning provision. Obviously excluded from the township were those not rich enough to buy a new home containing the required minimum size. At that time, this was not a sufficient consideration to cause the court to overrule the locality.

In the course of his opinion in that case, Chief Justice Vanderbilt made the following observations:

Has a municipality the right to impose minimum floor area requirements in the exercise of its zoning power? Much of the proof adduced by the defendant Township was devoted to showing that the mental and emotional health of its inhabitants depended upon the proper size of their homes. We may take notice without formal proof that there are minimums in housing below which one may

209

not go without risk of impairing the health of those who dwell therein. . . . But quite apart from these considerations of public health which cannot be over-looked, minimum floor area standards are justified on the ground that they pro-mote the general welfare of the community. . . . The size of the dwelling in any community inevitably affects the character of the community and does much to determine whether or not it is a desirable place in which to live. . . .

In a concurring opinion in this case, Mr. Justice Jacobs, embellished these sentiments:

The provisions with respect to two-story dwellings were influenced in consider-able part by aesthetic considerations which I believe to be entirely proper.

In the Point Pleasant case I recently expressed the view, to which I adhere fully, "that it is in the public interest that our communities, so far as feasible, should be made pleasant and inviting and that primary considerations of at-tractiveness and beauty might well be frankly acknowledged as appropriate, under certain circumstances, in the promotion of the general welfare of our people."

As much or even more controversy was raised ten years later by the case of *Vickers* v. *Township Committee of Gloucester Township*,[2] upholding an ordinance excluding all trailer camps within the locality. As in *Wayne*, again the court supported the community's decision on its aesthetics, wel-fare, and overall planning. It expressed sympathy for the feelings of local residents:

Trailer camps, because of their particular nature and relation to the public health, safety, morals and general welfare, present a municipality with a host or problems, and these problems persist wherever such camps are located. . . . Clearly trailer camps bring problems of congestion with all their attendant difficulties.

Viewed from the long run, as important as the ruling was the lengthy dis-sent of Justice Hall, who extensively discussed the matter of exclusion, anticipating the sentiments that were to become widespread in subsequent years. Given what appears to be the trend in that state, a similar opinion by Justice Hall in a case arising today would probably represent the majority opinion of that court.

One New Jersey Supreme Court case and three lower court cases, all de-cided in the 1970s, support this thesis, although none contain any language suggesting that the prior decisions are no longer the law of the state. In *DeSimone* v. *Greater Englewood Housing Corp. No. 1*,[3] Justice Hall wrote a unanimous opinion upholding the granting of a use variance allowing the construction of subsidized housing in a section zoned for homes. The case had been brought by local residents who protested the city's actions. It was clear that the court was no longer about to shield a municipality from prob-lems alleged to result from lower-cost housing:

We specifically hold, as a matter of law in the light of public policy and the law of the land, that public or, as here, semi-public housing accommodations to provide safe, sanitary, and decent housing, to relieve and replace substandard living conditions, or to furnish housing for minority or underprivileged segments of the population outside of ghetto areas is a special reason adequate to meet that requirement of N.J.S.A. 40:55–39(d) and to ground a use variance.

In *Molino* v. *Mayor and Council of the Borough of Glassboro,*[4] decided in a superior (lower) court of New Jersey, the locality had adopted a zoning amendment listing eleven conditions required for multiple-family construction. These included a limit of 70 percent of the units to one bedroom, costly provisions for recreation (such as 8 square feet of swimming pool or tennis court space for every 100 square feet of living space) along with such creature comforts as central air conditioning and automatic garbage disposal in each apartment, and a master TV antenna for the building. The ordinance was defended on the grounds that it would keep children out and thereby alleviate financial problems for the school; it was also argued that the ordinance would upgrade apartment construction and aesthetics and control population density. The court said that the provision on family size would offend the equal protection provision, and, in invalidating the ordinance, observed as follows:

The effort to establish a well-balanced community does not contemplate the limitation of the number in a family by regulating the type of housing. The attempt to equate the cost of education to the number of children allowed in a project or a community has no relation to zoning. The governmental cost must be an official concern but not to an extent that it determines who shall live in the municipality.

* * *

No municipality may isolate itself from the difficulties which are prevalent in all segments of society. . . . Zoning is not a boundless license to structure a municipality.

In *Oakwood at Madison, Inc.* v. *Township of Madison,*[5] a superior court found that a zoning ordinance was void in its entirety under the zoning-enabling legislation of the state. The township had adopted a zoning ordinance primarily to retard growth. It zoned most of the vacant land into two districts: R40, which required a minimum of one acre and 1,500 square feet of floor space for a single-family dwelling, and R80, requiring two acres and 1,600 square feet. Only five hundred to seven hundred multiple-family units could be erected under the ordinance; three bedrooms were not permitted and two bedrooms could constitute no more than 20 percent of the units. The township contended that it was seeking a balanced community, encouraging high- and moderate-income housing to balance its predominant low-income housing, and protecting drainage systems where high-density residential development might result in floods and surface drainage problems and interfere with and imperil underground water resources.

The court treated these arguments with dispatch:

In pursuing the valid zoning purpose of a balanced community, a municipality must not ignore housing needs, that is, its fair proportion of the obligation to meet the housing needs of its own population and of the region. Housing needs are encompassed within the general welfare. The general welfare does not stop at each municipal boundary. Large areas of vacant and developable land should not be zoned, as Madison Township has, into such minimum lot sizes and with such other restrictions that regional as well as local housing needs are shunted aside.

In a suit brought against the Township of Mount Laurel, decided in May of 1972, a Superior Court of New Jersey using largely equal protection reasoning declared the zoning ordinance invalid after finding that:

The patterns and practice clearly indicate that defendant municipality through its zoning ordinances has exhibited economic discrimination in that the poor have been deprived of adequate housing and the opportunity to secure the construction of subsidized housing; and has used Federal, State, County and local finances and resources safely for the betterment of middle- and upper-income persons. . . .[6]

Some of the plaintiffs in the suit alleged that they were individuals living in substandard housing in that locality and others contended they were former residents forced by local exclusionary practices to move to an adjacent municipality. The court ordered the Defendant municipality within ninety days after entry of the judgment to make an investigation and analysis of the housing needs for persons of low and moderate income with a view toward adopting a program for establishing housing, adding as follows:

The defendant shall, upon completion of the investigation referred to in the preceding paragraph, establish, to the extent possible, an estimated number of both low and moderate income units which should be constructed in the Township each year to provide for the needs as identified in the preceding paragraph.

The defendant shall, upon completion of the analysis set forth in the preceding paragraphs, develop a plan of implementation; that is, an affirmative program, to enable and encourage the satisfaction of the needs as previously set forth. Said plan shall include an analysis of the ways in which the Township can act affirmatively to enable and encourage the satisfaction of said needs and shall include a plan of action which the Township has chosen for the purposes of implementing this program. . . .

In this opinion, Judge Martino arrived virtually full circle from the earlier judicial reasoning in the state as he penetrated some of the zoning mythology:

Today when municipalities give reasons for the exclusion of certain uses, although they gloss them with high meaning phrases, they lack sincerity. It is not low cost housing which ferments crime, it is the lower economic strata of society which moves in, yet no ordinance would dare to raise that objection to prohibit them and expect to succeed. Local legislative bodies know better than to state that more low-income producing structures will mean a higher tax rate. This is what the Courts have abhorred as Fiscal Zoning. What local governing body would raise an objection to bringing a factory into a neighborhood because it would increase the population of the economically poor? While it may be an argument that it would affect property values and while it is proper to zone in certain instances against factories, it is improper to build a wall against the poor income people. . . .

* * *

There has been too much conservatism in the definition of the words which refer to one of the purposes of zoning, i.e., "to promote the general welfare." Some definitions would better apply to private welfare.

An analysis of the opinion by Pennsylvania Supreme Court in 1958 in *Bilbar Construction Co.* v. *Board of Adjustment,*[7] would hardly lead ·one to the conclusion that that court would, within seven years, begin a trend significantly restricting municipalities. The facts of *Bilbar* were not unusually unfavorable to the municipality; in question was the constitutionality of an ordinance establishing a minimum building site of one acre and 150 feet of frontage. The emphasis of the court stands out, not because it was unusual at the time (or even for courts today), but in contrast to what it has subsequently said and done. Due homage was paid *Berman* v. *Parker,* and the importance of aesthetic considerations, in determining the validity of zoning. The court asserted that:

A legislative enactment can be declared void only when it violates the fundamental law clearly, palpably, plainly and in such a manner as to leave no doubt or hesitation in the minds of the court.

These considerations seemed to vanish in a subsequent line of cases beginning with *National Land and Investment Co.* v. *Easttown Township Board of Adjustment,*[8] decided in 1965, which held a four-acre minimum lot size unconstitutional. The court redirected its attention from the rights of the municipality to the rights of would-be residents as well as that of the property owner, making the following statements which it has reiterated and reaffirmed in subsequent cases:

The question posed is whether the township can stand in the way of the natural forces which send our growing population into hitherto undeveloped areas in search of a comfortable place to live. We have concluded not. A zoning ordinance whose primary purpose is to prevent the entrance of newcomers in order to avoid future burdens, economic and otherwise, upon the administration of public services and facilities cannot be held valid.

* * *

The time must never come when . . . courts abdicate their judicial responsibility to protect the constitutional rights of individual citizens. Thus the burden of proof imposed upon one who challenges the validity of a zoning regulation must never be made so onerous as to foreclose, for all practical purposes, a land owner's avenue of redress against the infringement of constitutionally protected rights.

The contest was no longer between the "people" as represented by the municipality and the property owner: "people" had also been added to the property owner's side and this changed the balance. Use of the land would not only provide rewards for the landowner, but also for a good many others in the form of new housing and greater mobility. Using similar reasoning, the court in *Appeal of Kit-Mar Builders*[9] held two- and three-acre zoning improper and came to the conclusion that one-acre zoning was, in that situation, about the permissible limit. It had held earlier, in *Appeal of Girsh*,[10] that a zoning ordinance must provide explicitly for a district allowing apartment construction. None of these Pennsylvania cases involves low- and moderate-income housing, and cannot, therefore, be considered as products of judicial egalitarianism.

It is never difficult to formulate pretexts and excuses for the adoption of zoning restrictions, and in the recent cases cited above, the municipalities, in addition to the aesthetic arguments which had worked so well previously, came forth with arguments relating to the need for restricting development because of the burdens that would be placed upon water and sewer facilities, roads, and schools. It is difficult to remove the pretext from the real in these situations, but even assuming that the municipalities stated reasons were in fact true, these state courts had made a simple reply: a municipality cannot generally use zoning as an excuse to avoid added community cost. Otherwise it would curtail normal and natural growth. New communities would be able to force other and older developed communities to bear an undue portion of the burdens of urban life.

These cases suggest that when housing is involved in these states, it will be difficult for the municipalities to maintain restrictions that exclude people. Although they do not specify this, it should be noted that these decisions for cases involving housing, may have shifted the normal presumption of validity accorded an ordinance; the burden of proof may now rest with the municipality. It is interesting to note that this would be required normally in cases where the equal protection challenge is warranted; in those cases, the presumption operates against the legislation and the government must demonstrate some compelling justification, or the legislation will be overturned. The presumption also shifts on occasion in the usual due process inquiry. Thus, in Pennsylvania, the presumption is overcome and the burden shifts to the municipality whenever a challenged ordinance totally excludes an otherwise legitimate business from the municipality.[11] This may in effect be the rule in that state for zoning cases involving certain or any housing. Judge Hall's observation in the *Vickers* case appears consistent with this approach:

Accordingly it seems only fair to private citizens seeking judicial determination of their rights to require the municipality, with all its resources to assume the burden of going forward to justify its action when the challenged measure gives good possibility on the surface of going to a doubtful extreme.

Although the Pennsylvania cases appear to have reduced considerably the zoning prerogatives of municipalities, their actual effect may be considerably less. Thus in *Girsh,* the landowner who brought the suit sought to develop on his 17½-acre tract a high-rise building containing 280 units. What he accomplished instead was to establish an important precedent in the law of the state. When Nether Providence Township was required by the decision to establish apartment zoning, it complied, but not on the plantiff's property. It zoned for apartments four other sites where apparently less objection would be raised by local residents. There is, however, some doubt as to the suitability of these sites, particularly in comparison to the site involved in the litigation.

By contrast, it is interesting to note that in Illinois, which seems more favorably disposed toward municipalities, the court on similar findings probably would have issued as part of its decree an injunction restraining the municipality from interfering with the proposed development.

These cases did not disclose specifically whether the Pennsylvania court was using due process reasoning or relying on equal protection rationale, and both or either conclusion is warranted inasmuch as it found that the property was unreasonably restricted (due process) and that preferrential treatment was given different groups in the population (equal protection). In concurring opinions in *Girsch* and *Kitmar,* Chief Justice Bell used more traditional zoning reasoning to find that the restrictions had no substantial relationship to the usual requirements of health, safety, and welfare. For him the issue of the exclusion of people would seem to be one of the factors to be considered and evaluated. He stated that the use to which land will be put and the benefits to the "general welfare" of that use are some of the considerations appropriate in deciding whether the land has been validly restricted.

Cases in at least three other states favor the general tenor of these decisions (although, of course, there are many cases invalidating fiscal and density limitations). The most significant of these is *Bristow* v. *City of Woodhaven,*[12] decided by the Michigan Court of Appeals (an intermediate court), which held that a zoning ordinance excluding a mobile home park was not entitled to the presumption of validity. The trial court found that the zoning ordinance as a practical matter excluded mobile home parks from the community, although they could be established in one of the commercial districts by permission of the local board of zoning appeals. Said the higher court:

Since mobile home parks have, by virtue of state statute coupled with judicial precedence, been afforded a protective status, there is no longer a presumption of validity of an ordinance that operates toward their exclusion. Such protection of this particular land use is of increased importance in view of the massive nationwide housing shortage which necessitates a redefining of the term "general welfare" as applied to justify residential zoning. The term is not a mere catchword to permit the translation of narrow desires into ordinances which discriminate against or operate to exclude certain residential uses deemed beneficial. . . . Such zoning may never stand where its primary purpose is shown to operate for the exclusion of a certain element of residential dwellers.

In an Illinois case also involving a mobile home park, an appellate court, while not disturbing the status of the presumption of validity, stated that the exigencies caused by urbanized society must be considered in determining the relationship of the ordinance to the general welfare. The court held that the need for lower-cost housing "was an element which should be considered in determining the reasonableness of restrictive zoning ordinances."[13]

In *Board of County Supervisors of Fairfax County* v. *Carper*,[14] the supreme court of Virginia held in 1959 that two-acre minimum lot size restriction imposed on the western two-thirds of the county was invalid on the basis that the practical effect of the restriction would be to prevent low-income persons from living in that area. The county alleged that the restriction was necessary for a more economical operation of government and to prevent exhaustion of the water supply. The court observed that in enacting the zoning ordinance, the municipality had intended that it have an exclusionary effect and the evidence showed that this had been accomplished. The court found it significant that before the two-acre restriction was imposed, applications for subdivisions had been numerous, whereas after the enactment of the ordinance, there had been no such applications. "Such an intentional and exclusionary purpose" was found to bear no relation to the general welfare.

Considering the importance given housing in national priorities, it is possible that other states face similar judicial routes. Were it not for the environmental or ecological issues that enter into these cases, this judicial road would become more certain in other states. In many zoning controversies, the principal contestants have become those who seek more development and those who seek less. Sufficient zoning doctrine is increasingly available to allow the judges to use their own experience and background and propensities to pick and choose. The sentiments of the times make it almost inevitable that some judges will rule against development.

To summarize the significance of the recent New Jersey and Pennsylvania decisions, it may be said that certain changes in traditional zoning approaches have occurred. I shall proceed to make some categorization of these although no more may be warranted than the observation that the emphasis has shifted significantly for these courts from the primacy of local desires to the primacy of regional considerations. To accomplish this has required the alteration of some judicial rules. First, the presumption of validity for local zoning legislation may no longer be applicable in some or all cases involving housing. The locality may have the burden of justifying exclusion of any form of housing, whether subsidized or not. Second, again when housing is the issue, more judicial intervention in zoning can be expected. And third, whether the presumption of validity has shifted or not, housing problems of the area, region, or perhaps of the nation will be an important consideration in determining whether the ordinance has a reasonable relationship to health, safety, and welfare.

Nonetheless, however, at this stage in time *"Euclid* is, indeed, alive and well,"[15] and none of the cases cited has come close to terminating its existence. But its enemies are many (perhaps legion) and they wish and seek its judicial demise. The literature has brought forth a number of theories that would overturn *Euclid* and have the courts determine that much, if not all, of local zoning should be declared unconstitutional. Some of these positions will be discussed in brief subsequently.

Equal Protection: Voting Rights

This argument states that the zoning process denies nonresidents the right to vote in matters affecting their housing and its location. This, it is contended, is contrary to voting rights decisions of the Supreme Court under the equal protection clause "that the state may not deny the vote to persons substantially affected by the outcome of an election and capable of voting intelligently and responsibly in it." In presenting this thesis, a note in the *Yale Law Journal* synthesizes positions expressed in prior sections of this book:

Suburban control of metropolitan land development is a troubling reminder that the American idea of representative democracy has not yet been achieved. Suburbs alone regulate the use and development of most vacant land in metropolitan areas, yet this regulation has a pervasive effect upon the lives of people outside the borders of the suburbs. State delegation of control over vacant land use to suburbanites thus conflicts with a basic notion of representative democracy —that the governed should have a voice in the decision-making process.

This denial of representation is all the more serious because identifiable groups are likely to be permanently excluded from participation. Restrictive land use policies purposely exclude those who, if they had access to the ballot box, would vote to change current policies. Small and relatively homogenous groups, immune from political competition are thus able to perpetuate their power over other, generally poorer groups in the society.[16]

The Yale note proposes that the courts declare present zoning unconstitutional and enjoin enforcement of existing ordinances after a certain date, leaving final resolution of the problem to the legislature.

Equal Protection: Poverty and Housing

This argument contends that the equal protection clause should be extended to prohibit zoning that excludes the poor and near-poor. It assumes that the normal or classical due process approach in the zoning cases is one concerned with economic regulation of property and land and is, therefore, not applicable or appropriate to consider social and economic interests of those excluded. It suggests that the traditional judicial inquiry does not permit sufficient emphasis on questions of race, poverty, and housing.[17]

The burden would be cast upon the municipality to justify zoning ordinances that operate to exclude the poor, which seemingly applies to most if not all suburban ordinances and possibly to others as well. A note in the *Harvard Law Review* takes the position that under the equal protection clause:

A state or municipality may not enact zoning ordinances which generally operate to confine the poor to the deteriorating central city. This conclusion derives from a view of equal protection which holds that laws which isolate the poor in a way that impairs their social mobility, even though based on de facto rather than de jure lines are as invidious as those which discriminate according to race.[18]

Under this theory, a showing by a "low income" plaintiff that because of community zoning practices, he had been denied opportunity for employment and his children had been confined to inferior schools would create a presumption of unconstitutionality. This could be rebutted by a showing by the municipality that the ordinance was carefully designed to advance a public interest so important as to outweigh the infringement of these individual rights.

As suggested previously, efforts to enlarge the prohibitions of equal protection to include economic discrimination under zoning suffered a reversal on the national level in the *Valtierra* case. Since that decision, the two new justices who have been appointed to the Supreme Court are not likely to be favorable to overruling or distinguishing it in favor of an enlarging of equal protection. In my view, the situation in the state courts is much less certain. The Supreme Court of California in the *Serrano*[19] case may have commenced a new phase of equal protection activism with its decision invalidating that state's method of financing public education through the property tax. Education was designated in that decision as a "fundamental interest" of the state, but the logic of that case, notwithstanding the court's disavowals, may not be unusually strained to include housing as deserving of similar protection. However, much time may be required for the *Serrano* to be politically digested. (Housing may have to stand in line or alongside such other potential "fundamental interests" as health service, police and fire services, water supplies, parks and recreational facilities, transportation and welfare services, all matters which the *Serrano* court did distinguish from education.)

Substantive Due Process

Karlin, Horton, and Polster argue for a "resurrection" of *substantive* due process. It was this doctrine that was often used by the courts to strike down legislation in the New Deal period, and that had been left in a limbo by the justices who ultimately won that judicial battle. There has been other recent interest in it, including also its application to zoning.[20]

Karlin et al. contend that the cases which have been used in support of extending the equal protection clause to zoning become consistent and judicially workable only when considered in the context of substantive due process. They suggest that the courts are using substantive due process rationale but clothing it in equal protection terminology. A clearer line could then be drawn as to when the poor or less affluent are entitled to constitutional protection, and this would be only when a "fundamental right" was involved. This line of attack, they contend, could lead to the abolition of zoning:

The basic concern of a court when it applies substantive due process is to protect against a denial of access to those goods distributed according to need. In a society based on a system of government that is individualistic, competitive and market oriented, one of the most fundamental interests distributed according to need is the opportunity to realize the benefits of the system. What is more fundamental than the right of access to the market. Although such a guarantee would not assure the provision of goods, other than those distributed according to need, it would assure that everyone had the instrumentalities that make humanly significant action possible. In terms of zoning, this means access to the land market.[21]

For readers who want to know the difference between equal protection and substantive due process as applied to other significant questions of the day, there is no ready answer. It is understandable that lawyers now refer to the basic doctrine for many important decisions of recent years as "substantive equal protection."

There is certainly no dearth of judicial doctrine available to terminate the existence of all or most of local zoning. I propose in the following chapter to add still another.

14

Zoning, an Anomaly to the Rights of Property

I submit that zoning is not entitled to constitutional protection. It is not necessary; it is not desirable; it is detrimental. It has no relationship to public health, safety, and welfare, except, on the whole, an adverse one. It is regulation almost solely for the sake of regulation.

Nevertheless, even if all the above statements are accepted as correct, the courts will continue as always to adjudicate zoning, unless it is declared unconstitutional, on a case by case basis and probably to uphold most restrictions. This will happen because zoning trials are replete with fictions and charades that camouflage the real issues. It is not unlikely, therefore, that local restrictions will be upheld, when in fact they are detrimental and adverse to the public health, safety, and welfare. That this can occur should be of great concern in a society dependent on its courts to achieve a high degree of objectivity.

The following is a more recent scenario typical of that venerable play called "zoning" as produced and performed in courts throughout the land for the last forty-five years:

1. Nonresident owners petition to rezone their tract of twenty acres adjoining a single-family subdivision for a development of two hundred middle-income townhouses.
2. Objections are made at the public hearings by the adjoining homeowners and some others in the subdivision.
3. Solely because of this opposition, the planning commission and local legislature vote to deny the petition.
4. The nonresident owners file a lawsuit for the purpose of having the court overturn the local decision.
5. At the trial, each side presents a planner and some other witnesses to testify in its behalf. The trial court or an appellate court accepts some or much of the testimony of the municipality's planner, and, accordingly, rules that the plaintiff has not overcome the presumption of validity accorded the municipality, and dismisses the suit. In accordance with the law in this regard, no inquiry is permitted as to what really motivated the action taken by the local legislators.

The law books are replete with these cases, but, as a sports writer for a Chicago newspaper prefaced his stories about wrestling matches, these are stories for the drama pages, not the law books. Zoning is a tool of politics, not of planning. In this case as in most, the legislators refused to rezone the property for political reasons; good, bad, or neutral zoning or planning has

221

nothing to do with it, and almost everyone in the courtroom knows that to be the real situation. Yet days are spent in court contesting totally unreal and irrelevant questions of planning and economics.

The truth is that one group of property owners are able to deny others the use and enjoyment of their property. The objectors are an undefined group that may not even represent the will of most of the community or of an area. They are in effect exercising legislative powers never granted or delegated to them.

It is true that the rights of property ownership have been circumscribed within recent decades. I suggest, however, that it has bottomed out when a small group of property owners can deprive another of the right of property through state action—and the judiciary becomes a willing tool in this process.

This is the systematic operation of zoning. In the overwhelming majority of cases, the sole or dominant motivation is to accede to the political dictates of the issue. Local legislators could not be elected to or remain in office otherwise. Property rights and political rights are devoid of meaning when they are subject to the variables of the popular moods and caprices. If the local legislature were to adopt a law stating that a legitimate use of property will not be permitted when protested by an undefined number of adjoining and nearby homeowners, I doubt if it would be sanctioned by any court.

Camouflage should not make it otherwise. In other areas of law, the courts have pierced the veil. Professor Brest has stated:

That the rule is made manifest only through systematic application does not make it less "real"—or less harmful—than an overt regulation.
Courts generally have been willing to inquire whether a decision maker systematically employs an illicit or suspect operative rule and to enjoin the decision maker from continuing to apply it. . . . Determinations of this sort are at the core of decisions finding unlawful patterns of discrimination in jury selection, employment, voter registration, and pupil and teacher assignments.[1]

It may be argued that there are times when the legislators act purely and exclusively for "planning" reasons, and I assume this to be entirely possible. As we have seen, planning for zoning controls is highly subjective, no more than "educated" guesswork in the vast number of situations, and, even then, adequate or good for a limited time only. It is no more than an opinion at best as to an existing situation. That there *may be some possible* relationship between zoning and the local welfare hardly entitles zoning to supersede the right of property ownership as well as the welfare of a great many persons and communities that will benefit from its use. Moreover, the municipality can respond to the needs and requirements of the local "health, safety, and welfare" without resort to zoning. Cities can adopt specific ordinances when necessary, and the experience of Houston shows that they will.

Invalidating zoning restrictions on a case by case basis will not solve the problems and inequities. Zoning should be struck down on the basis that it inherently and almost invariably operates as a taking of property in violation of the due process clause of the Fourteenth Amendment. The *Euclid* case should be reversed.

A more stringent attitude on zoning by the courts will help many, but not the much greater number who do not seek relief in the courts and will continue to be subjected to illegal restrictions. As previously indicated, zoning trials are very costly in time and money—they are beyond the business risk of many of the most affluent developers. I can personally attest to the reluctance shown by both big and small property owners and builders to file suit against a municipality. Among other things, it may not be "healthy" to one's future undertakings in that municipality. For every case filed, there are many more that should be but never are nor will be. A municipality so determined can often ignore or emasculate court rulings when considering matters not actually involved in the litigation or the orders of the court.

The best or only solution for that large number of owners, builders, or developers who are effectively incapable of using the judicial process is for the courts to eliminate zoning. Otherwise, the right of property will remain no more than a platitude for large numbers of people. They have no recourse whatsoever for the inequities and tyrannies of local politicians and bureaucrats. And, it should be remembered, this includes many owners of small properties, lots, and acreage, whose values are largely controlled by the zoning process. Property ownership is not a privilege exclusively of the wealthy. Similarly, the overwhelming number of builders and contractors are small-business men. The results of the zoning elections should demolish forever the myth that less affluent property owners seek zoning controls to protect their interests.

Property Rights Under Eminent Domain

Property rights are still a meaningful concept in this country: reports of their demise are at the very least premature. Despite the enormous inroads made by zoning, fundamental constitutional protections against the actual taking of property by government are otherwise intact and have even been augmented in recent years. The Fifth Amendment of the U.S. Constitution and state constitutions contain provisions that no private property shall be taken for public use without just compensation. This is known as the law of "eminent domain." A governmental unit or some agency thereof must pay for the value of the property taken, as well as for all damages sustained to the value of the balance of the remaining property, when for example, it condemns a portion of the land for a road. The government has to make the owner whole by completely compensating him for his loss of property.

Within recent years, the traditional law of eminent domain has been enlarged by a doctrine known as "inverse condemnation," which requires that compensation be paid an owner of property where there has been no formal or physical taking of property but the owner has sustained loss as a result of governmental action, notwithstanding that it has not acted negligently. Thus, the government after having acquired the site for the road may thereafter be liable for any damage caused other property when it builds the road, despite the complete absence of fault on its part. Interestingly, all doubts seem to be resolved in the owner's favor; inverse condemnation applied to improvement cases "may simply embody an implicit hypothesis that practically any government decision to construct a public improvement involves, however remotely, at least some unforeseeable risk that physical damage to property may result."[2] Likewise, over the years the computation of "just compensation" has been enlarged and refined. For example, a governmental agency may now have to pay for the enhancement in value resulting to the condemned property from its own developmental activities. This will be illustrated subsequently.

"Regulation" and "Taking"

Certain property rights are therefore very much alive and even growing. Why then are the courts so acutely concerned about indemnifying a condemnee and so acutely unconcerned about financial loss caused by zoning? Why is one considered a "taking" and the other a "regulation"? This question occupies reams of scholarly pages, and there is no set formula to determine when regulation ends and taking begins.[3] The difference in treatment and result can be most arbitrary. Consider these three California cases:

1. In the *Holtz* case,[4] the court interpreted the eminent domain provision of the state constitution to require full compensation to the owner of an abutting property damaged when the public transit authority engaged in building activities on its property—without any showing of negligence on the part of the authority, something which would have been required for actionable liability in the case of the private builder. This was a case of inverse condemnation.
2. Property values in the vicinity of proposed new governmental projects often tend to rise upon the announcement and publicity attendant upon such projects. This is based on the assumption that the property will remain outside the project. If subsequently this property is itself condemned, should this increase in value be a proper element of the just compensation to be paid to the owner? These were the facts in the *Woolstenhulme* case,[5] and the court replied in the affirmative, contending that otherwise the owner would be denied the full market value of the property prior to the time it was pinpointed for taking.
3. Contrast this concern for property rights with a zoning case, decided some years prior also by the California Supreme Court,[6] upholding a zoning ordinance that permitted the owner's property to be used only for beach recreational activities, which could be operated on a fee basis. Involved in this

litigation was three-fifths of a mile of ocean frontage on which the owners then paid probably about $9,000 annually in taxes. The ordinance permitted no structures on the property except for lifeguard towers, open smooth-wire fences, and small signs. The owner sought to use the property for single-family residences, for which it had been zoned prior to the adoption of the ordinance involved in the litigation. The result of the decision was that the owner was deprived of the right to build on his property, and the public acquired an area of open space without cost except for fees the owner might charge bathers and others. There were questions raised whether the site would support buildings but this sort of concern could have been considered clearly a matter for regulation through building and structural requirements and not through zoning.

Or, consider the facts brought out in a 1968 New York zoning case in which the owners sought to rezone from residential to commercial a 14.5-acre tract at a major intersection in the Village of Old Westbury.[7] When 4.5 acres of the original 19 acres had previously been taken for road widening, the owner had received compensation in the sum of $105,800. In the zoning case, the court found that the balance of the land was worth from $200,000 to $225,000, as residential, and $1,500,000, as commercial. The other three corners of the intersection were commercially zoned and used, and a major department store (Bloomingdale's) had shown interest in the fourth corner, the site in question. Yet, the court refused to upset the residential zoning of the property, stating that the huge reduction in value caused by the zoning was not a decisive factor. Given the choice, the owner would obviously have preferred a reclassification rather than receiving compensation for the taking for the road. Nor will she find much consolation in the distinction that there was actual conveyance of ownership in the one situation and not in the other.

These cases may not be representative, and the California court, in particular, is noted for its reluctance to overrule zoning restrictions. Other courts may well have decided the zoning cases differently. But these cases do illustrate effectively the point that under one judicial category government must fully indemnify owners for losses to their property values which it occasions, while under another category, equal or much greater losses will not be compensated.

This important distinction in the law has had a not unexpected result. Zoning is being used as an escape hatch ("loophole"?) from the costs of eminent domain. There are many instances where government can achieve the same results through zoning or condemnation. Current efforts for environmental, scenic and conservation controls provide highly relevant examples of this. (Note also the discussion of the *Goldblatt* case in Chapter 12) One can safely predict which course even the most spendthrift governments will select. Many proposals have been made to require compensation to property owners subject to certain land use controls, but their success is unlikely because a considerable amount of current and proposed zoning is dependent on this exemption.

The current national land use bills before Congress appear to be predicated on the use of regulation as a substitute for condemnation. These measures contemplate reduction or elimination of development near airports, highway intersections, waterways, and other areas of so-called critical state and environmental concern. The areas will be controlled to enhance the use of these facilities, and the cost probably will be borne by those who happen to own land or property there.

Professor Allison Dunham presents this analysis of the issue:

To compel a particular owner to undertake an activity to benefit the public, even if in the form of restriction is to compel one person to assume the cost of a benefit conferred on others without hope for recoupment of the cost. An owner is compelled to furnish a public benefit just as much when his land is taken for the runway of an airport as when he is prevented from building upon his land so that airplanes may approach the runway. In the former the land owner is paid without question; in the latter there is an attempt from time to time to compel the land owner to furnish the easement of flight without compensation by restricting building. The evil of the latter system is that there is no approximation of equal sharing of cost or of sharing according to capacity to pay as there is where a public benefit is obtained by subsidy or expenditure of public funds. The accident of ownership or a particular location determines the persons in the community bearing the cost of increasing the general welfare. A further consequence of an attempt to obtain a benefit by means of a restriction is that the full cost of the public benefit is thereby concealed from those in our democratic society who are given the power of deciding whether or not they want to obtain a benefit.[8]

Nonetheless, one might argue that zoning originated at a time in this country when property rights were much more important in the scale of values than they are now, and was sanctioned by a Supreme Court which is seldom condemned for any hostility to property rights. The reason was simple: zoning was originally advocated and accepted as a means for preserving and enhancing property. It was a device for maintaining rather than for taking. The individual would simply not be permitted to use his property in a manner that would damage the property values of others. The analogy to the law of nuisance was invoked.

A normal and lawful use of property could at times be harmful. "A nuisance may be merely a right thing in the wrong place—like a pig in the parlor instead of in the barnyard."[9] The rights of property did not allow an owner to conduct a nuisance on his property to the detriment of others. But the law of nuisance did not go far enough; the majority of the court seemed convinced that zoning would provide additional protection for property.

But there was a significant defect in the analogy: The meaning of nuisance could be reasonably interpreted and confined. Similar safeguards would not be available when one of the interested parties, the local resident, was given great latitude to influence the decision as to what was and was not "adverse" use of another's property. "Adverse," "harmful," "incompatible," "undesirable" are words of art, highly prone to subjective interpretation, particularly when one has a partisan interest in the definition.

Unfortunately, time has shown that the more appropriate comparison is that presented in a taking of property by the state. When one's property is taken and used for a school, park, or highway, the properties of many others and the community as a whole are greatly benefitted. Yet, these benefits cannot rationalize any scheme to deny the owner compensation; any other result could be as appropriately termed a "stealing" as it is a "taking." Why, then, should the application of the term "zoning" change so drastically the consequence of a comparable action?

How strange and empty these words of the court in the *Holtz* case must be to literally thousands of property owners in zoned communities:

In other words, the underlying purpose of our constitutional provision in inverse —as well as ordinary—condemnation is "to distribute throughout the community the loss inflicted upon the individual by the making of the public improvements . . . to socialize the burden . . . to afford relief to the landowner in cases in which it is unfair to ask him to bear a burden that should be assumed by society."

There are many anomalies in the law, and a system of law could hardly function without distinctions that often strain logic and reason. Certain apples may become oranges in the eyes of the law and retain that status long after the original reasoning is shown to be defective. It is quite possible now to view the law of zoning in this context—as an aberration in the basic philosophy of the American law of property. The treatment of property rights in eminent domain is clearly consistent with the constitutional mandate, and their importance and necessity in an individualistic society. Zoning laws have proven themselves to be a serious departure from these tenets and philosophy. They are an anomaly in the law of property, contrary to significant meanings and values of this society.

Part V
Toward Zero Zoning

15 Eliminating the Zoning Ordinance

There are three ways in which zoning can be eliminated. First, the state legislature could repeal enabling legislation that authorizes the local government to adopt zoning ordinances. Second, the local legislature could repeal its zoning ordinance. Third, the U.S. Supreme Court interpreting the U.S. Constitution, could declare zoning unconstitutional for the entire country, and a state supreme court could hold zoning unconstitutional under its state constitution.

How drastic is this solution? Can zoning be eliminated without creating havoc for property owners and the real estate market? What will be the effect on the individual property owner? One of the problems of eliminating any kind of regulation regardless of how detrimentally it has operated, is that many legitimately have relied on it, and stand to lose upon its removal. The argument can be advanced that it may be better policy to retain the regulation rather than prejudice the interests of substantial numbers. This argument has its limitations, however, in that if immoderately utilized, it might preclude the change or elimination of any governmental controls.

It is my view that these fears are unwarranted with regard to eliminating zoning. There should be no more "chaos" than results when zoning ordinances are adopted or comprehensively amended. Overall, the detriments that may be sustained appear to be small and far less than the benefits to be received. In the preceding chapters of this book, I have shown the many benefits that would result from the elimination of zoning. This chapter shall be devoted to a discussion of the possible harmful effects of this course of action.

The adoption of a zoning ordinance or general changes in that ordinance may cost owners of land and real property in that community in the aggregate, many thousands of dollars. Furthermore, for property owners other than homeowners, the requirements or practical operations of zoning constitute a considerable hazard, in that, for one reason or another, restrictions are or may be adopted which will reduce the value of property. These losses are explained away on many grounds, one being that the values of homes will be stabilized and enhanced, and that this result tends to compensate the community for losses in other values.

The experience of Houston demolishes this proposition both with respect to the need for adopting an original zoning ordinance and repealing an existing ordinance. It shows that the market offers protection to homeowners in the absence of zoning, principally through restrictive covenants.

231

It also reveals that the consequences for most homeowners when covenants expire will not be adverse—which is highly relevant for communities that may no longer be "protected" by zoning.

Comprehensive "Zoning" Amendment: Repeal of the Ordinance

Planning or zoning theory requires that zoning ordinances be comprehensively amended periodically. It is said that almost every commentator on zoning suggests a need for periodic review and revision in order that the ordinance be kept up to date.[1] Even if "adequate" or "correct" in theory when adopted, an original ordinance or comprehensive amendment thereto will one day require extensive overhauling. Individual amendments in the text or of the use map will, over a period of time, require a coordination inherent in a comprehensive reevaluation. ". . . it is not only proper but highly essential that our municipal officers periodically review and update zoning regulations. Welfare of the people, present and future, will not permit a passive attitude on these matters. . . ."[2]

In the process of adopting a general or comprehensive amendment, many properties will be determined to be no longer suitable for their existing classifications, and will have to be reclassified. There may be changes in height, area and bulk requirements, and permitted uses may become special uses. Obviously there will be many changes in values as properties are reclassified or the provisions of the classifications changed. Even if one's classification is not changed, its value will be affected if the supply of that particular classification is increased or decreased. In the event the job is very thorough, or perhaps long overdue, the text and map of the new ordinance may have little relationship to those of the old. The effect on values can be quite significant.

Major amendments have been made in some cities several times within a decade: Memphis, Tennessee; Des Moines, Iowa; Richmond, Virginia; and Wichita, Kansas. Each made substantial amendments to their zoning ordinances six times between the years of 1920 and 1933.[3] Chicago and Cook County, in which it is located, each waited much longer periods, but the first comprehensive amendments adopted for both were very extensive and bore little resemblance to the original ordinances. And this appears to be true for many other cities.

Accordingly, an ordinance repealing in full an existing zoning ordinance and replacing it with specific ordinances directed at specific land use problems of the city can be viewed as operating in a manner analogous to a comprehensive amendment. It is common sense, if not planning theory, that if zoning has not worked well in the past and it is not likely to work well in the future, it should be discontinued. Certainly no one would argue that there should be regulation merely for the sake of regulation. That there would be some resulting variations in property values and protections should not of itself preclude repeal of zoning, since this is one of the overall results of any comprehensive (or even specific) changes that at one time or another would have to be adopted. Just as the provisions of a comprehensive amendment should endeavor to avoid severe losses in property values, so, too, some specific ordinances should be passed to avoid this from occurring upon the elimination of zoning.

Nor should the foregoing discussion be considered by the reader as an idle exercise in forensics. Some municipal officials have communicated to me their concern that zoning has severely impeded development of their city, and that future growth may depend upon its elimination. These are probably not unique positions—because their diagnosis is an accurate one, I assume it to be representative of many others. The problem is that publicly advocating this position will incur the political wrath of an important segment of the population, not necessarily, of course, or even probably, of a majority. In circumstances of this nature, it would seem appropriate to submit the question to the verdict of the entire electorate, rather· than possibly have minority control. Zoning substantially affects a city and its residents, and its existence should not be determined by the wishes of what may be a small minority. The voters should be asked by referendum or straw vote which one they favor, zoning or the alternative of a limited number of specific land use control ordinances. Zoning theory assumes public participation; and there is no more fundamental form of public participation than a referendum.

In Missouri, four counties that originally voted for planning and zoning authority subsequently voted it out. Under a statute of that state, counties may vote planning and zoning authority in or out at any general or special election. Jefferson County originally voted in planning and zoning in 1963, and voted it out in 1970 by a vote of 13,614 to 10,741 (56 to 44 percent). I do not have the numerical results for the other counties. They are Grundy, which voted in planning and zoning in 1966 and voted it out in 1968; Lafayette, which passed it in 1966 and repealed it in 1968; Phelps, which voted affirmatively in 1961 and negatively in 1968. In November 1970, Lafayette again voted down zoning 4,623 to 3,368. Zoning restrictions had not gone into effect in any of these counties at the time zoning authority was repealed. In apparently all but Phelps County, proposed regulations had been prepared, and became subject to considerable controversy.

What, then, should be the content of the ordinances that would control use of land and property upon the elimination of zoning? The experience of nonzoning provides a guide as to the ordinances that might be required. Houston has regulations controlling, among other things, setbacks, minimum lot size, parking, slaughter houses, mobile homes, and townhouses. An area of Galveston County, Texas, which is flood prone, is subject to an ordinance regulating the elevation of houses erected within that area. Houston, Baytown, and Pasadena enforce restrictive covenants. Some other aspects of land use are also covered in the building code and in traffic, subdivision and licensing regulations.

A city that eliminates zoning, however, confronts a problem not shared by cities that have never adopted it: how to provide protection for property values and for personal or business preferences established within and under the presumed security of zoning. This is primarily a problem of homeowners living in existing subdivisions not subject to restrictive covenants. The vast majority of future subdivisions would be restricted through covenants by their developers. Existing homeowners, however, in areas not subject to private restrictions who may have relied on zoning to exclude diverse uses from a subdivision and adjoining areas would no longer have this protection. Overall it should be much less concern for owners of or investors in vacant property. Many owners of improved properties might complain about the increased competition which might result—but then, zoning is not supposed to be a means for eliminating one's competition, or at least very few would publicly defend it on this basis.

There will be a change in values of unimproved properties whose values are dependent upon the scarcity created by zoning. Many vacant properties zoned for apartment, commercial and some industrial classifications will be reduced in price as the supply is increased. On the other hand, the values of some vacant properties now zoned for single family or industrial may be augmented. Some will benefit, others will not—as occurs in any comprehensive rezoning, and this is one of the risks zoning has created for property owners. One result is certain, however: the game of producing wealth through the beneficence of the city fathers thereafter will terminate.

The potential of added competition may also cause values of existing properties to be reduced. The benefits will go to other owners of property, including those to be erected. In the developing suburbs, the detriment to existing property owners (other than home owners) would seem to be minimal compared to the gains. With respect to the cities, it is difficult to understand how the absence of controls could be much worse than the current zoning scene. Moreover, it should be apparent from the experience of Houston that changes in existing properties generally do not take place immediately upon removal of controls; the process takes a considerable number of years for substantial changes in uses to occur allowing for a period of acclimation.

The experience of non-zoning has shown that commercial and industrial uses tend to locate and separate without compulsion much as they are supposed to do under the compulsion of zoning. Land values and other economic restraints are quite effective in excluding uses from areas where they would be harmful to values of commercial and industrial real estate, possibly more so than zoning. Adjoining owners may also enter into agreements to protect their mutual interests. Indeed, under zoning, owners of land and property zoned for multiple family, commercial and industrial uses constantly face the hazard that subtly or directly the ordinance will be amended in ways that will erode values.

Protecting the Homeowner

The elimination of zoning may appear to be more of a problem for homeowners than it actually is. Homeowners would be placed in much the same situation that homeowners in the nonzoned cities find themselves in when covenants for their subdivision terminate—except that many more would be affected at one time. As indicated in the discussion in Chapter 2, the consequences emanating from the termination of covenants are certainly not dire for most homeowners. There are considerable similarities in the termination of zoning. Upon the repeal of zoning, those in the more affluent subdivisions have or can obtain the knowledge necessary to impose restrictive covenants. In Houston, homeowners have created and imposed new restrictions upon the expiration of the old. (Examples will be presented in the last portion of this chapter.) This would probably occur for the bulk of the homes in the wealthiest areas, for these residents are generally exceedingly concerned about achieving maximum homogeneity and have the means to accomplish it. On the whole, the covenants that will be imposed in these areas would probably be more restrictive than zoning. A similar pattern may result in most middle-income subdivisions, although the covenants would be less restrictive than in the wealthier areas.

For homeowners at the lower ends of the economic scale, there is probably little harm that would result if the zoning controls were terminated. (This question was also discussed extensively in Chapter 2.) A limited number of commercial uses—probably no more than 5 percent of structures on local streets—might in time enter the subdivision, and most of which would provide services for local residents and thereby augment the viability of the area. (Occasionally, some industrial use might also develop.) Lower-income homeowners have limited mobility and obtain much service and convenience from stores and shops that have developed in the unrestricted subdivisions in the nonzoned communities. Most by far of these commercial enterprises depend almost entirely on patronage from local residents, and could not exist without their support and assent. Also benefitted would be older deteriorated areas that are desirable for multiple-family uses but that zoning retains for low-density usage. Values would increase and blighted structures would be replaced by new buildings.

There are also likely to be many single-family areas where the pressures for diverse uses are minimal or virtually nonexistent. Whenever I visit nonzoned areas, I try to ride through subdivisions that are unrestricted. I have usually found the Houston experience duplicated: A great many areas contain only homes despite the expiration many years past or non-existence ever of restrictive covenants. The explanation is also undoubtedly the same; minimal pressures for diverse uses.

To those most concerned about what would occur in the poorest areas —the Douglas Commission expressed some apprehension in this regard[4]— I suggest driving down the streets of Laredo, Texas, which has never adopted zoning. It is one of the least affluent cities in the country. In that city's poorest residential areas, which for the most part do not have paved streets, there are very few diverse uses. As elsewhere, commercial uses develop on the streets with heavy traffic. One can ride for very many blocks on interior streets without observing any commercial or industrial uses. It is apparent that the few that do exist serve residents of the area, and their scarcity indicates the absence of demand due to the poverty of the area.

A recent note in the *Southern California Law Review* proposed a means for protecting homeowners who would want to restrict their subdivision but would find the cost and time very burdensome. The note suggests that upon repeal of the zoning ordinance a regional governmental commission be established to promote the execution of restrictive covenants upon already developed single-family property. "The commission would accomplish its purpose by educating the public in the use of covenants and making expertise generally available to private individuals at no cost. By assisting land owners in contacting their neighbors and executing the bargained-for restrictions, the commission would serve a further function— that of bargaining agent or clearing house. In this connection, the commission could, based on its experience, develop standard form covenants and informational publications which would further diminish the expense and difficulties confronting land owners in existing neighborhoods who sought to protect their property."[5] The note also suggests that the covenants be enforced by the city as in Houston.

A major difficulty involved in covering the existing subdivisions with restrictive covenants is that complete success requires unanimous consent. A homeowner who does not consent to the restrictions will not be bound by them. The fewer the number of dissenters, the more assurance that the subdivision will remain homogeneous as it did under zoning. A recalcitrant homeowner does not, of course, mean that his property inevitably will be the site of a diverse use, inasmuch as, among other factors entering into the question, he may also be recalcitrant with respect to his price. Moreover, the price of a home would be excessive for many diverse uses, and the size of an individual lot may not be large enough. The greater threat to homogeneity would be presented by owners of vacant land who might have more opportunity to profit from a sale to some apartment or commercial developer. There are, however, some countervailing aspects to this possibility as is evident from the fact that many new homes have been constructed on vacant lots in long unrestricted areas of Houston (see Figs. 2–1, 2–2, and 2–3). Sometimes even older residences have been demolished to make way for the construction of new residences. The reason for this is the absence of demand in these areas for other uses.

Consequently, a substantial number of existing homeowners would not be adversely affected by the elimination of zoning. These would include the following:

1. Homeowners in subdivisions already subject to restrictive covenants.
2. Probably most of the more affluent homeowners, for they have the capability of establishing and imposing restrictions on their subdivision.
3. Many average-income homeowners who (possibly with the aid of the community) would enter into covenants.
4. Most of the least affluent who would probably benefit or not be affected.
5. Homeowners in older deteriorated areas that are in some demand for multiple-family use would benefit from new construction replacing blighted structures.
6. Homeowners who do not object to living in an area of mixed uses.

Table 15–1
Length of Ownership of Previously Occupied Houses

Year Property Acquired	Owners of Previously Occupied Homes as of April 1960	
	Number	Percentage
1959–1960 (part)	1,596,078	10.5
1957–1958	2,410,991	15.9
1955–1956	2,088,059	13.8
1950–1954	3,134,974	20.7
1945–1949	2,247,712	14.8
1940–1944	1,419,649	9.3
1939 or earlier	2,270,838	15.0
Total	15,168,301	100.0
Median no. of years owned		8.4

Source: 1960 Census of Housing; Vol. 5, *Residential Finance;* part 1, "Homeowner Properties"; table 1, p. 3.

In addition, homeowners who reside on major thoroughfares or in areas where there is major demand for multiple-family sites will find that the repeal of zoning has considerably augmented their property values. They might, however, prefer living in a single-family setting. Assuming that their neighbors do not agree to imposing restrictive covenants, there are still factors ameliorating their displeasure. First, changes will not occur very rapidly. It usually takes a considerable period of time before new uses develop in built-up areas. The cost of sites containing homes and of acquiring them in a group from individual owners will deter rapid change (see discussion on Montrose area in Chapter 2). Second, many homeowners tend not to live long periods of time in the same homes for various reasons having nothing to do with change in the character of property uses. Their discomfort, if any, may be short-lived and devoid of financial detriment (see Table 15–1).

Adverse monetary effects may be sustained by owners of homes backing up to those on major thoroughfares or adjoining or across a thoroughfare from an area that changes in character upon termination of zoning. The latter risk would be primarily that of owners of property on the perimeter of a subdivision. Inasmuch as there is much contiguity between single-family subdivisions in developed areas, however, most homes on the perimeter are contiguous to other homes.

What about partially developed areas? There would be considerable concern about adjoining acreage that is vacant. This question is particularly acute in areas where there is a substantial demand for multiple-family sites, and where almost every vacant tract is a potential site for dense development. More realistically, however, it should be understood that many of these sites have this potential solely because zoning has curtailed substantially the supply of land zoned for multiple-family use. If zoning were to be eliminated, there would be a much greater supply of sites, and many formerly highly potential sites would become much less so. In fact, some might no longer be suitable for multiple-family purposes because they are located in areas where actual market demand is not significant. Also, garden apartments and townhouses require much less land per unit than houses, perhaps one-third to one-fourth as much, and the demand can be satisfied on fewer sites. The 1970 census showed that about 49 percent of all housing units in Houston were renter occupied or for rent; yet less than 3 percent of total land was used for multiple family purposes and about 25 percent for single family.

It should be remembered that zoning is far from a foolproof technique to avoid "incompatibility" and "undesirability." Through the process of variations and amendments, many changes in use within and adjoining existing neighborhoods are annually allowed. Thus, the Douglas Commission notes that studies of three different communities in widely separated parts of the country have shown that "large numbers of patently illegal variances are granted every year."[6] The communities studied were Philadelphia, Pennsylvania; Alameda County, California; and Lexington County, Kentucky.

It may be contended that some limited form of zoning might solve these problems of homeowners. The purpose of such zoning would be to assure that a small minority of homeowners would not frustrate the desire of the vast majority within an area for restricting it. Zoning could still be removed from all other areas of the city and a modified form instituted for only those predominantly single-family. Each single-family subdivision or other specified area could be given the power by a two-thirds or three-fourths or more vote to restrict its area. However, significant problems would be created. How should the areas be selected? How big or small? Determining the boundaries may also determine the outcome of a vote on the provisions of the zoning or even whether there should be any zoning. Rich people and poor people disagree on the virtues of zoning. It might be legally questionable to create boundaries on the basis of income levels. Yet this would be essential to allow for a reasonable degree of self-determination.

Should these boundaries include or exclude the major thoroughfares or adjoining or nearby vacant tracts? If these are included, many of the problems inherent in zoning would remain and possibly be intensified because neighboring property owners would have even greater influence over contiguous vacant land than they do within the heterogeneity of the larger city.

Some of these problems would not be present if the boundaries were to be based strictly on subdivision boundary lines. This would, however, require a great number of individual elections even in a small community, and would still not necessarily solve the problems of major thoroughfares and vacant lands. It is my conclusion that greater problems would be created by such a limited form of zoning than would exist in its absence. However, to enable homeowners to have an opportunity to enter into covenants, an ordinance providing for a limited moratorium on use changes in single-family areas would seem an appropriate means of ameliorating possible harmful effects of "quick" removal of local controls.

Upon the repeal of zoning, homeowners will have less influence and power to control use of land, whether adjoining or nearby or distant, but this is precisely a major reason for eliminating zoning. Many homeowners will have to consider creating and imposing restrictive covenants within their areas and will not have the advantage of living in an area already covered by covenants or zoning. But this situation also has its advantages. If successful, homeowners will be much more in control of their immediate area than they would otherwise be. They can draft their covenants in a manner more consistent with the life style of the area and provide aesthetic and maintenance and even security controls which are also more suited to their needs and desires. Those homeowners who prefer some mixture of uses may be able to obtain these benefits, something which they could not accomplish at least to the same degree under zoning. Hence the repeal of zoning may lead to considerable decentralization of a city with respect to many important aspects of daily life. A degree of uniformity and conformity might be established as deemed appropriate and desirable by the residents of the area.

Any comprehensive rezoning inevitably causes changes in values, and benefits some and not others. Provided these changes meet the test of reasonableness, comprehensive amendments in zoning are essential to the credibility of zoning theory. The same reasoning should cause most American cities to repeal zoning in favor of a *limited* number of specific land use controls.

Imposing New Restrictions

As should be expected, there appears to be considerable activity toward creating new covenants in areas of Houston where covenants have expired or are soon to expire. I never gave much attention to the question prior to my last trip to Houston in January 1972. On that trip, I also travelled through another nonzoned city of about 40,000 population, Victoria, Texas, in which, I learned by chance, of one such experience. As far as I am aware, there is no agency that compiles statistics relating to the extent and success of these efforts in Houston to reimpose covenants, and, therefore, the information I have been able to obtain is necessarily limited, but it appears to be representative of what may be occurring on a greater scale. It is highly significant to this discussion for it discloses what may be expected to occur in many or possibly most single-family areas in the event zoning were to be eliminated.

In 1969, all of the then-owners of the sixteen lots in "Pool and Hoopers Addition to College Park," a subdivision in Victoria, executed and filed new covenants to run for a period of twenty-five years with automatic-extension provisions. The original restrictions for this subdivision had expired some years prior, and the imposition of new restrictions was prompted when construction of townhouses began on one of the two lots that had remained vacant. The other owners filed suit to enjoin this construction on the theory that they still enjoyed certain rights to prevent an owner from disturbing the homogeneity of the area despite the termination of the original covenants. The suit was dismissed when some of the owners purchased the two vacant lots and altered construction of the townhouses to allow greater conformity with the existing homes. Originally eleven units had been planned and only three were constructed under the new ownership. The new covenants allow only one single-family residence on each lot except the one on which the townhouses were constructed. This is an upper-middle to upper-class area.

I was able to obtain some information about six subdivisions in Houston where there have been efforts at establishing new covenants. Four of these (numbers 3 to 6 below) are at or near the 1600 block of Bissonet, and my single lead in the area led to several others. Values of homes in this area have appreciated substantially, possibly having tripled over the last ten years. Homes range in price from approximately $25,000 to more than $150,000. The area is highly desirable for multiple-family accommodations and contains some which were erected consistent with the provisions of certain of the covenants that had expired. Knowledge about the other two subdivisions (the first two reported below) came through some chance conversations and investigation of data.

1. "Garden Villas" subdivision is located in the southeastern portion of Houston across the road at its southeast corner from a corner of Houston's old Hobby Airport, at which scheduled commercial service was terminated in 1969. It was originally subdivided in the 1920's and its covenants were to expire on January 1, 1940, unless 75 percent of the then property owners agreed to extend them prior thereto to some later date. The required 75 percent of the owners agreed to extend the restrictions until December 31, 1969, and an extension to that date was effected and recorded in 1939. As originally platted, the subdivision contained 36 blocks of various sizes and an area of 89 separate sites not divided into blocks. The subdivision was restricted to single family use except for five blocks; the two at the southwest corner of the subdivision, the one at the southeast corner and the two south of Fauna. (The covenants authorized a "servant's house or room" to be rented to domestic servants. This provision probably accounts for many garage apartments in the subdivision, as will be indicated subsequently. A florist shop and poultry farm were also permitted uses on 20 sites on the north.) Figure 15–1 is a composite of several pages of the zoning maps contained in the 1962 proposed zoning ordinance for Houston and showing the subdivision and adjoining territory. The eastern boundary of the subdivision is Telephone Road, the western boundary is a railroad track (with an adjoining local street), the northern boundary is Sims Bayou, and the southern boundary for all but two blocks of the subdivision is Fauna Street. Telephone is the only major thoroughfare in or adjoining the sub-

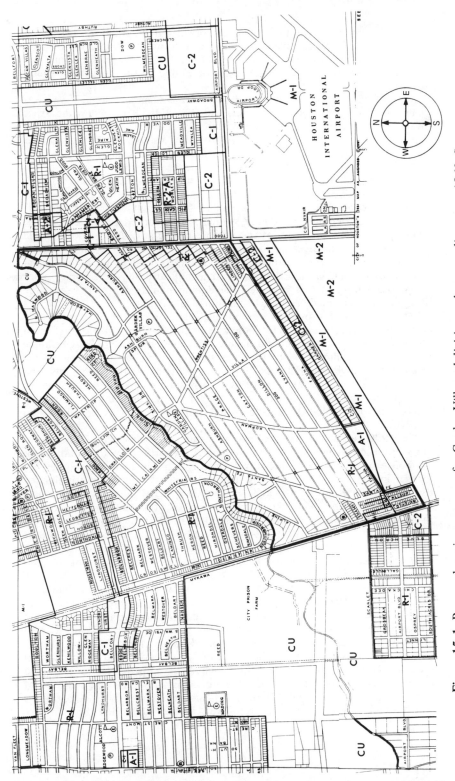

Figure 15-1. Proposed zoning use maps for Garden Villas subdivision and surrounding areas, 1962. Source: Houston Zoning Commission, *Recommended Zoning Ordinance*, 1962. Composite of maps 86, 87, and 95.

division. As indicated in Fig. 15–1, all of the area adjoining Telephone Road on the west would have been zoned C-1 commercial, and the balance of the subdivision north of Fauna single family R-1, except for some lots at the southwest corner. The area south of Fauna would have been zoned industrial.

Many of the original lots were relatively large ones and some have been resubdivided or conveyed in portions, and it is difficult to obtain the exact number of separate sites in the subdivision. Because precise accuracy in this respect is not essential for the purposes of this discussion, the figures that follow are submitted as reflective of the approximate situation in the subdivision. That portion of the subdivision restricted to single family use (including the sites that could be used for a florist shop and poultry farm) originally contained about 900 separate lots. In 1969 the owners of all or portions of over 680 of these lots (about 75 percent) executed an "Extension of Restrictions" agreement, which was recorded on December 31, 1969, the date of termination of the original restrictions. It provides that the restrictions then existing were to continue in effect for thirty years, both for the lots whose owners executed the document as well as all other lots in the subdivision. (It is most doubtful that legally any lots were bound other than those whose owners executed the document.) Except for three large sites, all lots were made subject to the prior restrictions.

Twenty-two of the original lots adjoin Telephone Road, and apparently only one of their owners executed the agreement. Excluding these lots, about 78 percent of the owners of the balance executed the extension. I estimate that about an additional 15 to 16 percent of building sites have been created through resubdivisions and conveyances of portions of the larger lots, and most of these new sites apparently were re-restricted, probably in about the same proportion as the original lots. A survey by the Houston Planning Department shows that there were a total of 1,028 houses in the subdivision in 1970.

The 1970 census showed the median value of owner-occupied homes in the subdivision to be $16,300. In the southern portions of the subdivision, the houses are frame and one-story; more expensive, two-story houses are located in the north and northeast areas. It is probably entirely populated by whites. Values do not appear to have been affected by the termination of the prior restrictions in 1969. Asking prices in May 1972 for vacant lots in the interior of the subdivision were reputed to be from $7,500 to $10,000. Values of homes were reported to range from $12,000 in the south to over $100,000 in the north. A vacant tract on the north had been developed in the late sixties into 13 lots, on which houses valued at about from $25,000 to $40,000 had been erected.

At least one business and a trailer "park" (on which only two trailers were parked in May 1972) were established in the 1970's on sites whose owners did not execute the extension of the covenants. The business is contained within a structure behind a house. This house and trailer park are located on interior streets, with the latter a short distance from Telephone Road. There are also some other trailers, garage apartments, and businesses on interior streets, virtually all or most of which developed prior to 1970 and involve in total about ten percent of the existing sites. The vast majority of these are garage apartments. (Under existing ordinances, individual trailers will probably not be able to locate on lots in the subdivision. See Chapter

2.) There are many strip commercial uses on Telephone Road which developed prior to 1970. It does not appear that the subdivision differed much in 1969.

2. The "Southwood Oaks" subdivision (in a southeasterly portion of Houston) consists of seven blocks; 49 lots in blocks 1 to 3, and 38 in blocks 4 to 6. Block 7 was not further divided. Subdivision plats were filed for blocks 1 to 3 in 1936 and for blocks 4 to 7 in 1940. All restrictions in the subdivision expired December 31, 1961. In 1964, owners of 9 of 13 lots in block 1, owners of 15 of 17 in block 2, and 18 of 19 in block 3 executed a document entitled "Restrictive Covenant Petition," restricting the lots to single-family usage without any termination date. The 1960 census showed the general area containing the subdivision to be predominantly black-occupied, and the median value of homes for the general area then was $16,500. This figure rose to $18,300 in 1970. Six lots of block 1 and ten lots of block 4 front on Southmore, a major thoroughfare. Five of the lots in block 1 fronting on Southmore were restricted as aforesaid, in 1964. As of April 1972, all of the lots in the subdivision appeared to be used for single-family residential, except for three lots in block 4, fronting on Southmore. Two of these lots contained a gas station and the other a washeteria, both located on corners. There was also a vacant tract on the unrestricted portion of the subdivision. All of block 7 is the site of a residence.

3. All thirty-five owners of houses in the "Cherokee Addition" executed a document imposing new covenants and had it recorded in December of 1959. These covenants expire in 1983 and can be extended. They revoked and replaced other and existing restrictions imposed by prior documents, including one which established restrictions expiring in 1966. The chronology of restrictions imposed on that subdivision is somewhat unusual. The original subdivider had never filed a document establishing restrictions, but they were contained in many individual deeds. Apparently some of the lots had never been restricted because of oversight. Most of the owners of the unrestricted lots subsequently entered into covenants. The new covenants (of 1959) rescinded all the existing covenants and created uniformity for all lots in the subdivision.

4. All of the owners of the fifteen homes on both sides of two streets in the south portion of what was formerly known as "West Edgemont" subdivision, on which covenants had expired about ten years prior, entered into new covenants in the early 1970s.

5. About 70 percent of the owners of the remaining thirty lots in "West Edgemont" subdivision executed new covenants in December 1969 and early 1970, which would, among other things, retain consistency with their old ones, that had allowed for garage apartments and duplexes. Robert I. Peeples, an attorney and president of the civic club, advised me (in May 1972) that he believed sufficient owners had executed the new covenants to assure stability of the area for residential use. Only three owners had actually refused, one of whom owned a vacant lot that was subsequently used for construction of expensive townhouses. Mr. Peeples indicated that a pattern of signatures had been obtained that probably would prevent those who did not sign from selling their properties for garden or high-rise apartments, since they lacked sufficient frontage to make such purchase feasible. He also indicated that the high cost of the homes coupled with the fact that they are on low-traffic streets would make it economically unfeasible for

purchase by a commercial user. The possibility of the home being used for business purposes seems remote in the more affluent areas.

6. "Edgemont Addition" subdivision consists of fifty-one lots owned by forty-four separate owners. Its covenants expire in 1975. A portion of the lots are on Bissonet, which is a major thoroughfare, and the balance on interior streets. The president of its civic club is Stuart Haynsworth, a lawyer, and he and his wife, Elizabeth, have led the efforts of the club to establish new covenants when the old ones expire. A letter of intent to renew and a document for "Restriction Renewal" were submitted to all owners. As originally drafted, the new covenants provided solely for single-family usage and would restrict all lots except those on Bissonet to one residence. These covenants expire in 1990 and automatic extensions are provided. As of May 1972, they had been successful in obtaining the consent of about 75 percent of the homeowners. The exceptions involve two areas: (a) Some of the owners on Bissonet have refused to sign the letter of intent (which is understandable, given that it is a major thoroughfare), and (b) the owner of a vacant parcel at a corner of the subdivision and of the house adjoining it have indicated refusal to enter into the new covenants. This vacant lot adjoins another subdivision whose covenants will expire in 1973.

In April 1972, an agreement was entered into with one of the owners of property on Bissonet for an amendment to the new covenants allowing the erection of expensive townhouses on that property.

Several property owners who live in other, less expensive subdivisions near "Edgemont Addition" voiced little concern to me about maintaining the same single-family character of their neighborhood. They either minimized the possibility that multiple-family use will enter the area or suggested that the effect if this did occur, would not be objectionable. I was told that the development of townhouses on some of the lots might even be helpful in maintaining the neighborhood. They pointed out that the townhouses would have to be expensive because of the high land cost, and that townhouses developed recently in the area (in "West Edgemont") apparently had sold for about $50,000 each, which at that time was more expensive than the value of nearby homes. The principal fear seemed to be of high-rise apartments. This does not seem to be a serious problem inasmuch as market conditions have been unfavorable to apartment high rises in Houston; parking requirements of the city (creating much difficulty on small sites) and possible sewer inadequacy on interior streets might be even greater deterrents.

In the lawsuit in Victoria previously referred to, the plaintiffs took the position that although the covenants had expired, the lot that was the subject of the litigation was still subject to a "negative equitable easement" and "implied reciprocal servitude." There is some basis in the law of some jurisdictions relating to reciprocal negative easements for this theory.[7] The possibility of such litigation may act as a deterrent to the purchase by a builder of property for other than single-family use.

Thus, to summarize, a controlled "rezoning" process is occurring in these areas and comparable changes would be likely to occur upon the elimination of zoning. It is "zoning" without zoning. The new restrictions may operate to modify the character of the area affected by the old ones. Some buildings and land may no longer be subject to restrictions, and as a result some uses will enter where previously forbidden. It is possible that if the pressures for different uses are great and "alien" uses develop on many of the properties no longer restricted, the effectiveness of the new covenants may be put to serious strain. But for most homeowners in the areas discussed, the new covenants will continue to maintain a similar life style in perhaps a more circumscribed setting.

This, then, is a price that would have to be paid for the elimination of zoning. Fortunately, it is a small one; actually minuscule when compared to the benefits.

16 Conclusion

It is time that we apply the clear and unmistakable lesson of the past fifty years: zoning has been a failure and should be eliminated! Governmental control over land use through zoning has been unworkable, inequitable and a serious impediment to the operation of the real estate market and the satisfaction of its consumers. And, as the experience of nonzoning in the city of Houston and elsewhere demonstrates, it is not even necessary for the maintenance of property values.

In attempting to solve certain problems of land use and development, zoning has created many greater problems for our society. When zoning restricts the operation of the real estate market, it also restricts the supply of housing. The federal government is spending gigantic sums in efforts, often futile, to overcome these consequences. When zoning curtails development, it likewise curtails business activity and badly needed revenues of local governments. Gigantic sums are also being spent to overcome *these* consequences. When zoning reduces competition, it inhibits the creation of a better environment with better living conditions.

It is absurd and tragic that the national goals of stimulating more and better housing and a desirable housing environment are being frustrated by local goals of limiting housing. It is equally inexcusable that federal policies to encourage business and development and competition are being impeded by local policies that operate to discourage them.

New zoning solutions abound, but they will have little or adverse effect unless they largely remove government from the control of land use. Governmental land use regulations at any level mean that politics and political power will continue making decisions for reasons that have minimum or no relationship to the best and most efficient use of the land, and that precious resource will continue to be wasted. In the absence of most governmental controls, the private sector is much more likely to utilize the land to provide better for the environmental and material needs of the people. In eliminating zoning, we shall be eliminating many of our pressing problems of land use.

Notes

Chapter 1

1. Udell v. Haas, 21 N.Y. 2d 463, 235 N.E. 2d 897, 900–901 (1968).
2. M. Brooks, *Social Planning and City Planning*, Planning Advisory Service Report No. 261, (American Society of Planning Officials, September 1970), pp. 28–33, 35–38.
3. Daniel R. Mandelker, *The Zoning Dilemma* (N.Y.: Bobbs-Merrill Company, Inc., 1971), p. 168.
4. Jacob Ukeles, *The Consequences of Municipal Zoning* (Washington, D.C. The Urban Land Institute, 1964), 22.
5. David Heeter, "Toward a More Effective Land-Use Guidance System," 4 *Land Use Controls Quarterly* (Winter 1970): 1–18.
6. Plaintiff's Brief, Village of Euclid v. Ambler Realty Co., 272 U.S. 365 (1926).
7. Los Angeles, Calif. *Citizens' Committee on Zoning Practices and Procedures: A Program to Improve Planning and Zoning in Los Angeles,* First Report to the Mayor and City Council, Summary Report 3, 5 and 6 (July 1968).
8. Jesse Dukeminier, Jr. and Clyde L. Stapleton, *The Zoning Board of Adjustment: A Case Study in Misrule*, 50 KY. L. J. 273, 322 (1962).
9. David J. Mandel, "Zoning Laws: The Case for Repeal," *Architectural Forum*, December 1971, pp. 58–59.
10. Allen D. Manvel, *Local Land and Building Regulations*, Research Report No. 6 (National Commission on Urban Problems) pp. 11, 17, 32–33.
11. Charles M. Haar, *Land Use Planning: A Casebook on the Use, Misuse and Re-Use of Urban Land* (Boston: Little, Brown & Co. 1959), p. 296.
12. Zoning Administration in Philadelphia, App.B, at A-8 (1957).
13. Fort Worth, Texas, City Planning Department, *Planning Fort Worth* (1962), p. 46.
14. Sidney Wilhelm, *Urban Zoning and Land Use Theory* (1962), p. 66.
15. Dukeminier and Stapleton, *ibid.,* p. 321.
16. Richard L. Wexler, *A Zoning Ordinance Is No Better Than Its Administration—A Platitude Proved*, 1 JOHN MARSHALL J. PRAC. & PROC. 74 (1967), contains data and references for (a) (c) (d), and (e) at 74, 75, 77, 78,n.19 (1967); information in (b) is from Comment, *Zoning Amendments and Variations, and Neighborhood Decline in Illinois*, 48 NW. U. L. REV. 470, 480 (1953).
17. " 'Ranchers "Face" Homesteaders' in Barrington Zoning Showdown," *Chicago Sunday Tribune*, 8 March 1970, Sec. 10, p. 8, col 4.

18. Note, *Zoning Variances and Exceptions: The Philadelphia Experience*, 103 U. PA. L. REV. 516 (1955).

19. Dukeminier and Stapleton, *ibid.*, p. 332.

20. Skrysek v. Village of Mount Prospect, 13 Ill. 2d 329, 148 N.E. 2d 721 (1958).

21. Ill. Rev. Stat., Ch 24, § 11–14–15 (1969).

22. E. C. Yokely, *Zoning Law and Practice*, 3d ed. (The Michie Co. Charlottesville, Virginia 1965), secs, 10–16, pp. 443–44.

23. Richard F. Babcock and Fred Bosselman, *Suburban Zoning and the Apartment Boom*, 111 U. PA. L. REV. 1040, n.3 (1963).

24. Richard F. Babcock, The New Chicago Zoning Ordinance, 52 Nw. U. L. Rev. 174 (1957).

Chapter 2

1. Much of the statistical information in this chapter has been obtained from the Houston Planning Department and Houston Chamber of Commerce.

2. Thomas M. Susman, *Municipal Enforcement of Private Restrictive Covenants: An Innovation in Land Use Control*, 44 TEX. L. REV. 741 (1966); Comment, *Houston Invention of Necessity: An Unconstitutional Substitute for Zoning*, 21 BAYLOR L. REV. 307 (1969). But see, Comment, *The Municipal Enforcement of Deed Restrictions: An Alternative to Zoning*, 9 HOUSTON L. REV. 816 (1972).

3. U.S., Fed. Housing Adm., *Protective Covenants for Developments of Single-Family Detached Dwellings*, Land Planning Bulletin No. 3 (Data Sheet 40, rev. April 1959), p. 1.

4. The surveys were made by Karl B. Stauss, then a graduate student of architecture at Rice University.

5. *Chicago Daily News*, 17 October 1941.

6. Note, *Amortization of Property Uses: Not Conforming to Zoning Regulations*, 9 U. CHI. L. REV. 477, 491,n.78 (1942).

7. Allen Foneroff, *Non-Conforming Uses*, cited in Jacob B. Ukeles, *The Consequences of Municipal Zoning* (Washington, D.C. Urban Land Institute, 1964), p. 38 (n. 5).

8. T. Nicholaus Tideman, "Three Approaches to Improving Land Use" (Ph.D. dissertation, University of Chicago, Dept. of Econ. 1969), pp. 39–44.

9. Note, *Zoning Variances and Exceptions: The Philadelphia Experience*, 103 U. PA. L. REV. 516, 531 (1955).

10. John P. Crecine, Otto A. Davis, and John E. Jackson, *Urban Property Markets: Some Empirical Results and Their Implications for Municipal Zoning*, 10 J. LAW & ECON. 79 (1967).

11. Houston, Texas, Citizen's Advisory Committee on Housing, City of

Houston Application to HUD for Grant to Plan Model Cities Program 110 (1968).

12. Jane Jacobs, *Death and Life of Great American Cities* (N.Y.: Random House, 1961), p. 15.

13. Walter Blum and Allison Dunham, *Slumlordism as a Tort: A Dissenting View*, 66 MICH. L. REV. 451, 457 (1968).

14. "Crystal Balling 101: Colleges now offer Courses on the Future," *Wall Street Journal*, 18 April 1972, p. 1.

15. Irvin Stander, "Land Use Controls in Houston, Texas," *The Legal Intelligencer*, 14 September 1967, finds the city unattractive; M. W. Lee, "Zoning: Myth or Magic," *The Real Estate Appraiser*, April 1964, p. 2, finds the city attractive.

16. L. R. Loggins, Deputy Chief Appraiser, and Fred Schreiter, Subdivision Appraiser.

17. Rice University, The Control Game Studio, 6 January 1969 (phase 1 research topics, Architecture 302b/502b).

18. U.S. Fed. Housing Adm., Div. Research & Statistics, *Data for States and Selected Areas on Characterstics of FHA Operations under Sec. 203* (Annual, 1957–1969). The figures reported are for the Standard Metropolitan Statistical Areas (SMSA) and not for cities alone. Over 75 percent of the Houston SMSA is not zoned, and this portion has accounted usually for at least 80 percent of the sales reported.

19. Karl B. Stauss was also employed to make sketches of land use. See note 4 above.

20. Wichita Falls, Tex., *Urban Transportation Plan 1964–1985,* vol. 2 (1964), fig 9.

21. Marmon, Mok and Green, "Development Plan for Pasadena, Tex., 1966 (1967) p. 77.

22. Bernard Johnson Engineers, *Summary Report of the Comprehensive City Plan of Baytown, Tex.* pt. 7 (1964), p. 32.

23. A map of major industrial districts of Metropolitan Chicago is contained in *Commerce,* July 1969, p. 27-IDG (industrial districts and major land developments). A land use map of Dallas and Fort Worth is contained in Texas Highway Dept. *Dallas-Fort Worth Regional Transportation Study,* vol. 2, fig. 5.1, pp. 40-41.

24. Bauske v. City of Des Plaines, 13 Ill. 2d 169, 148 N.E. 2d 584 (1957), rezoned 138 acres from residential to industrial. "The record shows that within 3,500 feet from the center of this tract (and of course, much closer to its borders) there are 1,016 residential buildings." Dissent of Justice Shaefer, id., p. 182.

25. Corthouts v. Town of Newington, 140 Conn. 284, 99 A.2d 112 (1953), permitted residential use for 18 acres out of over 600 acres zoned for industry in Newington, Connecticut.

26. John W. Reps, "Requiem for Zoning," *Planning* Chicago: ASPO 1964, 56, p. 59.

27. Thus, in Chicago, most of the demands of industry with respect to the restrictions of the proposed 1957 comprehensive amendment were met. Richard F. Babcock, The New Chicago Zoning Ordinance, 52 Nw. U. L. Rev. 174, n. 2 (1957). This should not be surprising, considering the importance of industrial development to any major city.

28. Dorothy Muncy, "Land for Industry: A Neglected Problem," *Harvard Business Review* 32 (1954): 51.

29. Identified in note 16 above.

30. However, defining the precise limits of the Central Business District is difficult in any city. Murphy and Vance, "Delimiting the CBD," *Economic Geography* 30 (July 1954): 189.

31. American Society of Planning Officials, *Problems of Zoning and Land Use Regulation* (Commission on Urban Problems, Research Rept. No. 2, 1968), 5.

32. Ibid., pp. 66–68.

33. O. Jack Mitchel and Doss Mabe, *Analysis of Components of Urban Form and Process*, Graduate Program in Urban Design 601a, Problem 2 (Rice University, 1969), p. 11.

34. Houston Center Promotional Brochure.

35. Charles S. Rhyne & Brice W. Rhyne, *Municipal Regulation of Signs, Billboards, Marquees, Canopies, Awnings and Street Clocks*, Model Ordinance Ann. Report No. 137 (National Institute of Municipal Law Officers, 1952).

36. See J. J. Dukeminier, "Zoning for Aesthetic Objectives: A Reappraisal," *Law & Contemporary Problems* 20 (1955): 218.

37. Robert Venturi & Denise Scott Brown, "A Significance for A&P Parking Lots or Learning from Las Vegas," *Architectural Forum*, March 1968, p. 37; Venturi, "A Bill-Ding-Board Involving Movies Relics and Space," id., April 1968, p. 75; Brown, "Mapping the City, Symbols and Systems," *Landscape*, Spring 1968, p. 22; Brown, "The Meaningful City," *AIA Journal*, January 1965, p. 27, John B. Jackson, "Other Directed Houses," *Landscape,* Winter 1956–1957, p. 29; and, J. M. Richards, "Lessons from the Japanese Jungle," *The Listener*, 13 March 1969, p. 339. For a commentary on the approach taken by these authors see, Vincent Scully, *American Architecture and Urbanism* (N.Y. Frederick A. Praeger 1969), pp. 240–43.

38. Such as J. J. Dukeminier, supra note 36, Edmund K. Faltermayer, *Redoing America* (NY: Harper & Row 1968); William H. Whyte, *The Last Landscape* (NY: Doubleday & Company, Inc. 1968).

39. Mason Gaffney, "Containment Policies for Urban Sprawl," ch. 10, in Stauber, ed., *Approaches to the Study of Urbanization* (1964), pp. 114, 124.

40. Texas Highway Dept., *Laredo Urban Transportation Study* (1964), fig. 9.

41. Texas Highway Dept., *Amarillo Urban Transportation Plan*

(1964), fig. 9; *Lubbock Urban Transportation Plan* (1964), fig. 9; *Abilene Urban Transportation Plan* (1965), fig. 9.

Chapter 3

1. Note, *Exclusionary Zoning and Equal Protection,* 84 HARV. L. REV. 1645 (1971).
2. Ibid., pp. 1668–69.
3. See Note, *Democracy in New Towns: The Limits of Private Government,* 36 U. CHI. L. REV. 379 (1969).
4. See Mahlon Apgar, "New Business from New Towns?" *Harvard Business Review* 49 (Jan.-Feb. 1971): 90.
5. Von Eckardt, "Are We Being En-Gulfed?", *New Republic,* 9 December 1967, 21, p. 23.
6. Note, *Snob Zoning: Must a Man's Home Be a Castle?* 69 MICH. L. REV. 339, 359–60, n.110 (1970).
7. U.S., Fed. Housing Adm., *Protective Covenants for Developments of Single-Family Detached Dwellings,* Land Planning Bulletin No. 3 (Data Sheet 40, rev. April 1959); *Land Development Manual* (National Association of Home Builders, 1969), p. 366.
8. Shelley v. Kraemer, 334 U.S. 1 (1948).
9. Note, see note 3 above, pp. 395–412.

Chapter 4

1. Mary Brooks, *Exclusionary Zoning,* Planning Advisory Service Report No. 254 (American Society of Planning Officials, February 1970), p. 3.
2. U.S., National Commission on Urban Problems, *Building the American City* (1969), pp. 211–13. Almost every major law review has discussed the subject within recent years, and the citations for notes and papers appears throughout the footnotes of this book.
3. Ibid., p. 214.
4. Note, *Large Lot Zoning,* 78 YALE L. J. 1418 (1969).
5. Norman Williams, Jr. and Thomas Norman, "Exclusionary Land-Use Controls: The Case of Northeastern New Jersey," 4 *Land Use Controls Quarterly* (Fall 1970): pg. 1, p. 25, table A.
6. President's Third Annual Report on National Housing Goals (U.S. Govt. Printing Office, 1971), p. 16.
7. *Ibid.,* pp. 16–17.
8. Bernard F. Hillenbrand, "A Fresh Look at Mobile Homes," *The American County* (December 1970), 8.

9. U.S. National Commission on Urban Problems, p. 216.

10. Williams and Norman, p. 10, table 2.

11. Ibid., p. 13.

12. The literature is surveyed in Frank Kristof, Filtration and Housing Policy Objectives, A Study for the Committee for Economic Development, Part I (Feb. 28, 1971).

13. John B. Lansing, Charles W. Clifton, and James N. Morgan, *New Homes and Poor People: A Study of the Chain of Moves* (Ann Arbor: Univ. of Michigan, 1969).

14. Such as Kristof, op. cit., pp. 24–28.

15. U.S., Fed. Housing Adm., *Analysis of the Houston, Texas, Housing Market as of June 1, 1968* (1969), app., table 3.

Chapter 5

1. U.S. National Commission on Urban Problems, *Problems of Zoning and Land Use Regulation,* Research Report No. 2 (American Society of Planning Officials, 1968), p. 69. The author was probably Dennis O'Harrow, the late executive director of ASPO.

2. Loc. cit.

3. The effect on schools of single family and multiple family construction has been subject to considerable study. The studies generally confirm the above analysis. George Sternlieb, Garden Apartment Development: A Municipal Cost-Revenue Analysis (1964); Wesley F. Gibbs, Supt., School District 68, Skokie, Ill. Development of a System for Predicting School Enrollment Using Selected Housing Factors (1966); Prince George's County, Maryland. Economic Development Committee, A Study of Income and Expenditures by Family Dwelling, Apartment and Business Units and Individual School Children for the Fiscal Year 1963–1964 (1963); Charles B. Hetrick, Assistant City Manager, Residential Land Use and Schools: A Study of Current Relationships for Park Ridge, Illinois (1964); American Society of Planning Officials, School Enrollment by Housing Type (ASPO Report No. 210, 1966.

4. Frank Kristof, *The New Zoning Ordinance and Privately Financed New Residential Construction in Manhattan*, Report to Department of City Planning, City of New York (12 April 1968), p. 9.

5. Anshel Melamed, "High Rise Apartments in the Suburbs," *Urban Land,* (October 1961), p. 1.

6. *Apartments in the Suburbs*, ASPO Information Report No. 187, (1964) pp. 4–5.

7. William A. Olson, "City Participation in the Enforcement of Private Deed Restrictions," *Planning*, 1967, p. 266.

Chapter 6

1. Judge J. Frank dissenting in Triangle Publications, Inc. v. Rohrlich, 167 F.2d 969, 982 (2d Cir., 1948); See Karlin, Horton, and Polster, *Zoning: Monopoly Effects and Judicial Abdiction*, 4 Sw. U. L. REV. 1 (1972).

2. Ronald H. Coase, Comment on paper delivered at 1971 Conference, Institute of Public Utilities, 5 November 1971.

3. Milton Friedman, "The Role of Government in Our Society" (Address delivered at Forty-ninth Annual Meeting of Chamber of Commerce of the United States, May 1961).

Chapter 7

1. Mr. Justice Black in Thomas v. Collins, 323 U.S. 516, 530 (1945).

2. Paul Goldberger, "Less is More—Mies Van der Rohe; Less Is a Bore —Robert Venturi," *New York Times Magazine,* 17 October 1971, pp. 34, 102.

3. Ibid., p. 35; See generally Vincent Scully, *American Architecture and Urbanism* (N.Y.: Frederick A. Praeger 1969), pp. 240–43, and other references in note 37 Chapter 2.

4. "The aim of the Pop Architect is to create a building (environment) that is meaningful to people . . . [not to] a handful of 'culturally superior' compatriots . . ." Virginia Wexman, "Pop, The New Architecture," *Soundings,* 44 (Summer 1971) 191, 199.

5. David M. Gooder, "Aesthetics and the Law," (Address delivered at the American Bar Association National Institute, June 2–3, 1967).

6. People v. Stover, 12 N.Y. 2d 462, 191 N.E. 2d 272 (1963).

7. Cadoux v. Weston Vol 33 Conn. L. Journal No. 35 Feb 29, 1972, p. 5

Chapter 8

1. Report of the National Commission on Urban Problems (Douglas Commission), *Building the American City* (1968); Report of the President's Committee on Urban Housing (Kaiser Commission), *A Decent Home* (1968); Report of National Advisory Commission on Civil Disorders (Kerner Commission) (1968).

2. Illinois, House of Representatives, *Findings and Recommendations of Zoning Laws Study Group* (1969); Massachusetts, Legislative Research

Council, *Report Relative to Restricting the Zoning Powers to City and County Governments,* June 1968. Bills have been introduced in Illinois, New Jersey, and Connecticut, and probably other states, for relief against exclusion of low- and moderate-income housing.

3. See discussion in Chapter 13.

4. Kaiser Commission, p. 139.

5. *Loc. cit.*

6. Linda and Paul Davidoff and Neil Gold, "The Suburbs Have to Open Their Gates," *New York Times Magazine,* 7 November 1971, pp. 40, 41.

7. Kaiser Commission, p. 136.

8. William A. Doebele, "Key Issues in Land Use Controls," *Planning,* 1963, p. 5.

9. Edward M. Bassett, *Zoning* (New York City: Russell Sage Foundation, 1940), pp. 47–48.

10. Ibid., p. 48.

11. Ibid., p. 50.

12. Baylis v. City of Baltimore, 219 Md. 164, 148 A.2d 429 (1959).

13. Bassett, p. 184.

14. Robert E. Michalski, "Zoning: The National Peril," *Planning,* 1963, p. 62.

15. David Heeter, "Toward a More Effective Land-Use Guidance System," *Land Use Controls Quarterly* 4 (Winter 1970), pp. 1, 13.

16. See Oakwood at Madison, Inc., v. Township of Madison, No. L-7502–70 P.W. (N.J. Super. Ct. opinion filed Oct. 27, 1971).

17. Heeter, *op. cit.*, pp. 16–33.

18. Edward C. Banfield, *The Unheavenly City* (Boston: Little, Brown & Company, 1968), pp. 41–42.

Chapter 9

1. See U.S., Congress, Senate, *Hearings before the Committee on Interior and Insular Affairs*, June 22 and 23, 1971, pt. 2.

2. Report Details of all urban zoning by Land Commission, *Honolulu Advertiser*, 19 February 1970, sec. B–4. See Eckko, Dean, Austin, and Williams, *State of Hawaii Land Use Districts and Regulations Review* (1969), pp. 9, 156–66.

3. *Honolulu Advertiser. op. cit.*

4. See Eckko, Dean, Austin, and Williams, p. 95, and Fred Bosselman and David Callies, *The Quiet Revolution in Land Use Control* (Council on Environmental Quality 1971), pp. 25–26.

5. U.S., Congress, Senate, Statement of Richard F. Babcock at Hearings before the Committee on Interior and Insular Affairs, June 22, 1971 pt. 2, pp. 394–95.

6. Florida Clears Stiff Land Use Bill, *Washington Post,* 20 April 1972.

Chapter 10

1. William Lilley III," Housing Report, Courts Lead Revolutionary Trend Toward Desegregation of Residential Areas," *National Journal,* 27 November 1971, pp. 2336, 2341 (chart).

2. Mary Brooks, *Exclusionary Zoning,* Planning Advisory Service Report No. 254 (American Society of Planning Officials, February 1970), p. 2.

3. See E. F. Roberts, *Demise of Property Law,* 57 CORNELL L. REV. 1 (1971).

4. National Commission on Urban Problems, *Building the American City,* p. 242.

5. Country Village Corporation v. Board of the Town of Hanover, Decided July 13, 1971 (88 units); Concord Homeowning Corporation v. Board of Appeals of Town of Concord, Decided Nov. 19, 1971 (60 units).

6. Dale F. Bertsch and Ann M. Shafor, *A Regional Housing Plan: The Miami Valley Regional Planning Commission Experience,* 1 Planner's Notebook (American Institute of Planners, April 1971), p. 1.

7. Ibid., p. 5.

8. Information contained in letter to the author, dated April 19, 1972, from Dale F. Bertsch, executive director of MVRPC and subsequent phone conversations. See also Craig, "The Dayton Area's 'Fair Share' Housing Plan Enters the Implementation Phase," *City* (January–February 1972), p. 50.

9. DeGroff Enterprises, Inc. v. Board of County Supervisors of Fairfax County, Va. No. 25609 (Cir. Ct. Fairfax County, Va., Nov. 11, 1971.)

10. The National Urban Coalition, *Report on Eighth Conference on Exclusionary Land Use Problems* (Held October 5, 1971), pp. 1–14.

11. Editorial, "People, Jobs and Housing," *Washington Post,* 6 July 1971.

12. "Forced Integration? Not in Fairfax,", *Wall Street Journal,* 29 September 1971.

13. See discussion in George Lefcoe. *The Public Housing Referendum Case, Zoning and the Supreme Court,* 59 CAL. L. REV. 1384, 1409 *et seq.* (1971). Donald Hagman, *Urban Planning and Development: Race and Poverty—Past, Present and Future,* 1971 UTAH L. REV. 46.

14. 402 U.S. 137.

15. 436 F.2d 108.

16. 401 U.S. 1010.

17. Valtierra v. Housing Authority of the City of San Jose, 313 F. Supp. 1 (N.D. Cal. 1970).

18. 402 U.S. 145.

19. Lefcoe, p. 1386–1390.

20. Statement of the President on Federal Policies Relative to Equal Housing Opportunity, June 11, 1971.

21. No. 71C 372, Eastern District of Missouri, Eastern Division (1971).

22. Crow v. Brown, 332 F. Supp. 382 (N.D. Ga. 1971).

23. Gautreaux v. The Chicago Housing Authority, 296 F. Supp. 907, *modified*, 304 F. Supp. 76 (N.D. Ill. 1969).

24. Decision of 5th Circuit on March 15, 1972. Citation unavailable at publication time.

25. 436 F.2d 908 (3d Cir. 1970).

26. "Subsidized Housing Rise in Suburbs Alarms Cities," *New York Times*, 24 January 1972.

27. "Proposal to Disperse Housing Snagged," *New York Times*, 24 April 1972.

28. Greacen, Houston, and Rogers, *Off-street Parking for Low-income Housing Projects,* Memorandum to Mayor Welch and City Council, Houston, Tex. (Sept. 1, 1971).

29. Advisory Committee to the Department of Housing and Urban Development, *Freedom of Choice in Housing* (1972), p. 10.

30. "New Law Aids Family Relocation," *Chicago Tribune*, 14 March 1971; "Tell Blacks Fear of White Areas," *Chicago Tribune*, 16 March 1971. See discussion Advisory Committee to HUD, p. 38.

31. Bernard J. Frieden, *Improved Federal Housing Subsidies: Summary Report* (Prepared for Subcommittee on Housing, Committee on Banking and Currency, U.S. House of Representatives, June 1971), p. 4.

32. U.S. Civil Rights Commission, *Homeownership for Lower Income Families* (1971), p. 41.

33. "Suburbs Resist New Demands for Subsidized Housing," *New York Times*, 10 April 1971.

34. Charles Biderman, "Shelter for Whom?", *Barron's*, 27 December 1971, p. 5.

35. Ibid., p. 13.

36. Frieden, ibid., p. 6.

37. See Defaults and Foreclosures, Correspondence between Senator Sparkman and Secretary Romney, U.S., Congress, Senate, *Congressional Record,* February 8, 1972, pp. S.1406–1415; Gurney Breckenfield, "Housing Subsidies are a Great Delusion," *Fortune,* February 1972, p. 136; Joseph P. Fried, "Any Hope for Housing?", *Saturday Review,* 12 February 1972, p. 44.

38. President's Third Annual Report on National Housing Goals (1971), p. 22.

39. "U.S. New Big Landlord in Decaying Inner City," *New York Times*, 2 January 1972; "U.S. Called Slumlord of the Future," *Chicago Tribune,* 24 October 1971; "Housing and Government: Official Criticism of Subsidy Program Is Growing," *New York Times*, 1 February 1972.

40. HUD Office of Research and Technology, "Direct Housing Assistance: An Experimental Program" (April 1972); See HUD letter, 5

November 1971, "Housing Allowance Experimental Program," Request for Proposal No. H–11–72.

41. See Henry B. Schechter, *Federally Subsidized Housing Program Benefits* (Congressional Research Service, Library of Congress, 1971), pp. 7–12; Colean, *Snare and Delusion,* Quarterly Economic Report (Mortgage Bankers Association of America, October 1970).

42. Ken Hartnett, "Who Is the Leading Slum Landlord?", *New Republic* (Dec. 11, 1971) pp. 11–13; "Housing Project Is Fortress of Dispair," *Chicago Tribune,* 25 October 1971; "Federal Housing Abandonment Blights Inner Cities," p. 1 *New York Times,* 13 January 1972; See notes 37 and 39 above.

43. HUD office of Audit, *Single Family Housing,* Audit Review of Section 235, (Dec. 10, 1971), pp. 65–72. See also Report on Audit of Section 236 Multifamily Housing Program, pp. 7–9.

Chapter 11

1. "Big Island Land Project: Sales Scheme—or for Real?" *Honolulu Star Bulletin,* 19 February 1970, p. A-2.

2. "No Bargain" Editorial, *New York Times,* 25 May 1972; "Development in Adirondacks Stirs Major Ecology Fight," *New York Times,* 23 May 1972, p. 37.

3. Alfred Balk, "Invitation to Bribery," *Harper's Magazine* (October 1966).

4. Linda Development v. Plymouth Township, 3 Pa. C. 334, 281 A.2d 784 (1971).

5. Jesse Dukeminier, Jr. and Clyde L. Stapleton, *The Zoning Board of Adjustment: A Case Study in Misrule,* 50 KY. L. J. 273 (1962).

Chapter 12

1. 272 U.S. 365 (1926).

2. Zahn v. Board of Public Works, 274 U.S. 325 (1927).

3. Nectow v. City of Cambridge, 277 U.S. 183 (1928).

4. Ambler Realty Co. v. Village of Euclid, 297 F. 308, 314–16 (1924).

5. Note, *The Constitutionality of Local Zoning,* 79 YALE L. J. 896, 912 (1970).

6. A phrase of Professor Philip B. Kurland, University of Chicago Law School, which he has used in explaining the role of the Supreme Court in our system of government.

7. 348 U.S. 26 (1954).

8. Ibid., pp. 32–33.

9. See E. F. Roberts, *Demise of Property Law*, 57 CORNELL L. REV. 1, 13–17 (1971).

10. 12 N.Y. 2d 462, 191 N.E. 2d 272, (1963).

11. 369 U.S. 590 (1962).

Chapter 13

1. 10 N.J. 165, 89 A.2d 693 (1952).

2. 37 N.J. 232, 181 A.2d 129 (1962).

3. 56 N.J. 428, 267 A.2d 31 (1970).

4. 116 N.J. Super. 195 (Law Div.), 281 A.2d 401 (1971).

5. No. L-7502-70 P.W. (N.J. Super. Ct. Opinion filed Oct. 27, 1971).

6. Southern Burlington County NAACP v. Township of Mount Laurel, No. L-25741–70 P.W. (N.J. Super. Ct. Opinion filed May 1, 1972).

7. 393 Pa. 62, 141 A.2d 851 (1958).

8. 419 Pa. 504, 215 A.2d 597 (1965).

9. 439 Pa. 466, 268 A.2d 765 (1970).

10. 437 Pa. 237, 263 A.2d 395 (1970).

11. Exton Quarries, Inc. v. Zoning Board of Adjustment, 425 Pa. 43, 228 A.2d 169 (1967); Beaver Gasoline Co. v. Zoning Hearing Board, 445 Pa. 571, 285 A.2d 501 (1971).

12. 35 Mich. App. 205, 192 N.W. 2d 322 (1971).

13. Lakeland Bluffs, Inc. v. County of Will, 114 Ill. App.2d 267, 252 N.E. 2d 765 (1969).

14. 200 Va. 653, 107 S.E. 2d 390 (1959).

15. Norman Karlin, Edward L. Horton and Lee M. Polster, *Zoning: Monopoly Effects and Judicial Abdiction*, 4 Sw. L. REV. 1, 32 (1972).

16. Note, *The Constitutionality of Local Zoning*, 79 YALE L. J. 896 (1970).

17. Lawrence G. Sager, *Tight Little Islands: Exclusionary Zoning, Equal Protection and the Indigent*, 21 STANFORD L. REV. 767, 784 (1969).

18. Note, *Exclusionary Zoning and Equal Protection*, 84 HARV. L. REV. 1645, 1650 (1971).

19. Serrano v. Priest, 5 Cal. 3d 584, 487 P.2d 1241 (1971).

20. E. F. Roberts, *Demise of Property Law*, 57 CORNELL L. REV. 1, 29–36 (1971).

21. Karlin et al., *op. cit.*, p. 42.

Chapter 14

1. Paul Brest, *Palmer v. Thomson: An Approach to the Problems of Unconstitutional Legislative Motive. The Supreme Court Review* (Chicago: University of Chicago Press, 1971), pp. 95, 111–12.

2. Arvo Van Alstyne, *Unintended Physical Damage*, 20 HASTINGS L. J. 431, 492 (1969).

3. See Donald Hagman, *Urban Planning and Land Development Control Law* (St. Paul: West Publishing Co. 1971), Chap. 14 § 180; Joseph L. Sax, *Takings and Police Power,* 74 YALE L. J. 36 (1964); Ross D. Netherton, *Implementation of Land Use Policy: Police Power v. Eminent Domain,* 3 LAND AND WATER L. REV. 33 (1968); Daniel Mandelker, *Inverse Condemnation: The Constitution Limits of Public Responsibility,* 1966 WISC. L. REV. 3 (1966); Arvo Van Alstyne, *Taking or Damaging by Public Power: The Search for Inverse Condemnation Criteria,* 44 S. CAL. L. REV. 1 (1970).

4. Holtz v. Superior Court of City and County of San Francisco, 3 Cal. 3d 296, 475 P.2d 441 (1970).

5. Merced Irrigation District v. Woolstenhulme, 4 Cal. 3d 478, 483 P.2d 1 (1971).

6. McCarthy v. City of Manhattan Beach, 264 P.2d 932 (1953).

7. Gardner v. Downer et al., 305 N.Y.S. 2d 252, 61 Misc. 2d 131 (1969).

8. Allison Dunham, *A Legal and Economic Basis for City Planning,* 58 COLUMBIA L. REV. 650, 665 (1958).

9. Euclid v. Ambler Realty Company, 272 U.S. 365, 388 (1926).

Chapter 15

1. Jacob Ukeles, *The Consequences of Municipal Zoning* (Washington, D.C. Urban Land Institute, 1964), p. 54.

2. Anderson v. Cedar Rapids, 168 N.W. 2d 739 (1969).

3. Ukeles, *op. cit.,* p. 55.

4. *Building the American City,* p. 220, (n. 23).

5. Note, *Land Use Control in Metropolitan Areas: The Failure of Zoning and a Proposed Alternative,* 45 S. CAL. L. REV. 335, 359 (1972).

6. *Building the American City,* p. 226.

7. See Sanborn v. McLean, 233 Mich. 227, 206 N.W. 496 (1925).

Bibliography

Babcock, Richard F., and Bosselman, Fred. *Suburban Zoning and the Apartment Boom.* 111 U. Pa. L. Rev. 1040 (1963).

Babcock, Richard F. *The Zoning Game.* Madison. Univ. of Wisc. Press (1966).

Bair, Frederick H. Jr. *Regulation of Modular Housing with Special Emphasis on Mobile Homes.* Planning Advisory Service. Report No. 271 American Society of Planning Officials (July–August 1971).

Balk, Alfred. *Invitation to Bribery.* Harper's Magazine (Oct. 1966).

Banfield, Edward C. *The Unheavenly City.* Boston. Little, Brown & Co. (1968).

Banham, Reynor, Barker, Paul, Hall, Peter, and Price, Cedric. *Non-Plan: An Experiment in Freedom.* New Society (Mar. 20, 1969) p. 435.

Bassett, Edward M. *Zoning.* New York: Russell Sage Foundation (1970).

Blum, Walter J., and Dunham, Allison. *Slumlordism as a Tort: A Dissenting View.* 66 Mich. L. Review 451 (1968).

Building the American City. Report of the National Commission on Urban Problems to the Congress and to the President of the United States. Paul H. Douglas, chairman. Washington, D.C.: U.S. Government Printing Office, 1968.

Coase, R. H. *The Problem of Social Cost.* 3 J. Law & Econ 1 (1960).

Comprehensive Plan of Chicago. Chicago Dept. of Development and Planning. (Dec. 1966).

Crecine, John P., Davis, Otto A., and Jackson, John E. *Urban Property Markets: Some Empirical Results and Their Implications for Municipal Zoning.* 10 J. Law & Econ. 79. (1967).

Davidoff, Paul and Linda, and Gold, Neil Newton. "Suburban Action: Advocate Planning for an Open Society," *Journal of the American Institute of Planners,* vol. 36 (Jan. 1970) 12–21.

Davis, Otto A. *Economic Elements in Municipal Zoning Decisions.* 39 Land Econ. 375 (1963).

Davis, Kenneth Culp. *Standing: Taxpayers and Others,* 35 U. of Chi. L. Rev. 601 (1968).

A Decent Home. Report of the President's Committee on Urban Housing. Edgar F. Kaiser, chairman. Washington, D.C.: U.S. Government Printing Office, 1969.

Dukeminier, Jesse Jr., and Stapleton, Clyde L. *The Zoning Board of Adjustment: A Case Study in Misrule.* 50 Ky L. Journ. 273 (1962).

Dukeminier, J. J. *Zoning for Aesthetic Objectives: A Reappraisal.* 20 Law and Contemporary Problems, 218 (1955).

Dunham, Allison. *City Planning: An Analysis of the Content of the Master Plan* 1 J. Law & Econ. 170 (1958).

Dunham, Allison. *Promises Respecting the Use of Land.* 8 J. Law & Econ. 133 (1965).

Dunham, Allison. *A Legal and Economic Basis for City Planning.* 58 Columbia L. Rev. 665 (1958).

Freedom of Choice in Housing. Advisory Committee to the Department of Housing and Urban Development. (Natl. Academy of Science—Natl. Academy of Engineering, Washington, D.C. 1972).

Freund, Ernest. *Some Inadequately Discussed Problems of the Law of City Planning and Zoning.* 24 Ill. L. Rev. 135 (1929).

Goldberger, Paul. *Less is More—Mies van der Rohe; Less is a Bore—Robert Venturi.* New York Times Magazine, (Oct. 17, 1971) 35.

Haar, Charles M. *In Accordance with the Comprehensive Plan.* 68 Harvard L. Rev. 1154 (1955).

Haar, Charles M. *The Master Plan: An Impermanent Constitution.* 20 Law & Contemp. Prob. (1955) 351.

Hagman, Donald. *Urban Planning and Land Development Law.* St. Paul. West Publishing Co. (1971).

Hearings Before the National Commission on Urban Problems. Hearings in Houston, Vol. 3, 131–175 U.S. Gov't Printing Office 1968.

Heeter, David, *Toward a More Effective Land-Use Guidance System: A Summary and Analysis of Five Major Reports.* Planning Advisory Service Report No. 250. Chicago: American Society of Planning Officials, (Sept.–Oct. 1969).

Jackson, John B. *Other Directed Houses,* Landscape, (Winter '56–'57) 29.

Jacobs, Jane. *Death and Life of Great American Cities.* New York: Random House (1961).

Karlin, Norman; Horton, Edward L., and Polster, Lee M. *Zoning: Monopoly Effects and Judicial Abdication,* 4 Southwestern Law Review (1972) 1.

Kristof, Frank. *The New Zoning Ordinance and Privately Financed New Residential Construction in Manhattan,* Report to Department of City Planning, City of New York (April, 1968).

Kurland, Philip B. *Equal Educational Opportunity: The Limits of Constitutional Jurisprudence Undefined,* 35 U. of Chi. L. Rev. (1968), 583.

Lansing, John B. Clifton, Charles W., and Morgan, James N. *New Homes and Poor People: A Study of the Chain of Moves.* Ann Arbor: Univ. of Mich. (1969).

Lefcoe, George. *The Public Housing Referendum Case; Zoning, and the Supreme Court.* 59 Cal. L. Rev. 1384 (1971).

Makielski, S. J., Jr., *Zoning: Legal Theory and Political Practice,* 45 Journ. of Urban Law 1 (Fall 1967).

Mandel, David J. *Zoning Laws: The Case for Repeal* Architectural Forum. 58 (December 1971).

Mandelker, Daniel R. *The Zoning Dilemma.* Indianapolis: Bobbs-Merrill Company (1971).

Manvel, Allen D. *Local Land and Building Regulations.* Research Report No. 6, Nat'l Commission on Urban Problems, (1969).

Melamed, Anshel *High Rise Apartments in the Suburbs* Urban Land 1. (October 1961).

Michalski, Robert E. *Zoning, The National Peril, Planning* (1963) p. 62.

Mixon, John. *Jane Jacobs and the Law—Zoning for Diversity Examined,* 62 Nw. U. L. Rev. 314 (1967).

Munro, William B. *A Danger Spot in the Zoning Movement.* 155 Annals of the American Academy of Political and Social Science 202 (1931).

Note: *Aesthetic Zoning: A Current Evaluation of the Law.* 18 U. Fla. L. Rev. 430 (1965).

Note: *The Constitutionality of Local Zoning.* 79 Yale L. Jour. 896 (1970).

Note: *Land Use Control in Metropolitan Areas: The Failure of Zoning and a Proposed Alternative.* 45 S. Cal L. Rev. 335 (1972).

Note: *Zoning Variances and Exceptions: The Philadelphia Experience.* 103 U. Pa. L. Rev., 516 (1955).

Olson, William A. *City Participation in the Enforcement of Private Deed Restrictions, Planning* (1967) 266.

Presdent of the United States' Third Annual Report on National Housing Goals. (U.S. Govt. Printing Office. 1971).

Problems of Zoning and Land Use Regulation. American Society of Planning Officials (Commission on Urban Problems, Research Report No. 2, 1968).

Reps, John W. *Requiem for Zoning, Planning* 56 (1964).

Richards, J. M. *Lessons from the Japanese Jungle.* The Listener. (March 13, 1969) 339.

Rothbard, Murray N. *Power and the Market* Menlo Park: Institute for Humane Studies (1970).

Sager, Lawrence Gene. *Tight Little Islands: Exclusionary Zoning; Equal Protection and the Indigent.* 21 Stanford L. Rev. 767 (1969).

Sternlieb, George. *Garden Apartment Development: A Municipal Cost-Revenue Analysis.* Rutgers—New Brunswick, N.J. Bureau of Economic Research (1964).

Stigler, George. *Director's Law of Public Income Redistribution* 13 J. Law & Econ. 1 (1970).

Toll, Seymour. *Zoned American,* New York City: Grossman Publishers (1969).

Ukeles, Jacob. *The Consequences of Municipal Zoning.* Washington, D.C. The Urban Land Institute (1964).

Venturi, Robert. *A Bill–Ding-Board Involving Movies, Relics and Space* Architectural Forum, (April 1968) p. 75.

Venturi, Robert and Brown, Denise Scott. *A Significance for A&P Parking Lots or Learning from Las Vegas* Architectural Forum (March 1968) p. 75.

Venturi, Robert and Brown, Denise Scott. *Ugly and Ordinary Architecture or the Decorated Shed* Part 1 Architectural Forum (Nov. 1971) 64; Part 2 (Dec 1971), 48.

von Mises, Ludwig. *Bureaucracy* New Rochelle: Arlington House (1969).

Williams, Norman Jr., and Norman, Thomas. *Exclusionary Land Use Controls: The Case of Northeastern New Jersey* 4 Land Use Controls Quarterly 1 (Fall, 1970).

Wolfe, Tom. *Electrographic Architecture,* Architectural Design, (July 1969).

Index

A